Multicultural Aspects of Sociolinguistics in Deaf Communities

Ceil Lucas, General Editor

Multicultural Aspects of

Sociolinguistics

in Deaf Communities

Ceil Lucas, Editor

GALLAUDET UNIVERSITY PRESS

Washington, D.C.

Sociolinguistics in Deaf Communities

A Series Edited by Ceil Lucas

Gallaudet University Press

Washington, D.C. 20002

© 1996 by Gallaudet University

Published 1996

Printed in the United States of America

ISBN 1-56368-046-7

ISSN 1080-5494

∞ The paper used in this publication meets the minimum requirements of American National Standard for Information Sciences—Permanence of Paper for Printed Library Materials, ANSI Z39.48-1984.

Contents

PART FIVE: SECOND LANGUAGE LEARNING

Editorial Advisory Board

Contributors

Jan Branson
National Institute for Deaf
  Studies and Sign Language
  Research
La Trobe University
Melbourne, Australia

Pietro Celo
Via C. Battisti 19
Verbania, Italy

Rhonda Jacobs
10810 Horde Street
Silver Spring, Maryland

Mala Silverman Kleinfeld
Gallaudet University
Washington, D.C.

I Gede Marsaja
Sekolah Tinggi Keluargan
  Indonesia Pendidikan
Singaraja, Bali, Indonesia

Susan M. Mather
Department of ASL, Linguistics,
  and Interpretation
Gallaudet University
Washington, D.C.

Don Miller
Department of Anthropology and
  Sociology
Monash University
Melbourne, Australia

Alejandro Oviedo
University of the Andes
Mérida, Venezuela

Sara Schley
Department of Psychology
Wellesley College
Wellesley, Massachusetts

Noni Warner
Gallaudet University
Washington, D.C.

Julie M. Wilson
Gallaudet University
Washington, D.C.

Introduction

This series, which began in 1995, provides an ongoing forum for current data-based research on the various aspects of sociolinguistics in Deaf communities around the world. The first volume contained papers revealing the variety and range of sociolinguistic issues currently facing Deaf communities in the United States, Canada, and the Philippines. The papers in this second volume provide fascinating accounts of communities in Bali, Indonesia; Venezuela; and Italy; and they extend our knowledge of multicultural communities within the U.S. Deaf community by looking at gay, lesbian, and bisexual signs; as well as analyzing how American Sign Language is used in dialogue, narration, and second-language learning.

It is my hope that the volumes in this series will help us expand our understanding of the richness and complexity of sociolinguistics in Deaf communities.

I am grateful to the contributors to this second volume and to the members of the advisory board for their hard work in putting this volume together. And as always, I also gratefully acknowledge Ivey Pittle Wallace, Managing Editor of Gallaudet University Press, who continues to have a sense of humor even after all of the hard work.

Ceil Lucas
Washington, D.C.

Part I **Variation**

Variation in the Deaf Community:

Gay, Lesbian, and Bisexual Signs

Mala Silverman Kleinfeld and Noni Warner

How one should speak or sign is becoming an issue of importance to users of American Sign Language (ASL) in the Deaf community today. Over the past decade, ASL signers, in keeping with current trends in language use, have adopted attitudes about the appropriateness of certain signs. These attitudes have in turn influenced people who use and interpret the language. This paper will focus on Deaf community members, both deaf and hearing, and the variation in their use of signs for gay, lesbian, and bisexual persons.

Within the U.S. Deaf community, more emphasis is being put on the acceptance of ASL as the language of Deaf people. Many people from all over the world are coming to the United States to learn ASL. In 1989, when Gallaudet University hosted The Deaf Way, an international Deaf conference, it was no surprise that, with all of the exposure to other sign languages, ASL should be influenced particularly at the lexical level. ASL adopted the native signs for some countries and, as a result, there are now two or more signs for such countries. For example, a sign resembling the Japanese Sign Language sign for Japan has been adopted by ASL signers and is now more commonly used than the original native ASL sign. The old sign in ASL for Japan was produced on the outer corner of the eye with a J handshape.[1] This sign was considered offensive

A version of this paper was presented at the Lavender Linguistics Conference at American University, Washington, D.C., on September 17, 1994, by Mala S. Kleinfeld and Noni Warner.

1. Handshape in this case refers to fingerspelling in ASL. The 'J' handshape mentioned here is the ASL form of the English letter 'J.' Generally, fingerspelling is used by ASL users to describe proper nouns. Some other users of ASL may use fingerspelling for vocabulary items that they do not know the signs for. When a user is not sure of the proper sign, then fingerspelling can be used. ASL uses a one-handed alphabet system, whereas some other sign languages, such as British Sign Language (BSL), use two hands.

to Japanese people in that it brought attention to the differences in their eyes, when compared with those of Americans. The choice of which sign to use appears to be based on the issue of political correctness. The newly adopted sign that ASL uses is produced with an L handshape on each hand that outlines the shape of Japan in the space in front of the signer's chest.

Similarly, in the eastern part of the United States, the sign GAY has traditionally been produced on the chin using the G or Q handshape. Within the past few years, a more neutral sign, #GAY,[2] has been adopted by many members of the gay culture. Its gloss is preceded by the crosshatch (#), which indicates that it is a lexicalized form of a fingerspelled sequence. It appears that the choice of these signs is also conditioned by attitudes.

Research in American Sign Language began only in 1960, which may account for the limited literature available regarding gay terminology and its variations. The purpose of the present study was to discover the current rules regarding ASL signs and the gay, lesbian, and bisexual community by looking at what signers have used before, what they use now, and the current attitude toward these signs within and without the language-using community. This study examines both Deaf persons and sign language interpreters. Because interpreters translate from the source language to the target language, it is important to analyze their choices for certain lexical items. Analyzing these choices, as well as Deaf persons' word choices will help us understand what signs are being used and in which settings they are being employed.

RESEARCH ON SPOKEN LANGUAGES

As in spoken languages, there are different types of variation in sign languages. In English for example, variational differences in vocabulary may depend on where one lives; these are known as regional dialects. Some differences among dialects are characterized by phonological differences in specific lexical items, whereas others differ on morphological or syntactic levels. For example, when a native New Jersey speaker says [kɔ] to indicate *car*, the pronunciation is phonologically different from that of someone on the West Coast who pronounces the term as [kar].

2. According to Battison (1979), this new sign was coined as a fingerspelled loan sign. The new term, *lexicalized fingerspelling*, is now used in place of *fingerspelled loan sign* and was introduced by Liddell and Johnson 1989.

Little research was obtained indicating the origins of terms used in the English-speaking gay community. Apparently, the term *homosexual* has been around since the early 1500s. It is seen as a clinical word, and many gay people prefer not to use it. *Gay* was first recorded in 1951, apparently as a shortened form of an earlier compound–*gay cat* meaning *homosexual boy* (Barnhart 1988). People within the homosexual community preferred this word, which has served as a symbol of pride ever since. It is said that *lesbian* was derived from the name of the Greek island Lesbos, in the northeastern Aegean Sea, which was occupied by a famous lesbian poet, Sappho (Barnhart 1988).

In *Signs of Sexual Behavior* (Woodward 1979), some variations of signs used in the Deaf community for the terms *gay* and *lesbian* are listed. Woodward, a hearing researcher, emphasizes that hearing people need to be cautious of their English-to-ASL translations. He stresses the importance of learning what is politically correct by asking Deaf people directly; his work serves as a collection of that data. Although some Deaf people are reluctant to show hearing people their signs for intimate terms, Woodward's book was published to benefit hearing professionals working with Deaf people. Much has changed since 1979 with regard to Deaf people openly discussing ASL with hearing people however.

William Rudner and Rachelle Butowsky conducted a survey at Gallaudet University in 1981, in which they interviewed twelve heterosexual males and females, ten homosexual males, and eleven homosexual females (all Deaf). Photographs of fourteen signs were shown to the groups in the study, and their English glosses were compared to those in other groups. Researchers studied the attitudes and connotations attached to each of the signs. Rudner and Butowsky found that the sign LESBIAN "was rated more negative by Easterners than by others" (Rudner and Butowsky, 43). They also stated that heterosexuals found this sign to be negative. "Homosexual women prefer to use another sign, G-A-Y WOMAN" (43). "The sign for the meaning 'gay' by tugging at an ear lobe with thumb and forefinger is universally understood by gay deaf persons (95%)" (40).

The Lavender Linguistics conference (1993) was a workshop in which approximately thirty-five members of the Deaf gay community from the areas of Washington, D.C., Virginia, and Maryland gathered for one day. The participants were divided into groups to discuss lexical signs commonly used in the gay community and the political correctness of these signs. Although the results of this conference have not been published, this present paper and the works it reviews are the most up-to-date information regarding the corpus of lexical sign data and politically correct attitudes.[3]

In *Sociolinguistic Aspects of the Black Deaf Community* (1989), Anthony Aramburo determined that the members of the Black Deaf community have their own corpus of lexical items not seen when they converse with non-members of the community. For example, the lexical item SCHOOL used by some members of the Black Deaf community is different from that used outside the Black Deaf community. The present study showed that the members of a community have a dialect that they use exclusively within the community. Register variation is also important. In *Toward a Description of Register Variation in ASL* (1989), June Zimmer demonstrated that messages differ at all levels (phonological, morphological, lexical, syntactic, discourse) and that the perceived differences are clearly related to register. The evidence of register variation was important in understanding sign choice in ASL and the various situations that demand a specific register.

METHODOLOGY

Informants

This research was geared toward thirteen hearing interpreters and twelve Deaf signers at Gallaudet University (see Table 1). The criteria for the Deaf informants were that there be an equal number of gay and straight people, and that they be fluent Deaf signers. The Deaf informants were selected from the faculty, staff, and students. There were six men (two gay, one bisexual, and three straight) and six women (three gay and three straight). The hearing group consisted of thirteen interpreters also employed at Gallaudet University. There were four males (two gay and two straight) and nine females (six straight, two lesbians, and one bisexual).[4]

3. This information was collected from a videotape of the conference, supplied by Clayton Valli. The conference was held for the Deaf gay and lesbian community and was held at the Old Post Office in Washington, D.C.

4. These labels of sexual orientation were taken from a background sheet that the informants filled out prior to the interview. However, the bisexual male and the bisexual female were placed in the gay/lesbian group for the purposes of this study.

TABLE I. *Informants' Demographics*

Subjects	Gender	Sexual Orientation	Age Acquired ASL/Years Interpreting	Geographic Location	Type of School	Family Status
1	M	S	10	CA		H
2	M	G	11	FL		H
3	F	S	3	WA		H
4	F	S	8	OH		HoH
5	F	B	2	FL		H
6	F	L	10	CA		H
7	F	S	2	IL		D
8	F	S	3	CA		H
9	M	G	13	IN		H
10	F	L	6	OR		H
11	F	S	15	MD/DC		H
12	F	S	15	IL		D
13	M	S	1	VT		H
A	M	G	at birth	NC	RES	D
B	M	G	age 3	MA	RES	H
C	M	B	age 3.5	WA	MS	H
D	M	S	at birth	NM	RES	D
E	M	S	age 11	MN	H/MS	H
F	M	S	at birth	MD/DC	RES	D
G	F	L	age 5	NY	RES/H	H
H	F	L	age 20	CA	H	H
I	F	L	at birth	WI	RES	D
J	F	S	age 15	CDA	H/RES	H
K	F	S	age 14	KY	RES/MS	H
L	F	S	age 5	PA	RES/MS	H

Note: M=male   L=lesbian
S=straight   D=Deaf
H=hearing public school   RES=residential schools
G=gay   MS=mainstream programs
F=female   H=hearing
HoH=hard of hearing   CDA=Canada
B=bisexual

It is interesting to note that only two interpreters were native signers. This proportion is a close approximation of the proportion of native signers among interpreters in the United States. At Gallaudet, approximately 10 percent of the interpreters are native signers. Six of the interpreters for this study hold certification from the Registry of Interpreters for the Deaf (RID).

Forty percent of the interpreters acquired sign language on the West Coast. Thirty percent learned sign language in the Midwestern states, and 30 percent on the East Coast. Of the Deaf people, all grew up Deaf, eight are native signers, and four learned ASL later in life, usually in their late teens. Two were from the West Coast, five from the East Coast, three from the northern Midwest, and the last two were from the South.

INTERVIEW PROCESS FOR DEAF AND HEARING INFORMANTS

The interviews were conducted separately by each researcher. All interviews/data collection sessions were videotaped. Pictures were used to elicit the production of lexical items by Deaf persons and to avoid the use of fingerspelling by the interviewer, so that the signers would focus on ASL and not be influenced by English (see Appendix A for description of photographs). The interpreters listened to an audiotape of a lecture incorporating several key lexical items (see Appendix B for the lecture).

During the eliciting of information, notes on specific lexical items were taken in order to refer to them during the interview section. Following the interpretation and description of photos, the informants discussed what they had signed and then were asked a series of questions:

1. Did they know of additional variants for those lexical items used in the lecture?
2. Why did they choose not to use the other variants during the interpretation or description of photographs?
3. Did they feel that some of the signs had any connotations attached to them?
4. Was one sign seen as more appropriate than another?

Attitudes about the "proper" sign choices play a significant role in the interpreting field, as well as for the Deaf people who are using the language twenty-four hours a day. Therefore, interpreters must be aware of how Deaf people feel about sign choices, especially those signs that may be taken as an insult to a community of people.

DATA

Within the lexicon of ASL, there are specific signs that describe gay persons and some aspects of their lives. This study found a great deal of variation when discussing the terms for gay people. There is strong evidence that some signs are not acceptable for use by nonmembers of the community. A variety of signs employed in the Deaf community were found and are shown in Figures 1–14.

The taxonomic tree in Table 2 clearly shows that ASL has quite a variety of signs that refer to the same term. However, in recent years, some of those variations have adopted a new meaning and can no longer be substituted for the original sign.

The results of our research are divided into three sections. The first section explores the differences in the interpretation of the eleven English words used by the two groups of informants.[5] The next two sections focus on what the researchers felt would benefit from intensive analysis: The first of these deals with the phonological variations for the sign LESBIAN, and the last section discusses the lexical variations of *gay*.

DIFFERENCES IN INTERPRETATION

During the course of data collection, we developed a list of eleven lexical items that were later referred to during the interviews. These items were BISEXUAL, BUTCH, COME OUT, DRAG, DYKE, EFFEMINATE, FAG (FAIRY), FEMININE, GAY, HOMOSEXUAL, and LESBIAN.

Following each English lexical item in this section, we present an explanation of an ASL lexical sign, the research data, and an analysis focusing on that particular lexical sign. The analysis will include similarities between Deaf and hearing groups, as well as participants' comments related to each sign.

5. A full description of these signs is printed in Kleinfeld and Warner (1994).

TABLE 2. *Taxonomic Tree for Terms Elicited in the Research*

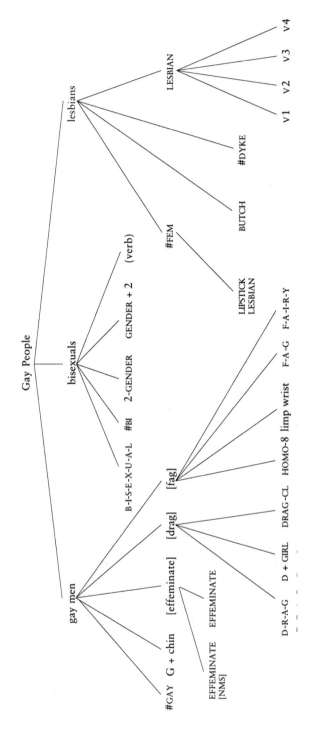

FIGURE 1. 2-GENDER ("bisexual")

Bisexual

Depending on the region in which a person learned to sign or interacted with gay individuals, the term *bisexual* varies. The first variant is
fingerspelling B-I-S-E-X-U-A-L. Some straight informants chose to fingerspell
bisexual; however, the most consistent sign among other persons in the
study was the lexicalized fingerspelled sign #BI. Another variation, 2-GEN-
DER, is produced by interpreters on the West Coast. They produce the
sign for bisexual with the v handshape contacting the side of the eye with
the index finger and moving downward to a bent v, ending contact at
the side of the mouth (see Figure 1). Other respondents from the West
Coast signed the numeral two plus the sign GENDER (2 + GENDER). People
who were trained on the East Coast considered these two signs to be
"ugly," "strange," and "awkward to produce."

The final variation of bisexual is a verb; however, many people who
produce it are unaware of its lexical classification. The sign is produced
at chest level with the weak hand facing inward toward the signer with
the v handshape and the dominant hand moving back and forth with a
bent v handshape (see Figure 2). This sign can also be produced with
both handshapes in a bent v formation (see Figure 3). The connotations
of this sign are that the dominant hand represents the bisexual and the
weak hand represents simultaneous partners. The sign is also considered
to be derived from the sign SLUT. Some informants agreed that this sign
functions as a verb and not a noun. It is deemed an inappropriate sign

FIGURE 2. A variation of BISEXUAL used as a verb

choice for labeling because it describes the action of a person and not the person himself or herself.

Butch/Dyke

The term BUTCH is fingerspelled by most straight informants. Most gay informants signed MACHO or B-U-T-C-H. The sign MACHO (see Figure 4) is

FIGURE 3. Bent V variation of BISEXUAL used as a verb

FIGURE 4. MACHO

also glossed as GANG to some people, who felt this sign was not appropriate for a lesbian. Ninety percent of the straight interpreters chose to
fingerspell B-U-T-C-H, rather than risk offending anyone. There appears
to be some confusion by all groups of people in regard to the appropriate connotation of this sign.

The concept of DYKE in English and ASL causes much difficulty with
regard to attitudes. Society does not view the term *dyke* in a positive way.
Confusion about what a dyke is, or what the term means, appears to be
similar in the Deaf community. Research has shown that the stylistic production of D-Y-K-E has become lexicalized into #D-(Y)-K-E (where the Y dips
and the K is not fully formed). There were no straight people in either
study (Deaf or hearing) who used the lexicalized fingerspelled #DYKE.

Drag

In the past few years, a new sign for *drag* has been borrowed from
Germany. Some gay interpreters consider the new sign DRAG-CL[6] in vogue
(see Figure 5) because it fits the person's glamorous life style. Before the
European sign was introduced, an initialized sign (D+GIRL; see Figure 6)
that was influenced by the English system was used by both Deaf and
hearing persons; otherwise, it was commonly fingerspelled. The D+GIRL
seems to be unappealing to those individuals who perform in drag shows

6. CL refers to a classifier handshape.

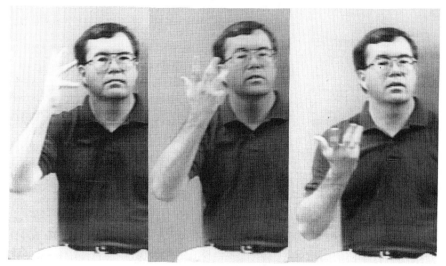

FIGURE 5. DRAG-CL

or dress in drag on occasion. Most of the gay males in both groups (and a few lesbians) produced DRAG-CL. All other informants, Deaf and hearing alike, chose to fingerspell D-R-A-G.

Effeminate/Feminine

These terms are frequently used in the gay community to describe characteristics of gays and lesbians. The sign EFFEMINATE (Figure 7), when used

FIGURE 6. D + GIRL ("drag")

FIGURE 7. EFFEMINATE

by Deaf informants in this study, describes feminine women, but for men it indicates effeminate behavior. The interpreters stated that EFFEMINATE refers to males only, and they never produced this sign to describe a female. The hearing subjects used #FEM to refer to women when describing a very feminine characteristic. A small percentage of the Deaf subjects used #FEM to refer to women. Deaf and hearing lesbians said they preferred #FEM over EFFEMINATE.

The terms for *fag* and *fairy* should not be used by the heterosexual community, according to the gay and lesbian informants. These terms are very derogatory when used by heterosexuals. They should therefore be used within the gay community only as a form of teasing, much like HOMO-8 (discussed in a later section, see Figure 8). When these terms are signed, the fingerspelling becomes lexicalized to #FAG and #FAIRY. These words may be signed in the same way as HOMO-8; furthermore, some may use the gesture LIMP-WRIST to indicate effeminate behavior.

Homosexual

Many of the informants fingerspelled H-O-M-O-S-E-X-U-A-L. Another variant is HOMO-8. If the term *homosexual* were labeling a group of people, such as in the lecture, some of the gay and straight informants said they would use other variants. It was very clear among the gay informants that *homosexual* is considered a medical term and not equivalent to *gay;*

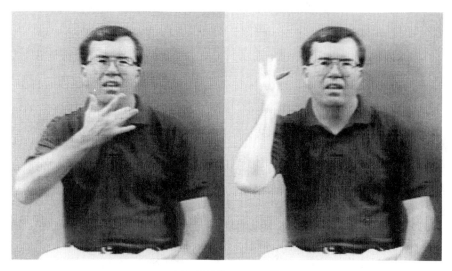

FIGURE 8. HOMO-8

those persons generally chose to fingerspell this term. Some used the compound G+chin⌢LESBIAN or LESBIAN⌢#GAY (lesbigay) to show respect for both genders. There is a parallel here between the terms *homosexual* vs. *gay* and the terms *hearing impaired* vs. *Deaf* within the Deaf community. *Hearing-impaired* is a medical term that refers to a person's audiological status and tends to have broad coverage. *Deaf* is a cultural term that refers to a person's cultural status within the Deaf community and tends to be more specific. (The terms *gay* and *homosexual* will be discussed later.)

Come Out

One facet of life in the gay, lesbian, and bisexual community is "coming out," or openly recognizing oneself as a homosexual or bisexual. There has been a strong trend in recent years to come out. The same holds true for Deaf members of the gay community. As interviews were conducted, several signs and their associated social attitudes emerged. In talking with informants, one discovers there are numerous attitudes about which sign is correct. First of all, there are different meanings for coming out. One can be coming out to oneself, in which case most persons would use the sign glossed as ADMIT (either one- or two-handed), plus a labeling sign such as LESBIAN or GAY. This sign is very popular among signers from the West Coast. Another sign combination is ANNOUNCE plus an

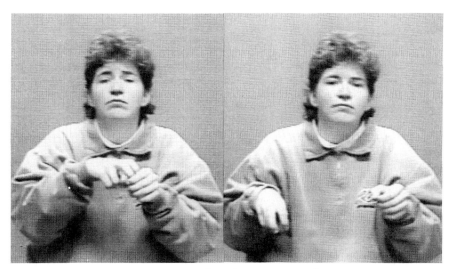

FIGURE 9. RESIGN signed to mean *coming out*

identifier such as GAY or LESBIAN. These signs were used by straight and gay persons alike. The interpreters who used these signs felt they represented a conceptual translation. These signs have been designated politically correct and accepted by Deaf persons in the community.

A general term for coming out is a sign that is glossed as RESIGN (see Figure 9). The interpreters who were surveyed stated that this uses the base sign for CLOSET, changing the dominant hand to show the movement of coming out. Deaf and hearing informants felt this sign choice was not only English-based but also insulting to gay people because of its iconic imagery.

Another general sign used by deaf and hearing people on the East Coast is 2H-OPEN⌒COAT (see Figure 10). One straight female claimed that it portrayed gay people as "people who will take their clothes off without hesitation." She preferred the sign ADMIT or ANNOUNCE.

With regard to attitudes toward the sign COME⌒OUT, more research is required. There are too many different opinions to formulate a hypothesis about which is correct.

PHONOLOGICAL VARIATIONS FOR *LESBIAN*: DESCRIPTIONS

The first set of signs consists of the phonological variation for the term LESBIAN. Videotapes, questionnaires, and background sheets of informants

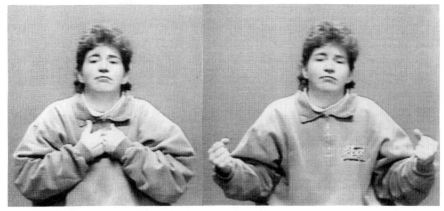

FIGURE 10. 2H-OPEN-COAT is another general sign for *coming out*

from a 1994 article by Kleinfeld and Warner were further analyzed to investigate the usage of the four variants of the sign LESBIAN. Further interviews with some informants provided a stronger foundation for our findings.

Phonetic notations[7] for the four variants of LESBIAN[8] appear in Figures 11-14. The taxonomic tree in Table 3 shows the variations of LESBIAN.

The first photo shows variant 1 (V1), which is produced at the chin with an L-shaped handshape contacting the chin with the web of the thumb and index finger. The production of this sign has a Movement Hold (M-H) structure, as described by Johnson (1994). It is important to compare the movement in V1 to that of V2. This sign is produced in the same fashion as V1, except that the movement of the sign is M-H-M-H, which is present in a majority of nouns in ASL (Johnson 1994). Figures 11 and 12 appear to be the same except for the nonmanual signals that accompany V1. V2 is the sign depicted in all of the sign language dictionaries and books that have discussed this sign. This is known as the citation form for LESBIAN.

The third variant (V3) is produced with the same handshape as V1 and V2, except that the contact point is at the joint of the index finger

7. Liddell and Johnson's (1989) and Johnson's (1994) phonological notation system was used to notate each variant and will be used throughout this paper.
8. Analysis of the variations of LESBIAN was taken from Kleinfeld (1994a).

TABLE 3. *Taxonomic Tree for the Variations of* LESBIAN

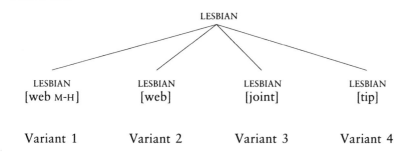

LESBIAN

LESBIAN [web M-H]	LESBIAN [web]	LESBIAN [joint]	LESBIAN [tip]
Variant 1	Variant 2	Variant 3	Variant 4

Variant 1

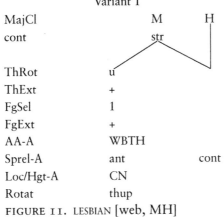

MajCl		M	H
cont		str	
ThRot	u		
ThExt	+		
FgSel	1		
FgExt	+		
AA-A	WBTH		
Sprel-A	ant	cont	
Loc/Hgt-A	CN		
Rotat	thup		

FIGURE 11. LESBIAN [web, MH]

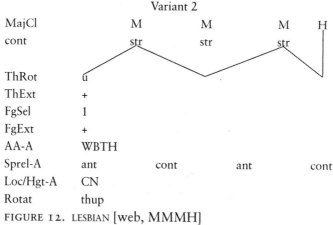

Variant 2

MajCl	M	M	M	H
cont	str	str	str	

ThRot	ú
ThExt	+
FgSel	1
FgExt	+
AA-A	WBTH
Sprel-A	ant	cont	ant	cont
Loc/Hgt-A	CN
Rotat	thup

FIGURE 12. LESBIAN [web, MMMH]

or the middle phalanx (see Figure 13). This sign's structure also follows the M-H-M-H pattern. (MHMH is the lexical form for V_2, V_3, and V_4 before phonological processes have been applied. The final production is MMMH.) The range of contact for this sign can shift from the proximal bone to the middle bone of the index finger.

The final variant, V_4 (see Figure 14), is produced with the pad of the index finger contacting the chin; all other features are exactly like those in V_1 through V_3. The structure of the pad version is M-H-M-H, and the contact can range from the middle bone through the distal bone to the tip or pad of the index finger. Table 4 shows the compilation of the informants' usage of the variants for LESBIAN.

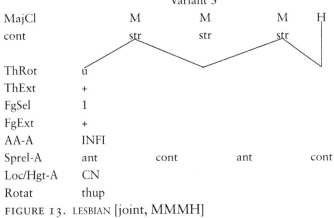

	Variant 3			
MajCl	M	M	M	H
cont	str	str	str	
ThRot	ú			
ThExt	+			
FgSel	1			
FgExt	+			
AA-A	INFI			
Sprel-A	ant	cont	ant	cont
Loc/Hgt-A	CN			
Rotat	thup			

FIGURE 13. LESBIAN [joint, MMMH]

DATA ANALYSIS

Only one respondent, a straight female, (J), produced V1. V2 was produced by three straight females (#7, K,L), one lesbian (#10)[9], one bisexual male (C), and one straight male (D). V3 was produced by five straight males (1,13, D,E,F,), five straight females (3,4,8, J,L), five lesbi-

9. #10 labels herself as a lesbian, yet she does not socialize with signers that are gay, and her production of LESBIAN along with her perceived meanings shows strong verification that she is not in fact a member of that community.

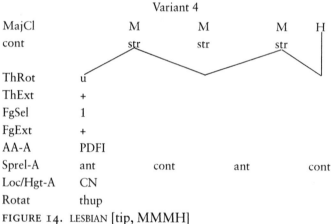

Variant 4

MajCl		M		M		M	H
cont		str		str		str	

ThRot	u				
ThExt	+				
FgSel	1				
FgExt	+				
AA-A	PDFI				
Sprel-A	ant	cont		ant	cont
Loc/Hgt-A	CN				
Rotat	thup				

FIGURE 14. LESBIAN [tip, MMMH]

ans (5,10,G,H,I), and three gay males (A, B, C). V4 was not produced by any straight males; however, four straight females (4,11,12,K), one of whom also produced V3, four lesbians (5,6,G,H), and four gay men (2,9,A,B) produced V4. Three straight informants (4,11,12) have been in the interpreting field much longer than the other three female interpreters and have evidently increased their knowledge of signs and their usage.

As researchers, questions emerge for us: Is it important to know whether the informants chose those particular variants over others? If so, why? Are the informants selecting certain variants for particular situations, or are they influenced by the observers' paradox (Labov 1972)? Or does the register of a particular setting influence their sign choice?

TABLE 4. *Signs Produced by Informants for* LESBIAN

Respondents	V1 (web, MH)	V2 (web)	V3 (joint)	V4 (tip)
Straight male		D	1,13,D,E,F	
Straight female	J	7,K,L	3,4,8,J,L	4,11,12,K
Lesbian female		(10)	5,(10),G,H,I	5,6,G,H
Gay male		C	A,B,C	2,9,A,B

Note: Letters refer to Deaf informants; numbers refer to interpreters. (See Table 1.)

To obtain answers, we examined responses to a number of questions during the interview process. For example, we asked: "You used this particular sign LESBIAN (we showed which variant they had used). Do you know of any other ways to sign that?" If the person was unclear about what we were asking, the question was restated: "You used this particular sign LESBIAN. Have you seen this sign?" (Another variation of the sign was shown.)

Table 5 shows that most of the informants are aware of all existing variants. Interestingly, though, the straight males' knowledge appears to be more limited. Of the males, only one straight male (F) knew all variants; three straight males (1,13,D) knew of only two variants, V2 and V3, although neither of the hearing males signed V2 in the lecture portion of the study. One straight male knew only V4 (F). One bisexual male, (C), also did not know all the variations, perhaps due to his sexual orientation (not being as involved with the gay community).

The more experienced straight female interpreters (4,11,12) knew all four variants, whereas the interpreters who had been in the field only a

TABLE 5. *Knowledge of Variation by Informants for the Sign* LESBIAN

Respondents	V1 (web, MH)	V2 (web)	V3 (joint)	V4 (tip)
Straight male	F	1,13,D,F	1,13,D,E,F	F
Straight female	4,11,12, J,L	3,4,7,8,11, 12,J,K,L	3,4,8,11, 12,J,K,L	4,11,12,K
Lesbian female	5,6,G,H,I	5,6,(10), G,H,I	5,6,(10), G,H,I	5,6,G,H,I
Gay male	2,9,A,B	2,9,A,B,C	2,9,A,B,C	2,9,A,B

Note: Letters refer to Deaf informants; numbers refer to interpreters.

few years (3,8) knew of only V2 and V3, a pattern similar to that of the straight male interpreters. The four gay males (A,B,2,9), two lesbian female interpreters (5,6), and all deaf lesbians knew all four variations, except for #10, who knew of only two (V2 and V3). In the interview portion of the study, #10 informed the researcher that she "didn't know much about gay or lesbian things." Table 5 thus demonstrates that sign usage is not based on knowledge alone. Many of the signers knew more varieties than they used.

The last grouping of data shows the connotations of the variants that appear to determine why some interpreters chose one sign over another. Table 6 indicates the connotations that interpreters reported for each variant.

Table 6 was constructed after a review of the videotapes and questionnaires and a follow-up meeting after the researchers had compiled the data. This collection of data helped uncover the connotations of the specific variants. We asked the informants to indicate if they attached a positive (+), neutral (∅) or negative (-) meaning to each variant. We also asked whether the signs that they hadn't chosen had any connotations and whether that was their reason for not choosing them.

One Deaf straight male (F) labeled V_1 and V_2 negative, considering V_1 to have strong stereotypical labels attached to it. Another Deaf straight male (D) said that V_2 was neutral, bordering on negative. Both males agreed that V_3 was neutral, while the third Deaf straight male (E) said that V_3 was positive. F was the only one who stated that V_4 was positive. One of the hearing straight males (13) said that V_2 and V_3 both had positive connotations, and he saw nothing wrong with signing either one. The other hearing straight male only mentioned V_3 as being positive. Five straight male only mentioned V_3 as being positive. Five straight females (4,11,12, J, L) considered V_1 and V_2 to be negative and V_3, positive. One straight Deaf female (K) thought V2 negative as well but said she had learned that she should sign V_4 because it was positive and respectful. She considered V_3 to be neutral, as did seven other straight females (3,4,7,8,11,12,L). The same three straight females (4,11,12) who had knowledge of all four variants also agreed on the meanings of and connotations associated with each variant (V1 and V2 negative, V3 neutral, and V4 positive). These three females also stated that their sign choice would not be influenced by register.

There was some confusion as to the appropriateness of V2 for the three other straight females. Because this is the citation form used in dictio-

TABLE 6. *Attitudes of Informants Toward Variations of* LESBIAN

Respondents	V1 +	V1 ø	V1 −	V2 +	V2 ø	V2 −	V3 +	V3 ø	V3 −	V4 +	V4 ø	V4 −
Straight male	F	13	D	F			1,13, D,F E			F		
Straight female	4,11, 12,J, L	7,8	3	4,11, 12,J, K,L		J,L	3,4,7, 8,11,12, K,L			4,11, 12,K, L		
Lesbian female	5,6, G,H,I	10	6	5,6, G,H,I		10	5,6, G,H,I			5,6 G,H,I		
Gay male	A,B, 2,9			A,B, C,2,9			A,B, C,2,9			A,B, 2,9		

Note: Letters refer to Deaf informants; numbers refer to interpreters.
+ = positive meaning
ø = neutral meaning
− = negative meaning

naries, the two interpreters with only 2 or 3 years of experience seemed to feel that "if it is in the dictionary, then it must be right," whereas #3 chose to be neutral about both signs that she knew. This interpreter (#3) stated that she has never been in a situation that required the use of these types of signs and that she would not accept an assignment of this nature because she didn't feel comfortable with all of the meanings. All of the lesbian and gay informants (with the exception of #10 [see footnote 6]) agreed that V1 was a sign with negative connotation that is used to describe a stereotypical lesbian as seen by the heterosexual society. V1, with its M-H structure, gives the sign more emphasis and is usually accompanied by the negative nonmanual signals shown in Figure 11. Within the gay community, this variant is used as in-group teasing in which members call one another a dyke or indicate that someone is macho or a lesbian with pride. There is a strong tendency to associate this sign's meaning to that of oral sex, due to the phonetic form of the sign. Therefore, informants who were members of the gay community viewed this sign as very derogatory if signed by an outsider. They stated that V_2 was also negative, whereas V_4 was positive.

Given the choice between V_1 and V_2, V_2 is more acceptable to members of the gay community because they realize that this is what all the sign language dictionaries print and that the majority of sign language instructors teach it as the citation form. This creates a problem because the majority of teachers, hearing or Deaf, will probably teach V_2 as the sign for lesbian. After all, this is the sign that appears in all dictionaries and is used by Woodward (1979) and Rudner and Butowsky (1981). Because this is a sensitive issue, it would be advisable to incorporate this research into the ASL curriculum.

If ASL students become interpreters or members of the Deaf community, and a gay person sees them producing this variant (V_2), the gay person will probably question whether the signer is closed-minded, homophobic, or just straight but ignorant of the preferred sign choice. This may present a level of discomfort for the gay individual. There are no instructional materials that inform straight people of connotations associated with this sign; as a result, they may never have had the opportunity for this kind of input if they have not interacted with gay people.

Members of the gay community and people who support them and interact with them say that they feel comfortable using V_3 as a general label for lesbians. This sign is seen as very respectful if used by either a straight person or another gay person. This sign can be regarded as neutral or positive, but most interpreters surveyed evaluated it as neutral.

V_4 is the most acceptable variant in all situations promoting gay and lesbian rights. This sign is seen as the most appropriate, and perhaps the most politically correct, variant for LESBIAN. This sign appears to be moving away from its iconicity related to oral sex. All those who are aware of the existence of this sign label it as the most positive.

A safe sign to use is V_3 (see Figure 13), which is said to be very neutral in describing a woman or group of women who are lesbians. A random survey of people on the Gallaudet campus, not knowing their sexual identity or hearing status, showed that they generally sign LESBIAN with the joint contacting the chin (V_3).

V_4 (Figure 14) was seen as the sign that the majority of gay males and lesbians prefer to use. Some lesbians in the Washington, D.C., area–Deaf and hearing alike–stated that when a straight person signs using the web, (V_1, V_2), they sense a negative stigma attached to that sign and may be unsure of the person's opinions of lesbians. Lesbians who are somewhat more feminine than others prefer to use the tip version to describe themselves. Some of these women call themselves *lipstick lesbians* and associate the web with describing a dyke.

In conclusion, the hearing informants seem to be very aware of the proper ways of labeling a person or a characteristic of a member of the gay community. Those who were members of the gay community felt that they knew the politically correct signs and were confident in interpreting in any situation that called for those lexical items to be used. There was one female interpreter, however, who felt she knew what was appropriate, when, in fact, some of her choices conformed more to those of the straight informants. Register did not prove to be a deciding factor with the informants. We predict that, if a situation is formal and gay persons are in attendance, the speaker, if male, will sign G+chin. However, we must look further into this theory in both gay men and lesbian women. One might assume that if an interpreter is gay, he or she would naturally know the "right" signs to use. As this study indicates, however, it takes only one person to show that this is not always the case.

We are not aware of any studies on this topic that are geared toward interpreters. This area of linguistics is very new to the Deaf Community, and more studies will be beneficial to the interpreting field. Interpreters relay information to many Deaf individuals; therefore, it is imperative that they become aware of changes in the language as they surface.

VARIATIONS OF THE TERM *GAY*

This section deals with the three variations of the lexical item *gay:* G+chin, #GAY, and HOMO-8. Following the same format for LESBIAN, these items are analyzed for production, knowledge, and attitudes. (Keep in mind that letters represent Deaf people and numbers represent Hearing people.)

Gay

When the term *gay* appeared either in the audiotape or with the photos, there were two productions. The first is a *g* or *q* handshape contacting the chin with the index finger and thumb (see Figure 15; henceforth,

TABLE 7. *Sign Usage Produced by Deaf Informants for* Gay

Respondents	G+chin	#GAY	HOMO-8
Straight male	D,E	D,F	
Straight female	J,K,L	K,L	
Lesbian female	H,I	G,H,I	
Gay male	A,B,C	A,B,C	

G+chin). The second variation is a lexicalized fingerspelled sign (Liddell and Johnson 1989) G-(A)-Y[10] (henceforth #GAY), formerly referred to as a fingerspelled loan sign (Battison 1979). Compared to other signs, #GAY was used by the largest majority of each group (for usage, see Table 7).

Some lesbian informants said they refer to themselves as #GAY and not by one of the variations for LESBIAN. Their reason was that this sign applies to both men and women, although they do occasionally call themselves V3 or V4. Most straight people mentioned that they were taught by others (gay people, school system, family) that to say the next variation was negative and that #GAY is considered a more appropriate sign in recent years. This introduces us to the next variant. HOMO-8 (Figure 8) is considered a very derogatory sign for *homosexual*, and no one in

FIGURE 15. G + chin

10. Parentheses are used for letters that are not produced in the lexicalized fingerspelled sign.

TABLE 8. *Knowledge of Variation by Informants for* Gay

Respondents	G+chin	#GAY	HOMO-8
Straight male	1,13,D,E,F	1,13,D,F	1,13,D,E,F,
Straight female	3,4,7,8,11,12,J,K,L	4,8,11,12,J,K,L	3,4,7,8,11,12,J,K,L
Lesbian female	5,6,10,G,H,I	5,6,G,H,I	5,6,10,G,H,I
Gay male	2,9,A,B,C,	2,9,A,B,C,	2,9,A,B,C,

Note: Letters refer to Deaf informants; numbers refer to interpreters.

either the Deaf or hearing group produced this sign. However, some Deaf straight males and one Deaf straight female said they would use this sign among straight friends. It was believed by gay Deaf informants that it should not be used by straight people, regardless of their acceptance by members of the gay community. The use of this sign in ASL is analogous with the English word *fag*. When spoken, the term has very strong negative connotations and is accompanied by a strong negative attitude. Both gay and lesbian informants would use this variant only with other gay persons in the community as in-group teasing or mocking. All interpreters said that they would never use this sign in an interpreting situation unless the speaker meant it to be derogatory. If an individual wants to use this term in a respectful manner, he or she would use either of the compounds mentioned on page 16 or #GAY to include the entire community (see Table 8).

Most people felt that #GAY is a friendly sign when referring to gay males (females, too, in some cases) and the gay community. The gay males from the Lavender Linguistics Conference (1993) stated that #GAY is used to identify others, but, if they were to identify themselves (first person), they would use G+chin. G+chin is seen as an in-group sign; gay men prefer that straight people (either Deaf or hearing) use #GAY. Some gay people take offense when a straight person uses G+chin, and negative connotations are sometimes perceived.[11] Table 9 shows the attitudes of the informants regarding the variations for GAY and HOMOSEXUAL.

There is some controversy in both the straight and the gay communities as to what #GAY refers to. Both hearing and Deaf informants could not agree on a single meaning for #GAY. Most used it to refer to the community, whereas few used it to refer to males only.

11. This is a small pool of informants, and the signs or attitudes shown in this section could be regional variation.

TABLE 9. *Respondents' Attitudes Toward Variants for Gay*

Respondents	G+chin +	G+chin ø	G+chin −	#GAY +	#GAY ø	#GAY −	HOMO-8 +	HOMO-8 ø	HOMO-8 −
Straight male		1,13, D,E,F		1,13,F		D		1,13, D,E,F	
Straight female	3,7,J	K	8,11, 12,L	4,8,11, 12, J,K		L		3,4,7,8, 11,12,J,K,L	
Lesbian female	10	6,I	G,H	5,6, G,H,I				5,6,10, G,H,I	
Gay male		A,B,C		2,9,A,B,C				2,9, A,B,C	

Note: Letters refer to Deaf informants; numbers refer to interpreters. Gay males' and lesbians' responses depend on who is producing the sign, but G+chin and #GAY are both seen as positive by all gay persons.

+ = positive meaning
ø = neutral meaning
− = negative meaning

When we discuss gay issues, social rules tell us to use those signs that carry the least potential for conflict. #GAY carries the fewest negative connotations of all the signs discussed above and crosses the boundary comfortably between gay and straight. V1 is the least emotionally charged of the three variations of the sign LESBIAN.

The trend seen in the use of #GAY versus G+chin and the various locations and meanings for LESBIAN may indicate a wish to use those signs that produce the smallest negative reaction. Rules and social mores define and shape language use of such highly charged material.

CONCLUSION

Our research has only touched upon the issues of variation in ASL related to the gay community. More research with a larger number of informants needs to be done. From our studies at Gallaudet, it appears that the two signs considered most acceptable and most widely used are

12. Mala S. Kleinfeld, the researcher for the hearing interpreters, surveyed some certifyied interpreters at the National Center on Deafness at California State University, Northridge, during a three-week period in July 1994.

#GAY, V3, and V4. However, according to the background forms filled out by participants, people from Washington state, Los Angeles, and other parts of the West Coast do not use #GAY and have a very neutral attitude toward G+chin. Is it possible that these signs are limited to the East Coast or even to Washington, D.C.? Perhaps #GAY is simply a regional variant. Although these are plausible conclusions, the researchers believe that #GAY may become the standard. It is spreading swiftly at Gallaudet and the surrounding area, and as Deaf people travel to different parts of the United States to attend conferences or events, signs of this nature will become more widely used. #GAY had not appeared in the California State University at Northridge as of July 1994 (Kleinfeld 1994).[12] However, interested parties may begin to use #GAY after discussing the research done at Gallaudet.

In both the hearing and Deaf groups, there is some confusion about whether #GAY refers to men only or to the entire community. We are unable to answer that question at this point and do not feel comfortable hypothesizing about its semantics.

Heterosexual people today tend to show more respect and open-mindedness toward the gay community, and from what we have seen, straight people are more willing to ask people in the gay community which signs are preferred. People are becoming more culturally sensitive to and aware of the derogatory connotations of certain signs. For example, according to all the persons in this study, HOMO-8 is no longer acceptable outside of the gay community.

In the section on phonological variations of LESBIAN, we discussed the significant differences in the production of this sign. We suggest that a more concentrated study on this topic would be beneficial for users of ASL.

REFERENCES

Aramburo, A. J. 1989. Sociolinguistic aspects of the Black Deaf community. In *The sociolinguistics of the Deaf community*, ed. C. Lucas. San Diego: Academic Press.

Barnhart, R. E., ed. 1988. *The Barnhart dictionary of etymology*. New York: H.W. Wilson Company.

Battison, R. 1979. *Lexical borrowing in American Sign Language*. Silver Spring, Md.: Linstok Press.

Johnson, R. E. 1994. American Sign Language morphology. Gallaudet University Department of Linguistics and Interpreting. Lecture notes.

Kleinfeld, M. S. 1994. Variation among sign language interpreters: The case of LESBIAN. Unpublished manuscript. Georgetown University, Washington, D.C.

Kleinfeld, M. S., and N. Warner. 1994. Prescriptivism in the deaf community relating to gay, lesbian, and bisexual signs. In *Communication forum*, ed. Elizabeth A. Winston. Washington, D.C.: Gallaudet University School of Communication.

Liddell, S., and R. E. Johnson. 1989. American Sign Language: The phonological base. *Sign Language Studies* 64:195–277.

Rudner, W. A., and R. Butowsky. 1981. Signs used in the Deaf gay community. *Sign Language Studies* 30:36–48.

Woodward, J. 1979. *Signs of sexual behavior: An introduction to some sex-related vocabulary in American Sign Language*. Silver Spring, Md.: T.J. Publishers.

Zimmer, J. 1979. Toward a description of register variation in American Sign Language. *The sociolinguistics of the Deaf community*, ed. C. Lucas. San Diego: Academic Press.

The Pictures Used to Elicit Responses During Data Collection Interviews

The following were shown to the Deaf informants. The pictures came from greeting cards and postcards obtained from Lambda Rising, a gay bookstore in Washington, D.C.

1. two "feminine" women in a bathtub, kissing each other
2. two "butch" women, separate, each looking the part of a tough person
3. two "feminine" women hugging each other
4. one woman with short hair, in men's cotton pants, sitting on a motorbike
5. one woman with short-cropped hair with a widow's peak, wearing a leather jacket
6. two men with a boy in middle, family-like picture, wearing T-shirts titled "gay father" and "gay stepfather"
7. two men, one holding the other, the other holding flowers, both looking at each other
8. one man in high-heeled shoes, lifting a dumbbell
9. one man dressed like a woman with a blonde wig, dress, and frilly scarf

APPENDIX B

Model Lecture

"GAY AND LESBIAN YOUTH IN CRISIS"

Lesbian and gay youth grow up with several strikes against them before they even discover or name their sexual orientation. At a young age, children observe society's dislike and disapproval of homosexuals. Children learn that they may not fill society's expectations of the heterosexual.

Often these youth are afraid to come out in fear of not being accepted because of the negative stereotypes that society has for homosexuals. The community of gays, lesbians, and bisexuals is still a community of people, not sick, unfit weirdos that should be condemned to hell!

It is understandable that it would be difficult for a parent to look at their son dressed up like a drag queen, or to look at their daughter in men's clothing all the time. However, the community goes way beyond just sexual orientation. Being gay is not a bedroom issue only; these people are gay twenty-four hours a day. Within the community there are different groups of individuals. As mentioned earlier, there are the gay men, lesbian women, and bisexuals. There is a lot of controversy in both the heterosexual and homosexual communities as to the validity of a bisexual. Is it just a phase, or can a person actually be attracted to both sexes? We will not attempt to answer this question today.

What about the gays and lesbians in the community who dress a little different? The femmes who are referred to as lipstick lesbians, who often wear dresses, have long hair and long nails and wear makeup and high heels: Do people on the streets label them *lesbian?* Not usually. They are "invisible" and could live amongst straight people without being considered as any different. On the opposite scale, there are the butches who may dress in men's clothing and have short hair. Or the dykes, who may be like a butch, but wear men's cologne, undergarments, body piercing, and may not shave any body hair. These may be generalizations, but without statistics, and we can draw conclusions only on what we have seen.

What about a man who dresses like a GQ model and perhaps has a higher pitched voice than most? Do we call him a fag, fairy, or effeminate? More than likely he will be labeled that way, but how do we know what role he plays in his homosexual relationship? He may be very manly or macho in his personal life and we would never know. In fact, it is really none of our business, just as the people walking down the street would offend you if they made assumptions about your personal life just because you may be different from what they expected.

Part 2 **Multilingualism**

Everyone Here Speaks Sign

Language, Too: A Deaf Village

in Bali, Indonesia

Jan Branson, Don Miller, and I Gede Marsaja
with the assistance of I Wayan Negara

This article introduces the people and sign language of a very special village in north Bali, in eastern Indonesia. Like the community of Martha's Vineyard, this village has a substantial hereditary Deaf population that uses sign language, a language known and used freely by hearing members of the village. Unlike the sign language of Martha's Vineyard, the sign language of this Balinese village has emerged within the confines of the village. Most importantly, the population and the language are alive and well. What follows is an initial report of an ongoing research project into the village sign language and the relationships among its users. The village sign language is referred to in the village as *kata kolok* ("deaf talking"), although *basa kolok* ("deaf language") was also used occasionally. The term *kata* refers to the dynamic act of talking, in contrast to the more abstract concept of language (*basa* in Balinese and *bahasa* in Indonesian).

The study of this language will not only enrich sign language linguistics by providing knowledge of a pristine and thoroughly Deaf sign language, but it also effectively challenges many current orientations toward sign languages and toward the nature of language itself. So, for example, whereas sign language linguists and Deaf people themselves have known without doubt for some time that sign languages are independent languages, the kata kolok, like the Mayan Sign Language reported by Johnson (1994), refutes once and for all statements such as that by Walter Ong (1982) that "The basic orality of language is permanent." His claim that:

Wherever human beings exist they have a language, and in every instance a language that exists basically as spoken and heard, in the world of sound. . . . Despite the richness of gesture, elaborated sign languages are substitutes for speech and dependent on oral speech systems, even when used by the congenitally deaf. (p. 7)

is completely disproved. The sign language of the kolok is not only rich and fully developed as a language but is in no way derived from or dependent on the oral language of the village, despite the fact that it has developed over many generations in intimate association with a hearing community. The languages might well show similarities through the sharing of a common culture, through both being integral to the same sociocultural practice, and through the influence of bilinguals, especially hearing members of Deaf families. The sociolinguistic situation in Desa Kolok ("Deaf Village," as we have called it here and as it is sometimes referred to colloquially) is particularly intriguing. This is not only because it provides an opportunity to study a pristine and thoroughly Deaf sign language but also because it provides for the comparative study of the link between language and culture in two languages, both of which are nonliterate and operate in the same sociocultural environment. One is a sign language, and the other, an oral language. A comparative study in such a controlled environment provides for the possibility of deciphering the impact of different social, cultural, and sensory factors on the form of the village sign language. In an earlier article (Branson and Miller 1992), we discussed the need to question the categories and oppositions that were so often taken for granted in work on sign languages. For example, we pointed out that the opposition between sign languages and sound languages, or between sign languages and oral languages, is too often regarded as absolute. Sign languages and oral languages in nonliterate societies may in fact have more in common syntactically than do oral languages in nonliterate societies and oral languages in literate societies. These issues will only be touched on here but our aim is to lay the groundwork for further papers that investigate these issues in detail. In following through in practice of some of the theoretical issues discussed in detail by Branson and Miller (1992), we demonstrate above all the fundamental need for sign languages to be analyzed within their sociocultural contexts.

Robert Johnson (1994) has outlined the early stages of a study of a Yucatec Mayan village in Mexico where a substantial Deaf population uses a Mayan Sign Language that is known and used by the hearing villagers as well. We will discuss the similarities and differences between the Yucatec Mayan village and the Balinese village. The situation studied by Johnson and his colleagues certainly provides vital comparative material.

DESA KOLOK

Desa Kolok, as we call the village here, is in the foothills of north central Bali, not far from the old Dutch capital of Singaraja. The main focus of agriculture is the production of rice, cassava, maize, turmeric, coconuts and mangoes. The village has two administrative subdivisions (*dusun*)[1] and contains twelve patrilineal, patrilocal clan groups *(dadia).* The 43 kolok are spread through both dusun and eight of the twelve dadia. Although there are only 43 kolok in a village of more than 2,000 people, they have been part of village life far beyond living memory and have a rightful and taken-for-granted role in village life. The kolok children play happily and naturally with the hearing children, all signing. Adult men and women, Deaf and hearing, go about the business of village life together, aware of sensory difference but unperturbed by it and unhampered in their communication with each other, given the ready access to the village sign language.

This does not mean that Desa Kolok is a Deaf paradise. It is the real world. To point to the free communication among villagers, Deaf and hearing, and the ready acceptance of the kolok as full members of the village does not imply that life is unproblematic. It does not mean that all hearing villagers are competent signers. It does not mean that the children and adults do not make fun of each other and that aspects of deafness may not be seized upon as the basis for teasing. But so are many

1. The tern *dusun* was introduced by the Indonesian government in 1979 and replaced the local term *banjar* (see Nordholt 1991). The desa and dusun levels of day-to-day government have little to do with the administration of local customary behavior *(adat)* but are concerned with secular administration, in which the officials act as agents of the state. The level at which the administration of adat appears to be most active is in the banjar councils and in the clan *(dadia)* councils.

other characteristics. For instance, the Balinese have a reputation for poking fun at each other, for laughing at misfortune and for highlighting peculiar physical characteristics in nicknames and name calling (a misshapen mouth, a long nose, and so on). It is a reputation that they seem to live up to throughout the island. But what is important is that the Deaf villagers interact freely and equally with other villagers. Their deafness does not appear to marginalize them socially. It is the widespread access to and knowledge of the kata kolok that mitigate the marginalizing effects of their sensory difference.

THE KATA KOLOK: THE SIGN LANGUAGE OF DESA KOLOK

The sign language of the village is a full-fledged language, extremely rich in the registers associated with village life. The language has evolved entirely within the context of the village over a very long period of time. Memory takes the Deaf population back eight generations to known ancestors (150-200 years), but village mythic tradition takes it back much further to about the eleventh century.

There had been no outside signing influences until a few years ago when one kolok was sent to the Deaf School (SLB Negeri Bagian B—Regional Special School, Section B) in Singaraja. He left after two years. Four very young kolok from the village are currently enrolled at the school, and a former pupil of the school has recently married a village girl. When the former pupil (the man who has married in) uses any signs or fingerspelling from the school, the other kolok dismiss it and see it as irrelevant. At the school, the young villagers stick together and cope with an atmosphere of intense linguistic confusion as the school attempts to introduce Signed Indonesian, Sistem Isyarat Bahasa Indonesia (Indonesian Language Gesture System), developed by a committee and published in 1994 (Departemen Pendidikan dan Kebudayaan 1994). But that is another story. The television news has recently included a small insertion of a Signed Indonesian interpreter in the bottom right corner of the screen. The signing incorporates the large quantities of (one-handed) fingerspelling and the complete lack of facial expression characteristic of signed manual codes. The signing is unintelligible to the village kolok.

The kata kolok employs classifiers, topicalization, and aspect and has a productive lexicon. The use of space is wide and rich, and facial expression is dramatic and complex. Name signs are common and are based on bodily characteristics: a facial scar, protruding mouth, sagging breasts, distinctive hair. Mimesis is well developed.[2] As mentioned earlier, the registers associated with village life are extremely rich, as rich as any sign language. So, for example, discussions about agricultural production, market transactions, family life (childhood, adolescence, marriage, parenthood, parental responsibility, old age, death, burial, and cremation), religious ceremonies, and village affairs inspire intense lucidity. Of fundamental sociolinguistic importance is the fact that even the most iconic of signs are contained by, and thus understandable only within the con-

2. Although this is not the place to launch into theoretical discussions of the way linguists and others have regarded the iconic and mimetic aspects of sign language, the following brief note is important. At least since Ferdinand de Saussure put forward his structural model of language, there has been a range of premises that have become doxic in relation to the way language is understood and defined. Of particular importance has been his assertion that the units of meaning in language (its signs) are arbitrary and that these signs, usually words, have no intrinsic meaning and are not linked to their referents in any necessary way. The arbitrariness of its signs thus becomes the definiens of language.

Some sign language signs have an iconic or mimetic aspect. Where mime is particularly prominent the meaning may be apparent even to someone who has no knowledge of sign language at all. In cases where there is an iconic element, the iconicity may not be apparent until the meaning is known. Here the arbitrary element is certainly present but is mitigated by the visual iconicity of the sign. How then are these iconic and mimetic aspects of sign language affected by doxic assumptions about the arbitrariness of "signs" (used in the Saussurian sense)? A frequent response to the use of mime in particular is to respond with the idea that mime is not language because it is not arbitrary. The same is true of the iconic aspects of sign language. Because mime and iconicity are virtually impossible in sound-based languages in their oral form, apart from onomatopoeia, and absent from most written forms (hieroglyphics and ancient forms of Chinese writing are picture images and thus either direct visual representations or strongly iconic forms), the mimetic aspects of the sign language are often regarded as apart from the language itself, rather than integral to it. To acknowledge that mime was language would somehow devalue its linguistic status. In more extreme cases, because mimesis is integral to sign language, sign language has frequently been defined as not really language, but "gesture," lacking the arbitrariness intrinsic to the concept of language.

text of, the cultural orientations of the villagers. Thus the telling of stories about ducks uses the classifier for a duck in ways that relate directly to the distinctly Balinese way of herding and moving large groups of ducks. The sign for marriage represents the headdress worn by the bride in the marriage ceremony. Other signs reflect the masked figures of religious ceremonies, and others represent culturally distinct aspects of the process of production and consumption. Telling jokes and storytelling in the kata kolok require no prompting and are appreciated by all villagers. The Balinese oral tradition is alive and well through the kata kolok.

THE PLACE OF THE KOLOK IN DESA KOLOK

The kolok are integral to the life of the village, participating fully in its social, economic, political and religious life. The hearing members of the community are referred to as *inget,* and, as one inget villager put it, "kolok + inget = *masyarakat"* ("Deaf + hearing = community"). This use of inget appears to be a village development, a local transformation of a more general Balinese word. It can be translated, like its Indonesian equivalent *ingat,* as "to remember," but it appears in the context of the village to refer to the particular kind of awareness that hearing people have. Linda Connor mentions that the word *inget* was used by the spirit medium Jero "to refer to the experience of returning to ordinary awareness from possession" (Connor et al. 1986). The word *engsap,* usually translated as "to forget," was "used by Jero to refer to some possession experiences" (Connor et al. 1986) and is in fact used widely in Bali to refer to the experience of going into a trance. The connotations of *inget* are therefore much more complex than the English verb *to remember* and indeed much wider and more complex than the Indonesian word *ingat.* What is clear is that the distinction between Deaf and hearing villagers concentrates on dimensions of sensibility, on differences in the way the world is sensed. In Indonesian conversations with village officials and educated villagers, inget tends to be replaced by the Indonesian word for "normal," which introduces a whole new range of connotations associated with normality vs. pathology. These concepts of normality and pathology are not relevant to the inget understanding of, or interaction with, the kolok in the village. There is no sense in which the kolok are regarded as additional to the community and certainly no sense in which they are regarded as pathological. To understand their participation, we must place the villagers and their village within the context of Balinese social and cultural life and in particular in the context of village life in this part of north Bali.

BALI: MYTH AND REALITY

Bali is often pictured as the archetypical paradise, a land of lush picturesque rice terraces and majestic volcanoes, inhabited by a smiling, graceful people naturally oriented toward dance, music, and the arts. Politicians, novelists, Western artists and some anthropologists have helped to construct this singularly romantic image of Bali.[3] The great Indian statesman, Jawaharlal Nehru, referred to Bali as "the morning of the world." In building such an image, the dramatic ceremonial, hierarchical religiosity, and majesty of the kingly courts of south Bali have been presented as the way of life of Bali as a whole, as though there were a singular and uniform Balinese culture, a singular and uniform Balinese way of life. But the reality is, or rather the multitude of realities are, very different. Although Bali is indeed a picturesque and dramatic island, it is by no means socially, culturally, or linguistically uniform. The intensely hierarchical society of the southern plains and foothills contrasts with the essentially egalitarian societies of the north and the hills. The common Balinese language shared by the people of the plains, north and south, contrasts with the very different languages of the so-called Bali Aga (original Balinese) villagers in the hills. The reliance on Brahman priests for religious expertise and ceremonial sanctification, most intense in the south, contrasts with the widespread rejection of Brahman authority elsewhere. And throughout Bali, local interpretations of custom vary markedly from village to village.

In spite of this reality, Balinese religion, society, and culture have often been represented in the literature as uniform and essentially timeless (see, for example, Hooykaas 1973). There has been no appreciation of the nature of practice, of the transformation of culture through the stra-

3. For more general discussion of these images of Bali and their sources, see Vickers 1989.

tegic practice of society's agents as they creatively interpret ideals and relationships and in the process shape and transform their culture. The people we describe here are not predictable role players but rather sociocultural strategists. Their strategic practice is structured but not determined by their sociocultural environment, by what Bourdieu has called their "habitus," their dispositions toward each other and the world around them[4] (see Bourdieu 1991; Miller and Branson 1991). They are neither mechanistic puppets nor calculating game players. Their behavior does not involve obedience to rules; it does not "presuppose a conscious aiming at ends or an express mastery of the operations necessary to attain them and [yet is] . . . collectively orchestrated without being the product of the orchestrating action of the conductor" (1977, 2).

Once we grasp such a view of strategic agents operating through and transforming culture, we can transcend the simplistic schemes that have dominated anthropological and sociological writing. Ideologies are no longer either sets of rules and regulations oriented toward order, or reflections of the material conditions of existence; kinship is no longer a clear unambiguous field of rules and terminologies; and culture is anything but a field of symbols with clear unambiguous referents. In considering behavior in Desa Kolok, such a perspective is vital, for in this Deaf Village we find habitus very different from other villages in the area. The strategic practice of Desa Kolok has generated a very special environment. The dispositions of its villagers toward each other, toward humanity, and toward language have been strategically molded to include the kolok, their language, and their sensibilities as essential features of the community.

MARRIAGE, DESCENT, AND INHERITANCE

Whereas village life is shaped by a wide range of informal social and cultural processes as people strategically orient themselves toward each other through shared, although often controversial, values, some village activities are also formally coordinated through a range of councils

4. Bourdieu's concept of habitus refers to "systems of durable, transposable dispositions, structured structures predisposed to act as structuring structures, that is, as principles of the generation and structuring of practices and representations." (Bourdieu 1977, 72).

associated with different aspects of village life. Membership of councils is available only to married adults, who, when married, become *medesa (krama desa)*, "those who sit as village members." In much of Bali, the individual cannot participate in decision making or inheritance unless made complete through union in marriage with the opposite sex (the *nareswari* principle). Few kolok actively participate on these adat councils despite the fact that they are full and equal members with inget. Those few who do are married to inget wives and use family members as interpreters of spoken conversations. But what is important is the fact that the married kolok are formally full members of the village and are entitled to participate in decision making. As married members of the village, whether married to other kolok or to inget, they are in no sense different in terms of village status. At the dusun level, in the administration of secular village affairs, the kolok are particularly active. As we drove into the village one morning, kolok were particularly active in the coordination and enthusiastic performance of *gotong royong,* community labor on the approaches to the village and in the village streets.

These conclusions are affirmed when we look at marriage and inheritance. There is no stigma attached either to being kolok or to marrying a kolok in Desa Kolok. Marriages between kolok and inget are completely acceptable and were not considered unlucky or problematic by the inget we spoke to. They, like other marriages, are *jodoh,* "God's will." When talking with villagers from Desa Kolok in the company of Balinese from nearby villages, we were interested to note that the villagers from other villages were very surprised that a marriage with a kolok was not considered problematic. These other villagers pushed the villagers from Desa Kolok saying "but surely it must be considered unlucky to have your daughter marry a kolok?" But the inget of Desa Kolok were adamant that it was not and that in Desa Kolok, the kolok were normal and fully-fledged members of the village, valued as such. The villagers from elsewhere could not conceive of kolok being ordinary members of the community. This situation also contrasts with the situation reported by Johnson for the Yucatec Mayan village, where "it is difficult for a deaf man to find a wife. None of the deaf women are married; and they all say it would be impossible to find a husband" (Johnson 1994, 108). In the Mayan village the Deaf community is neither as large nor as strictly localized as in Desa Kolok, and there is no indication in Johnson's report of the generational depth of the deaf population of the Yucatec Mayan village.

The reactions of neighbors and the contrasts with the Yucatec Mayan village confirm that in Desa Kolok, where kolok villagers have been part of the community for generations and thus a normal part of the villagers' experiences from birth, there have developed attitudes and behavior patterns special to the village. The kolok, their language, and their sensibilities have become part of the village experience. In Bourdieu's terms, life with the kolok is integral to the habitus of the villagers of Desa Kolok.

Property is inherited through the male line, passing to all the married sons. In Desa Kolok, whether a father or a son is kolok or inget has no influence whatsoever on inheritance rights. If the eldest son of an inget is kolok, as long as he is married to a kolok or an inget, he will inherit the family home and share in the family property. No matter what the identity of parents or children, kolok or inget, the same inheritance and marriage rules apply.

WORK AND EDUCATION

The kolok work in a wide range of occupations. Some farm their own land, some are sharecroppers *(nyakap),* and some are daily laborers *(buruh),* working on farms, working around the village, and carrying water for gardens from the river. Some women sew. Seven of the kolok men run a business making the food tempeh from soybeans, a business set up with assistance from the state, labeled as aid to the disabled. As far as the state is concerned, the kolok are disabled. As far as the villagers are concerned, the assistance has been warranted because the kolok are poor and their access to education is severely limited.

The village primary school *(sekolah dasar),* SDI, opened in 1951. Basic literacy in Indonesian has therefore been available in the village to the last three generations of villagers. However, the kolok have never gone to the village school. The teachers are state employees who are charged with teaching a set curriculum through the Indonesian language. There has been no place there for the kolok and their language. There is, however, a residential school for Deaf students in Singaraja, established in 1957 by a private foundation and taken over by the state in 1968.[5] None

5. The signing influences in the school are complex, with Dutch, American, and local, though undefined, influences present. The sign language used among the 71 children currently is very different from the kata kolok of Desa Kolok.

of the kolok of Desa Kolok had attended the school until a few years ago. The kolok said that the school had little relevance for them. It took valuable labor away from their families, and, if they did go to the school, they would still end up doing the work they were doing now. Many inget agreed and wished there were some way the kolok could receive basic education in the village like other villagers, but they stressed that the kolok were in no way less intelligent or capable than the villagers who had been to school. They pointed out that the education received by the kolok was received within the family, from neighbors, and through apprenticeship within the village. They were not regarded as uneducated, and there was certainly no sense in which the kolok of Desa Kolok were seen as "dumb."

There is, however, an increasing concern among the kolok of the need for basic literacy if they are to operate small enterprises such as the tempeh production effectively. These concerns reflect the relatively recent importance of secular literacy in the lives of the villagers in general and have particular significance for the quality of kolok participation in the life of their village.

THE CHANGING LINGUISTIC ENVIRONMENT

Since Indonesian independence there has been a massive expansion of formal schooling in Bali and an associated expansion of the assumption of the need for schooling and literacy among the population at large. The literacy associated with formal schooling is very different from the literacy of the pre-Dutch period, a concept of literacy that lives on in certain aspects of Balinese life.[6] Today, the new literacy encompasses more

---

We visited the school on a number of occasions, took extensive video of the signing among the pupils, and are currently involved in a joint research project on the school with STKIP Singaraja. The teachers in the school have picked up their signing in the context of the school. One out of the 22 teachers is Deaf, a former pupil of the school. A dictionary of Signed Indonesian was published last year (1994), and a copy is used as a reference work at the school (Departemen Pendidikan Dan Kebudayaan 1994).

6. For a detailed discussion of the current system of schooling in Bali and of the various literacies operating in Bali, see Branson and Miller (1984, 1991). For a more general discussion of the cross-cultural study of literacy, see Street (1984).

and more of the routine of daily life. Government records, newspapers, printed notices, text on television, and popular reading materials all permeate village life to some degree. Business activity is increasingly associated with the keeping of written records and agreements.

But until relatively recently, the language of everyday interaction for the vast majority of the population was common Balinese, an oral, not a written, language. There was no Indonesian language. And everyday life was organized through an oral, or more correctly, a nonliterate, culture. What effect does the lack of literacy have on the shaping of language and culture? What do we mean by an "oral culture"? First, it must be understood that the use of the term *oral* in this context refers to the fact that languages in these societies are only spoken, not written. Students of these nonliterate cultures have ignored or misunderstood sign languages (see quote from Ong on p. 40) and thus referred to nonliterate cultures as oral cultures. In fact, many of the qualities thought of as distinctive of oral cultures and their languages will be very familiar to students of sign languages and of Deaf culture. Despite his ignorance of the nature of sign languages, Walter Ong, in his discussion of "orality and literacy" (Ong 1982), provides an excellent summary of the distinctive qualities of nonliterate cultures and languages.

Ong begins his discussion of the "psychodynamics of orality" with two basic observations that:

1. without writing, words have no independent existence. "They are occurrences, events" (31);

2. the retention and retrieval of knowledge requires the shaping of language use to assist memory. Thus, oral language has a "mnemonic base," and "mnemonic needs determine even syntax" (34), with the necessary use of set expressions and fixed formulae, heavily patterned. Ong regards this mnemonic base as opening the way to an understanding of "further characteristics of orally based thought and expression" (36).

These "further characteristics of orally based thought and expression" are, according to Ong, as follows: They are "additive rather than subordinative" (37), with all events given equal status. They are also "aggregative rather than analytic" (38), the language characterized by the use of epithets, parallel terms, phrases, and clauses–"not the soldier, but the brave soldier" (38)–using "a load of epithets and other formulary baggage" (38), giving the things and events referred to concrete identity in myth or experience. The focus is on traditional and totalized knowledge: "An oral culture may well ask in a riddle why oaks are sturdy, but it does so to assure you that they are" (39). He adds later: "Colorless personalities cannot survive oral mnemonics. To assure weight and memorability, heroic figures tend to be type figures" (70). The oral culture is, according to Ong, constantly "redundant" or "copious" (39), requiring constant repetition of what has just been said. The language is voluble and fulsome. It is also "conservative or traditionalist" (41) with high energy expended on conserving knowledge.

All these qualities relate to the fact that "oral" thought and expression remain "close to the human lifeworld" (42): "Oral cultures must conceptualize and verbalize all their knowledge with more or less close reference to the human lifeworld" (42). There are no abstract statistics or facts, for all knowledge is anchored in human or quasi-human activity. In its interpretation of experience, particularly linked to its mnemonic base, oral language is "agonistically toned" (43), for "orality situates knowledge within a context of struggle" (44), for example, reciprocal name calling (flyting/fliting in linguistics). In tune with the life world, the stress is on interpersonal relations. The relations are constantly redramatized, given life: "the other side of agonistic name-calling or vituperation . . . is the fulsome expression of praise" (45). Thus "oral" knowledge is "empathetic and participatory rather than objectively distanced" (45), expressive of the need for "close, empathetic, communal identification with the known" (45). Oral "cultures are also 'homeostatic'" (46), for "oral societies live very much in a present which keeps itself in equilibrium or homeostasis by sloughing off memories which no longer have present relevance" (46). Meaning has constantly to be affirmed within real life situations. "The oral mind is uninterested in definitions" (47). Meaning is always actual, in the present. Those aspects of the past that are retained in archaic form are those that are part of the present as such, for example, in the performance of myths, theater, legends, and so on.

Thus above all, oral knowledge is "situational rather than abstract" (49). Ong adds that oral pronouncements are always in context and not simply in word. "The oral word . . . never exists in a simply verbal context, as a written word does" (67). Concepts are constantly contextualized. With regard to abstraction, he also points out that even if people engage in moral and ethical statements via the assessment of the influence of one experience, such as myth or ritual, on other experiences, such as morality in everyday life, the reasoning is still not abstract. There is no linear abstract thinking.

Ong also points to the importance of the bodily hexis. "Oral memory has a high somatic component" (67), stressing the importance of body, gesture, cues, and so on in oral performance, as cues to memory.

The spoken Balinese of the inget villagers and the culture of the village expressed (and still to a very large degree express) these characteristics. Balinese is a very expressive language, full of onomatopoeia (words that sound like the actions or animals they stand for). The use of classifiers is extensive, far more so than in Indonesian, and time is constantly contextualized. The kolok thus operated, and for much of the time continue to operate, in a wider cultural environment in tune with their own language, where visual cues are important, where the drama of everyday life is enjoyed and expressed, where contextualization of knowledge is fundamental, where the present is primary, where memory is basic to social interaction and constantly reinforced, and where abstraction is minimal. The kata kolok, a nonliterate language like all sign languages, coexisted with the spoken nonliterate language of the inget, both operating within the framework of a shared non-literate culture of everyday life, in the case of Desa Kolok, shaped not only by the wider oral culture, but given its own distinctive qualities by the constant interaction between the kolok and inget.

LITERACY IN BALI

What then of literacy? The Dutch did not bring either education or literacy to Bali. Most Balinese lived in social environments with a clear division between a small literate elite and a majority of nonliterate commoners (see Miller and Branson 1989; Miller 1982, 1983). Literature was varied, ranging through poetry, sacred texts, and medicinal texts associated with healing. Above all, literacy was associated with access to power, to the sacred. Whereas the sacred Hindu texts, the *wedas*, were the province of trained Brahman priests alone, including women, literacy itself was not. The stress was on initiation into the mysteries of literacy through a teacher (guru) and was open to non-Brahman and to women as well as men.

The emphasis on being an initiate as opposed to a layman as a precondition for access to literacy and texts highlights a fundamental Balinese belief: Letters have a divine origin and are imbued with divine and supernatural potency. Writing and reading, therefore, are sacred activities that cross the threshold of the divine and the supernatural (Rubenstein 1984, 2).

As we have discussed in detail (Miller and Branson 1989), the Balinese Hindu cosmos embodies the constant struggle between forces of creation, sustenance, and destruction. Human beings tread warily in a world that can move from plenty to plague and pestilence in an instant. Their survival depends upon the control of the awesome powers that surround them, through a maze of ritual in which they are dependent on those with "spiritual power" *(sakti)*, the initiates. Those with sakti are always as potentially dangerous as they are protective and thus to be treated with respect. Integral to their power is thus their very specialized literacy, a literacy not primarily oriented toward the transfer of information but toward the experience and harnessing of power. In this context, literacy is itself not simply, or even primarily, a medium but a contextualized experience, an aspect of an oral, nonliterate culture. Literacy was practiced and understood in terms of the oral culture that encompassed it.

THE NEW LITERACY AND THE TRANSFORMATION OF CULTURE

The reverence for traditional literacy remains strong, a reverence that gives added legitimacy to the architects of modern Indonesian education. But the literacy of these architects of Indonesian modernity is a new literacy. The new literacy of the school, the office, and the media challenges and seeks to transform the oral culture of everyday village life. Literacy is regarded as an abstract medium, devoid of spiritual significance, for the communication of information. Ideally it is available to all. Increasingly it is regarded as a skill that all effective people should have. To be nonliterate is no longer to be part of the vast majority and one with your fellow villagers. To be nonliterate is to be illiterate. Accompanying the spread of literacy is the spread of the national language, Indonesian, the main language of modern literacy in Bali (although Balinese texts in both Balinese and Roman script are increasingly available, and Balinese language is taught in schools as a written language).

For the kolok, access to literacy and Indonesian is severely restricted. In the one school to which their children have access, the Deaf school in Singaraja, the orientation is toward literacy in Indonesian, via oralism, now to be complemented with a manual coding of written Indonesian, a Signed Indonesian that seems certain to generate many of the problems associated with the use of Signed English and other signed versions of dominant written languages in the West (see Branson and Miller 1993). The linguistic and cultural atmosphere within which the kolok operate is therefore changing toward expectations that are increasingly difficult for them. A few of the young kolok are becoming basically literate and are beginning to bring to the village a range of linguistic influences that might well impact upon the indigenous sign language, the kara kolok, linguistically, culturally, and socially. For the moment, however, the language remains relatively untouched by outside influences and is respected and used by the villagers, kolok and inget.

CONCLUSIONS: THE KATA KOLOK AND THE SOCIOLINGUISTICS OF SIGN LANGUAGES

The kolok therefore have the same rights and village obligations as inget and participate with them in the performance of economic, political, and ritual tasks. They are in the main poor and their access to educational opportunities is restricted. Their active and effective participation in the life of the village is integrally linked to the village-wide familiarity with and use of sign language. It is combined with the village orientation toward the kolok as full, unproblematic members of the village with whom they engage in the full range of social relationships, free of the prejudices that characterize approaches to deafness in nearby villages.

The significance of the Desa Kolok situation for the study of sign language and for sociolinguistics in general is enormous. As an autonomous, locally developed, independent language associated with a known hereditary population, the sign language of the village provides an unprecedented case study of the development of sign language. In this regard, the Desa Kolok situation contrasts with the Yucatec Mayan situation, for there the sign language was not confined to the village and its source was not known (Johnson 1994, 106).

The Deaf villagers of Desa Kolok were certainly not waiting for hearing people to come along and teach them sign language. Here in the hills of north Bali, we see the long-term development of a Deaf population that became a valued, integral part of a community. Here the mysterious processes of language development occurred in the medium of sign. Here sign language became a natural medium of communication for Deaf and hearing alike. Here the Deaf villagers emerged from the stigma attached to deafness elsewhere in Bali and became valued and understood friends, relatives, and neighbors. Here we can see what happens when Deaf people are not rejected as pathological but are appreciated both for and independently of their difference. For studies of disability, for studies of the management of difference cross-culturally, the village of Desa Kolok provides a unique case study.

Although historical evidence points to the development of full-fledged sign languages long before the emergence of formal Deaf education (see Branson, Toms, et al. 1995), there remain doubts in the literature about the sources of sign languages and indeed about whether the signing used by Deaf people in the historical record, such as de L'Epée's pupils when he first met them, constituted a language. The historical cases of Deaf communities with distinct sign languages, such as the original sign language of the migrants to Martha's Vineyard from Kent in England in the seventeenth century, or the sign language of the Deaf courtiers at the court of the Turkish Emperor in about the seventeenth century also,[7] remain largely unknown and have the question mark of historical proof hanging over them. The skeptics can call on lack of detailed factual knowledge to support their prejudices. But the sign language of Desa Kolok, the kata kolok, reinforced by the material currently being collected by Johnson in Mexico, leaves us with no such doubts.

With knowledge of the kata kolok, we can turn to sign languages

7. According to Sibscota:
    49. Cornelius Haga Embassadour to the Emperour of the Turks sent thither by the States of the United Provinces did once invite all those Mutes to a Banquet (as I observed from the relation given me by the most Noble and Worthy Dr Brinkins Senator of Hardervick) where there was not a syllable heard yet they did exchange several discourses as is usual at other Treats which the Embassadour understood by an Interpreter on both sides by whose assistance he himself did discourse with the Mutes upon all subjects. (1670, 42-4)

It should be noted that Sibscota's work is in fact a loose translation of excerpts from a 1660 publication by Anthony Deusingen (see the note to the Scolar Press facsimile and Lane 1984, 69 and 424 [fn 11]).

throughout the world, confident of the depth of their history, confident that sign languages can and do emerge naturally within the context of communities where groups of Deaf people have come together. These languages have been appropriated and transformed by hearing teachers, not invented by them.

REFERENCES

Bourdieu, P. 1977. *Outline of a theory of practice*. London: Cambridge University Press.
————. 1991. *Language and symbolic power*. London: Polity Press.
Branson, J., and D. Miller. 1984. Education and the reproduction of sexual inequalities in Bali. In *Women and education*, ed. R. Burns and B. Sheehan. Australia and New Zealand Comparative and International Education Society (ANCIES).
————. 1991. Schooling and the imperial transformation of gender: A poststructuralist approach to the study of schooling in Bali, Indonesia. In *Comparative education*, ed. R. Burns and A. Welch. New York: Garland Press.
————. 1992. Linguistics, symbolic violence and the search for word order in sign language. *Signpost* (summer): 14–28.
————. 1993. Sign language, the Deaf, and the epistemic violence of mainstreaming. *Language and Education* 7(1): 21–41.
Branson, J., J. Toms, B. Bernal, and D. Miller. 1995. Understanding fingerspelling in a linguistic context. In *Sign language research 1944*, ed. H. Bos and T. Schermer. Hamburg: Signum Press.
Connor, L., P. Asch, and T. Asch. 1986. *Jero Tapakan: Balinese healer, an ethnographic film monograph*. Cambridge: Cambridge University Press.
Departemen Pendidikan dan Kebudayaan. 1994. *Kamus Sistem Isyarat Bahasa Indonesia*, edisi pertama. Jakarta: Departemen Pendidikan dan Kebudayaan.
Hooykaas, C. 1973. *Religion in Bali*. Leiden: E.J. Brill.
Johnson, R. E. 1994. Sign language and the concept of deafness in a traditional Yucatec Mayan village. In *The Deaf Way*, ed. C. Erting et al. Washington, D.C.: Gallaudet University Press.
Lane, H. 1984. *When the mind hears: A history of the deaf. New York: Random House.
Miller, D. 1982. The Brahmin/Kshatriya relationship in India and Bali. *South Asia* 5(1): 54–60.
————. 1983. Hinduism in perspective: India and Bali compared. *R.I.M.A.* (December): 36–63.

Miller, D., and J. Branson. 1989. Pollution in paradise: Hinduism and the subordination of women in Bali. In *Creating Indonesian culture,* ed. P. Alexander. University of Sydney: Oceania Monographs.

————. 1991. Pierre Bourdieu. In *Social theory: A guide to central thinkers,* ed. P. Beilharz. North Sydney: Allen and Unwin.

Nordholt, H. S. 1991. *State, village and ritual in Bali.* Amsterdam: VU University Press.

Ong, W. 1982. *Orality and literacy.* London: Methuen.

Rubenstein, R. 1984. The magic of literacy. Paper presented at the Fifth National Conference of the Asian Studies Association of Australia.

Sibscota, G. 1670. *The deaf and dumb man's discourse; or A treatise concerning those that are born deaf and dumb, containing a discovery of their knowledge or understanding; as also the method they use, to manifest the sentiments of their mind.* London: H. Bruges, for W. Crook. (Also available as a Scolar Press Facsimile, The Scolar Press Limited, Menston, England 1967.)

Street, B. V. 1984. *Literacy in theory and practice.* Cambridge: Cambridge University Press (Cambridge Studies in Oral and Literate Culture).

Vickers, A. 1989. *Bali: A paradise created.* Ringwood: Penguin Books.

Part 3 Language in Deaf Education

Bilingual Deaf Education

in Venezuela: Linguistic Comments on

the Current Situation

Alejandro Oviedo

Since 1985 Venezuela has developed intriguing experiments in deaf education. That same year, the Dirección de Educación Especial[1] (henceforth, DEE), the office that directs education policy for the almost fifty public schools for the deaf all over the country decided to change from its oralist practices to a bilingual model, which implied a major transformation whose consequences are still not well understood or defined.

According to DEE's decision, the public schools for the deaf had to eliminate all oralist practices and began to use sign language as the medium of instruction. That decision brought forth two main goals:

1. To ensure that deaf schools became places where children learned sign language as their first language at an early age. Usually these children had found it necessary to wait until they were teenagers

This investigation was supported by grant H221-92-C from La Universidad de Los Andes.

1. I have based certain elements of the study upon decisions made by DEE. I feel it is necessary to make certain comments regarding this source: there are few written essays by DEE on the bilingual model, and none have been published or circulated outside the central office. Thus, I have not documented sources from the DEE. I based my reconstruction of the process used by the Venezuelan Bilingual Model upon data from personal communications maintained since 1989 with several specialists responsible for the Venezuelan Bilingual Deaf Education Policy (Dr. Carlos Sánchez and Professors Miriam de Luján, Carlos Pérez, and Ileana Vázquez). Furthermore, I worked from 1989 until 1992 as a linguistic expert assessing teachers in Venezuelan deaf schools on bilingualism, which allowed me to obtain information directly from the schools.

(when then they would enter into the adult deaf community) to receive full acquisition of their first language.[2]

2. Once deaf children acquired their natural language (sign), they began developing abilities in written Spanish. Literacy in Spanish may be the best opportunity for the deaf community to improve their situation within the Venezuelan hearing society.

In the early nineties,[3] in a study presented at a conference in Mérida, I claimed that the bilingual model was not following the expected path (Oviedo 1991). My conclusion was that, in deaf schools it was possible to recognize two different languages: Spanish, the language of the teachers,[4] and Venezuelan Sign Language (henceforth, VSL), the language used by deaf children. It was also possible to see that the teachers had no command of VSL, and the children had no command of Spanish: our deaf schools were not bilingual. Teachers communicated with children through a contact code, whose basic characteristics were a mixture of VSL's phonological and morphological features with a spoken Spanish syntax.

In this chapter I discuss these claims, focusing on the first obstacle to the development of bilingual deaf education in Venezuela, namely, that teachers do not have a full command of VSL. Therefore, they cannot assume proper educational roles. I contend that the only way bilingual deaf education can achieve its main objectives is to have teachers who are fluent in VSL.

HISTORY

Since its early days in 1958,[5] deaf education in Venezuela has been based upon oralist principles. According to these principles, deafness

2. This was because most deaf children in Venezuela are born to hearing parents, who are unable to give them a natural linguistic environment.

3. Those conclusions were reached in the III Curso de Actualización Linguistics, Mérida, Venezuela, 1991.

4. All Venezuelan teachers of deaf children are hearing. I refer to this in my study.

5. In 1958 the first private educational institution for deaf children was founded–Instituto Venezolano de Audición y Lenguaje (I.V.A.L.). Four years later, the Ministry of Education founded the first public schools for deaf children in Caracas. Since then, initiatives have been made in all of Venezuela for deaf children (Soto 1993).

should not be considered an insuperable problem for integration into the hearing society. It was thought that a deaf person could reach an acceptable proficiency in any oral language if he or she were adequately trained. And as a result, schools directed their efforts toward this goal.

In Venezuelan oralist schools, deafness was seen as a disease, a clinical problem that could be overcome by adequate therapy (Sánchez 1990). Consequently, deaf children received a tiresome training in order to produce acceptable versions of Spanish sounds. This training involved lipreading exercises, whose aim was to give deaf children the spoken Spanish input that deafness denied them. In addition, teachers prohibited children the use of any gestural code because it was seen as detrimental to the process of learning Spanish.

In spite of teachers' efforts, the results of these educational practices were always negative. Only those children with mild-to-moderate hearing losses, which thus permitted them to receive auditory signals, could obtain a certain grasp of spoken Spanish. The rest of the children were never able to accomplish this even with help from adequate technology. Children with more severe hearing losses though not completely deaf developed a deficient oral Spanish, which gave them little possibility of success within the regular educational system. Moreover, since the curricular content of basic education was constantly overlooked in favor of an effort to teach oral Spanish, this situation led to a deficit of basic educational necessities. Furthermore, and most seriously, is the fact that these children were denied full acquisition of their first language throughout their entire school years.

In 1985, following years of studies regarding the status of deaf schools, the DEE radically changed the educational scheme. The new proposition, the Bilingual Model, was inspired partly by a number of investigations undertaken in Europe and the United States, which recognized the natural characteristics of languages that sign languages also possess, and partly by an international educational movement based on studies defending the need to use sign language as a first language for deaf children. In the Bilingual Model, which is different from the oralist conception, the problem of deafness is not clinical by nature, but rather linguistic: The peculiarities of deaf communities are similar to those of any community having a different language. In Venezuela these ideas were backed by a series of investigations carried out by Venezuelan specialists, concentrating especially on Venezuelan Sign Language (VSL) (Pietrosemoli 1987).[6] The Bilingual Model started to be applied with three principal guidelines:

1. Abandon all training practices in the use of oral Spanish.
2. Make VSL the official language of deaf schools.
3. Use VSL to teach written Spanish. The simultaneous use of VSL and written Spanish in deaf schools justified the name *bilingual* in the new educative scheme.

While attempting to achieve these changes, two problems were encountered:

1. All teachers in Venezuela were hearing and were unfamiliar with VSL.[7] All had been educated in the oral method, and their work experience had also been restricted to this environment. Up until this change, sign language had always been considered harmful and was even prohibited in schools.
2. A high percentage of deaf students from these schools was not fluent in VSL. This was because their contact with gestural codes had been, up until that point, limited to brief moments. This occurred, for instance, when teachers failed to watch the children, who then felt free to use gestural communication.

These two facts became the two principle obstacles to reaching the objectives of the new educational model. The solution proposed by DEE authorities was the integration of deaf adults from each city into school activities (social events, sports, and so on) and the hiring of some of them as teaching assistants, thus bringing VSL into the classroom.

The achievement of educational objectives in deaf schools depended on the adoption of VSL as the language for all school activities. This meant that teachers became bilingual in Spanish and VSL and that students acquired VSL as their first language.

This apparently occurred in the first years following the change to the bilingual model. The initial reports of the DEE indicated that, at least in

6. Starting from studies by Lourdes Pietrosemoli (1987, 1989), the name VSL began to be used for this sign language.

7. This problem stems from the fact that all teachers must possess university degrees; this requirement excludes the deaf population, which has not received a sufficient education from the oralist schools, which in turn prevents them from attending universities.

elementary classrooms, students and teachers communicated with each other by means of a gestural system, and they left aside the attempt to develop oral Spanish, with the purpose of concentrating on educational content by means of the gestural system. The expectations of the DEE were that at this initial stage, the teachers would become bilingual, and deaf children would finally achieve a full acquisition of VSL. Once this was accomplished, it was expected that written Spanish would be used in the classroom.

In the early nineties, the DEE conducted a general evaluation of several deaf schools in Venezuela. The study demonstrated that deaf children, in spite of expectations, had not begun to use written Spanish as a learning method. Although they could recognize the significance of certain Spanish words written apart from the general text and could construct basic phrases, these children were not capable of understanding simple literature, nor were they able to coherently codify any type of written information (Sánchez 1993).

CURRENT RESEARCH

I have corroborated the validity of two hypotheses based on the informal observations already mentioned: First, I hypothesized that the gestural code used by teachers was distinct from that used by children. Second, I hypothesized that the gestural code used by children was VSL, whereas the teachers used a hybrid contact code consisting of Spanish and VSL.

This research is based on a comparison of a series of signed narrations from hearing teachers and deaf students from La Escuela Ofelia Tancredi de Corredor, and from deaf adults from the community, narrations that took place in Mérida. All of the narrations were signed, starting with an observation of a fragment from the Charlie Chaplin movie, "The Circus."

The subjects were four teachers, four deaf children, and seven deaf adults. All observed a fragment of the movie and were instructed to relate with signs what scene had been displayed. Each subject narrated the story alone and apart from the group and had no contact with the rest of the group until all had finished. The narrations were videotaped, transcribed, and then analyzed.

The basic limitation of this study is that VSL has received until now no more than partial and isolated descriptions, primarily in Pietrosemoli's (1987, 1989, 1990, and 1991) and Oviedo's (1990, 1991) studies. These studies refer mainly to the typological form of VSL, aside from references to various types of sentences in VSL. As a result, very few criteria are available to help decide whether a particular structure may be classified as corresponding to the VSL norm. For this reason, the field of analysis was restricted and oriented exclusively toward the strategies used in the narrations. This approach allows the presentation of information related to argumental roles (Givon 1984). In addition, Ahlgren and Bergman's (1990, 1992) model of analysis for narrative signed texts for Swedish Sign Language was followed.

The reason for choosing this topic is that, in a current investigation, I have determined that when users of VSL narrate, they use eye contact with their interlocutor to introduce new argumental information. Eye contact also helps to distinguish narrative fragments of the narration from descriptive fragments as well as from the comments of the narrator regarding what is being said. This strategy, which coincides with that described by Ahlgren and Bergman for Swedish Sign Language, was utilized as comparative criteria for the different narrations. Furthermore, I compared the grammatical use of gaze direction in order to introduce references to the arguments into the narration. This tactic, related to the grammatical use of the signing space, has been described thoroughly by Ahlgren and Bergman for Swedish Sign Language (1990, 1992). The present study has determined that these strategies are also used in VSL.

In order to explain this research, I present transcriptions[8] of three fragments that correspond to the first sentences of the narrations signed by a hearing teacher (narration #1), by an eighteen-year-old deaf adult (narration #2), and a ten-year-old deaf child, a student in her third level of elementary school.

The abbreviations used in the transcriptions are as follows:

a = above
+C = eye contact signer-addressee
−C = no eye contact signer-addressee

---

8. The transcriptions initially used equivalent Spanish words or phrases according to the VSL sign. The English translation followed the same criterion: I wrote the semantically equivalent phrases or words in English for each VSL sign.

d = downward
fw = forward
Gaze = gaze direction
l = left
r = right

Narrative 1 (hearing teacher)

1. "The story begins in a place that seems to be a circus."

	+C–C	+C	–C +C	+C
Gaze:	fwr/r	fwr	a/fwr	
Hands:	STORY	BEGIN	CIRCUS	SEEM

2. "Chaplin walks nearby and takes off his cap."

	–C +C	+C –C	+C	–C +C	–C
Gaze:	dr/fwr	dr	fwr	dfw/fwr	dr
Hands:	WALK	CHAPLIN	TAKE-OFF-A-CAP		WALK-NEARBY

3. "There are a lot of people (the public) who see him and

	+C	–C	–C	–C	–C
Gaze:	fwr	r	fw	r	
Hands:	PUBLIC	PEOPLE (x3)	SEE	APPLAUD APPLAUD	

applaud happily."

	+C
Gaze:	fwr
Hands:	HAPPY

4. "They applaud Chaplin. He starts silently to climb."

	–C	–C	–C	+C –C +C –C
Gaze:	r	r /l	d	fwr r /fwr/a
Hands:	APPLAUD	CHAPLIN	SILENTLY	START CLIMB

5. "The people see him with attention and applaud."

	–C –C	–C –C	+C
Gaze:	r ar		fwr
Hands:	PEOPLE (x2) SEE	PAY-ATTENTION	APPLAUD

Narrative 2 (young deaf adult)

1. "A man with a beard is walking."

	–C	+C
Gaze:	r/fw	fwr
Hands:	WALK (prox. r- dist.fw)	MAN BEARD

2. "He greets those around him."

	–C	–C	–C
Gaze:	ra	la	ra
Hands:	GREET (ra)	GREET (1a)	GREET (ra)

3. "He is in a circus."

	+C
Gaze:	fwr
Hands:	CIRCUS

4. "He walks and greets those around him."

	–C	–C	–C
Gaze:	ra	la	d/fw
Hands:	GREET (ra)	GREET (la)	WALK (prox. fw -dist. fw)

5. "He greets those around him again."

	–C	–C
Gaze:	la	ra
Hands:	GREET (la)	GREET (ra)

6. "He bows and walks."

	–C	–C
Gaze:	r	d/fw
Hands:	BOW (fw)(x2)	WALK (prox. fw -dist. fw)

7. "Chaplin walks and greets those around him."

	–C	–C
Gaze:	d/fw	lfw
Hands:	WALK (prox. fw -dist. fw)	GREET (lfw)

8.　"The public applaud him."

	_____ −C
Gaze:	1d _____
Hands:	APPLAUD

9.　"He climbs with a cord."

	_____ −C		_____ −C	_____ −C	+C	_____ −C
Gaze:	ra		ra	fwa	fwr	fw
Hands:	CLIMB (fw-r fw)		CLIMB-WITH-A-CORD

10.　"All is ok."

	_____ +C
Gaze:	fw _____
Hands:	OK!

11.　"Then he walks."

	_____ −C
Gaze:	d/fw _____
Hands:	walk (prox. fw- dist. fw)

Narrative 3 (young deaf girl)

1.　"There is a gymnast..."

	_____ +C
Gaze:	fw _____
Hands:	GYMNAST　　　GYMNAST

2.　"...who climbs with a cord. Then..."

	_____ −C	+C	_____ −C	
Gaze:	1fw	fw	a	
Hands:	CLIMB-	WITH-A-CORD (a)	THEN	

3.　"...walks."

	_____ −C
Gaze:	dfw _____
Hands:	WALK

4.   "Above him someone breaks something."

	−C		+C
Gaze:	ar	fwr	d
Hands:		BREAK [something]	

5.   "The gymnast presents his hat, making a bow."

	−C
Gaze:	r
Hands:	PRESENT-THE-HAT (r)

6.   "An object falls..."

	−C	−C
Gaze:	ar	/dr
Hands:	THROW [something]	

7.   "...into the gymnast's hat."

	−C
Gaze:	dr
Hands:	HOLD-THE-HAT

8.   "The gymnast takes an object out of the hat..."

	−C
Gaze:	d
Hands:	TAKE-OUT-OF-THE-HAT [something]

9.   "...and throws it toward the left."

	−C
Gaze:	l
Hands:	THROW [something]

10.   "The object falls onto the forehead of a person who

	−C
Gaze:	(closed eyes)
Hands:	HIT-THE-FOREHEAD

is under the gymnast."

11.   "This person summons the gymnast."
            –C
Gaze: ar
Hands: SUMMONS (a)

12.   "The gymnast answers, making a bow with his hat."
            –C
Gaze: ld
Hands: BOW-WITH-HAT (. . .)

Comparison of the Narratives

USE OF VISUAL CONTACT BETWEEN NARRATOR AND INTERLOCUTOR ("+C")

The use of visual contact between narrator and interlocutor ("+C") occurs clearly in the discourse of the two deaf narrators as a grammatical strategy. Its functions are to introduce new argumental information and to introduce nonnarrative information in the narration (comments, flashbacks, descriptions, and so on). In the child's narration, the corresponding signs of the definition of the protagonist (narration #2, sentence 1) and the definition of the space of the narration (item, sentence 3) appear to be accompanied in complete duration by "+C." This happens again in the young girl's first sentence (narration #3, sentence 1), when the character of the gymnast is introduced. The introduction of nonnarrative information is found in sentence 10 of narration #2.

Out of these contexts, the deaf narrator systematically avoids eye contact with the interlocutor. When "+C" is registered in other contexts (narration #2, sentence 9; narration #3, sentence 2), it is only a glance, a brief contact that does not last as long as the manual sign.

In the teacher's narration, this systematic use of "+C" does not appear. In sentence 1, for example, this characteristic accompanies manual signs that correspond to verbs in their total duration and appears at least in part during the nominal signs (STORY and CIRCUS) of the same fragment. This scheme is different from that found in the sentences that follow (in the verbs of sentences 2 and 3, for example). They are also accompanied by brief interrupted "+C" (such as TO WALK and TO TAKE-OFF-THE-CAP) or appear marked as –C (in the verbs TO WALK-NEARBY, TO SEE, and

TO APPLAUD). In regard to the same pattern, the nominal information does not follow the initial scheme (consider, for example, the distinctive values of "C" for the names CHAPLIN, PUBLIC, HAPPY, and PERSON [sentences 3 and 4]).

GRAMMATICAL USE OF GAZE DIRECTION

Such differences of the use of the characteristic "+C" have other important grammatical consequences that can be observed in the texts. I have verified that, in narrative VSL texts, standards are demonstrated that are similar to those described by Ahlgren and Bergman (1990, 1992) in narrative texts of Swedish Sign Language. In narration #2, for example, the deaf adult defines her protagonist with "+C." From the beginning of the spatial placement of this character, she used gaze direction (and also signs of modifiable movement) to define the placement of the narration's secondary characters in relation to the space occupied by the protagonist. In the selected fragment, the second character, the public (mentioned for the first time), plays a passive role in sentence 2 due to the orientation of the gaze and the hands (in the verb GREET). The subject in sentence 2 is still the "MAN-BEARD" (Chaplin), the one who greets the public. The narrator is aware of this because there was no indication that the subject had been changed. He greets the people found above and all around him (right to left). This operation permits the narrator to locate the public. In sentence 8, the public plays an active role by means of the verb APPLAUD. The gaze is then directed downward because this appears to be the relative location of Chaplin (the object of the applause) with respect to the public, who then applaud. The change of gaze direction implies a change in the active role, which is not required to be manually lexicalized.

In narration #3 by the young girl, one observes similar strategies. In sentence 1 of the transcribed fragment, the gymnast is introduced as the protagonist by "+C," which accompanies that sign. The narration will thus be arranged from the gymnast's perspective. Starting from this point of view, the rest of the participants will be located (and defined) in the story. When, in sentence 4, the narrator looks upward, she is locating above her another character (marked immediately with "+C") in a position relative to the gymnast. That other character is the one who

9. In the movie, Chaplin is high up on the post, waving to the public, before he begins walking on the tightrope. While waving a hat in his hand, a monkey—

performs the action TO BREAK (something).[9] Then, the gaze is directed downward (where the gymnast is located in relation to the character who breaks something). As a result, the gymnast is again put in the position of the subject and then performs the verb TO PRESENT-THE-HAT (r) (sentence 5) with the gaze toward the right. Then the gaze is directed upward again, just above the place where the hat is located; meanwhile, the hand indicates that something is thrown from this position and falls on the hat (dr) toward where the gaze is simultaneously directed (sentence 6). The upward gaze indicates that the object was thrown by the same character who is above the gymnast. The gaze remains above the hat in the following sentence (7), whose subject is the gymnast (compare with sentence 5). The subject takes an object out of the hat and throws it toward the left. In sentence 10, the object falls onto the forehead of another character, located below and to the right of the gymnast. This is defined by the trajectory of the object that comes from the right and hits the other character's forehead and by the victim's later statement to the person above him and to his right (sentence 11). In sentence 12, the look is directed to the left and bottom (ld). The sign BOW-WITH-HAT is made, which indicates that it is the gymnast who apologizes to the victim for dropping the object.

Due to the grammatical use of gaze direction in VSL, there is no need to lexicalize manually all arguments of the narration. Rather, it is enough to establish a particular place for them in space, a position relative to the protagonist (if located in the same narrative space as in the selected fragments). Each subsequent time, it is necessary to refer to them, orienting the gaze toward their location(s).

In the teacher's narration, the information related to the arguments is introduced following other strategies. At the beginning of the narration, for example, the introduction of the public is lexicalized with two manual signs: PUBLIC and PEOPLE. The gaze is directed then toward the right, which allows a VSL-user to suppose that the public is located in this position (to the right of the protagonist, Chaplin). In turn, the VSL-user would expect to find Chaplin to the left of the public. However, the gaze direction during the signing of the verbs TO SEE, TO APPLAUD, and PAY-ATTENTION, (sentences 3 and 5) is oriented to the right; therefore, there is no formal mark to indicate that Chaplin (who should be found to the left) is the

---

above him and on the same post—breaks a piece of fruit and lets it fall down into the hat.

object of those verbs. The teacher does not make use of the gaze direction to introduce arguments; as a result, she must lexicalize them manually. Thus, each time the subject of the sentence changes, she must articulate the corresponding sign: CHAPLIN (sentences 2 and 4) and PEOPLE (sentences 3 and 5).

The teacher's discourse makes evident an incomplete knowledge of the grammatical strategies of VSL. Unable to exploit fully the syntactic uses of gaze direction and eye contact with the interlocutor, she uses the grammatical strategies of Spanish (mention of complete nominal phrases or pronouns) for the introduction of arguments.

ADDITIONAL RESEARCH

Regarding the obstruction of information by the contact code, I performed a series of tests to establish in some form the measure of this roadblock between students and teachers. The analysis of one of these tests is enlightening.

The story as transcribed was read by a teacher from the school, who later signed a version of the story in front of a group of three of her fellow teachers and four deaf children.

A Road Full of Mud

Two priests walked together one time through a road full of mud. It had rained heavily for hours.

When arriving at a certain point, they encountered a pretty girl dressed in a white silk dress. The girl tried to find a point where she could cross the road but could not find it.

One of the priests, seeing a place, told the girl "Let's go" and, lifting her in his arms, carried her to the other side of the mud.

The other priest, who observed everything, remained silent, and both priests immediately continued on their path. They walked a few hours more in the rainfall until they found a place where they could stay for the night. Then the priest who had seen his friend help the girl could not stand the silence anymore and exploded: "We as priests must not get close to women especially if they are young and beautiful. Why did you help her cross the road?"

His partner hearing this answered simply: "I left the girl there. But I ask, 'do you still carry her with you?'"

Each person who had witnessed the signed version of the story then retold their own version. The children were filmed using VSL, and the teachers used written Spanish. The following transcriptions exhibit a considerable difference between the re-told versions and the original story:

The Teachers' Versions

"A child." A child was found in a puddle of very dirty water. Then a priest arrived and said, "Why were you there?"[10] Later a woman in a white soft dress arrived and took away the child. The priest asked the woman, "Why did you take the child away?" and she answered, "To clean and take care of him." The priest was taken by surprise by the woman's attitude.

2

"The story was about a priest.

A mommy went shopping with her little children, but it was raining. She began to walk down the street and saw a dress. She said, 'How pretty.'

The lady bought a lot of clothes. She asked help from a gentleman because the suitcase was very heavy."

3

"November

A story.

This story is called...

Once upon a time a priest who crossed a road came upon a river and saw that it was very dirty. At this moment a woman appeared who had to cross the river. The priest kindly offered his help, and he said it did not matter, he would carry her in his arms. And so he did. Later on the same road, two priests were walking, and they came upon

10. The translation was attempted in its original state, which, because of simple grammatical errors, was difficult to translate and, as a result, is difficult to follow.

another person who wanted to cross the river, and both offered their help. One asked the other, why did he always help people cross the river, and he answered, because finally, he had already died."

Two of the Children's Versions

I

"Went...how do you say? a priest in a road, seeing, looking for something."
__?__
GO NAME   PRIEST   GO   SEE.r ROAD   SEE.r   LOOK-FOR.r-fw

"The road was dirty. It was raining. The priest's dress was dirty. The priest was looking for something."
ROAD   DIRTY   RAIN   DRESS   DIRTY LOOK-FOR.r-fw-l

"He said: My dress is dirty. He was looking for something."
DIRTY   DRESS   DIRTY SAY LOOK-FOR. r-fw

"Then the priest got another priest in the dirty road."
INDEX.fw   PRIEST   OTHER PRIEST SEE OTHER ROAD DIRTY

"He was looking at dirty road. It was raining very much."
_____!_
GO   SEE   DIRTY   RAIN   SO-MUCH

"One priest saw the other one. The end."
SEE   OTHER PRIEST   END.

2

"There was a woman with a dress on a road. A priest..."
ROAD   WOMAN   DRESS   PRIEST

"I forgot it ... The priest bore in silence"
FORGET (x3)   BEAR   SILENTLY

"He bore. He carried the woman in silence, bearing."
BEAR   CARRY.r-l   SILENTLY   BEAR

"The priest talked about that. The end."
SAY   END.

CONCLUSIONS

The analysis of the narratives corroborates my initial presuppositions. First, the sign code utilized by Mérida school teachers is different (in important characteristics) from the code used by deaf students. On the other hand, narrative strategies used by deaf school children correspond to those of deaf adults in Mérida, thus proving that these children share the same sign code (VSL) used by deaf adults.

From these conclusions, I make two clear statements on the linguistic reality that exists today with regard to the Bilingual Model in the Mérida Deaf School:

1. VSL has been acquired by the student body at the school. This verifies one of the principle hypotheses that the DEE had formulated by implementing the Bilingual Model: namely, that deaf children adapt fully to a natural sign language, which was not guaranteed by the oralist model.

2. The teachers have not developed a command of VSL that permits them, in a restricted definition of bilingualism,[11] to be accepted as bilingual individuals. Instead of assimilating VSL, the teachers seem to have formed a distinct sign code, which may be classified as a "contact code" (characterized by Lucas and Valli 1989) that intermixes Spanish and VSL grammatical elements.

11. With this we want to make clear that we followed a definition of bilingualism relative to the ability to produce discourse equally acceptable in whatever languages are considered (Bloomfield 1933; Weinrich 1974; Hormann 1972; Romaine 1989). A less restricted definition, (such as the proposal by Mackey 1968 cited in Romaine 1989), stated that the existence of different levels of bilingualism would allow classification of the teachers as "bilinguals of a certain level," according to their knowledge of grammatical components of VSL. This is not the place to develop an argument with respect to the notions of bilingualism. We opt to assume a restricted definition because, in order to perform the necessary duties that correspond to the role of teachers in the school, teachers have not attained an acceptable command of VSL. In spite of their abilities to use basic sign language skills, they are not bilingual insofar as what the new education model requires.

The use of this contact code constitutes a fundamental obstacle in order in achieving the two objectives that pursue the bilingual model of deaf schools in Venezuela: offering regular education in sign language to deaf children and helping them become efficient users of written Spanish. The obstacle exists because the contact code seems to solve basic communication problems (situations), such as those that involve giving orders or simple instructions. Therefore, because teachers and deaf children appear to communicate, these schools continue to exist, and, as a result, only an apparent—not an actual—completion of the schools' basic duties has been achieved in recent years. In addition, the contact code impedes, by virtue of its characteristics, teachers and children understanding each other when it is necessary to transmit more complex kinds of information than orders and simple instructions; all scholarly curricula contain such complex information.

In accordance with the earlier analysis, an important difference between VSL and the teachers' contact code is that the latter makes no use of certain nonmanual signals that introduce argumental information (therefore, not utilizing grammatical space). The teachers, in agreement with Spanish grammar, opt to lexicalize this information manually. This is, in my judgment, an insuperable linguistic obstacle that prevents deaf children from understanding their teachers. And if deaf children do not understand their teachers adequately, the teachers are prevented from performing their main role in the school. This will continue to occur as long as the flow of information between the teachers and deaf children is obstructed.

REFERENCES

Ahlgren, I., and B. Bergman. 1990. Preliminaries on narrative discourse in Swedish Sign Language structure. In *Current trends in European sign language research: Proceedings of the third European congress on sign language research*, ed. T. Vollhaber. Hamburg: Signum-Verlag.

———. 1992. Reference in narratives. In *Perspectives on sign language structure: Papers from the fifth international symposium on sign language research*, ed. I. Ahlgren, B. Bergman, and M. Brennan. Durham, England: The University of Durham and International Sign Linguistics Association.

Bloomfield, L. 1933. *Language*. New York: Holt.

Givon, T. 1984. *Syntax: A functional-typological introduction.* Amsterdam: J. Benjamins.

Hoffmann, C. 1991. *An introduction to bilingualism.* London: Longman.

Hormann, H. 1977. *Psicología del lenguaje.* Madrid: Gredos.

Johnson, R., S. Liddell, and C. Erting. 1989. Unlocking the curriculum: Principles for achieving access in deaf education. Washington, D.C.: Gallaudet University. (Pietrosemoli [1990] contains a Spanish translation.)

Liddell, S. 1996. Tokens and surrogates. In *Perspectives on sign language structure: Papers from the fifth international symposium on sign language research,* ed. I. Ahlgren, B. Bergman, and M. Brennan. Durham, England: The University of Durham and International Sign Linguistics Association.

Lucas, C., and C. Valli. 1989. Language contact in the American deaf community. In *The Sociolinguistics of the deaf community,* ed. C. Lucas. San Diego: Academic Press.

Oviedo, A. 1990. Ser o no ser en Lengua de Señas Venezolana: Estructura de las oraciones con verbos estativos de la LSV. (mimeo)

———. 1991. La interacción lingüística en las escuelas de sordos venezolanas. (mimeo)

———. 1992. *La lingüística de las lenguas de señas. Clave (1).* Caracas: Asociación Venezolana para la Enseñanza del Español como Lengua Extranjera. ·

Pietrosemoli, L. 1987. Evaluación sobre el lenguaje gestual. (mimeo)

———. 1989a. I Seminario de Lingüística de la LSV. Materiales de apoyo. (mimeo)

———. 1989b. *Señas y palabras.* Mérida: Universidad de Los Andes.

———. 1990. *El aula del sordo.* Mérida: Universidad de Los Andes.

———. 1991. La Lengua de Señas Venezolana: Análisis lingüístico. (mimeo)

Romaine, S. 1989. *Bilingualism.* Oxford: Blackwell.

Sánchez, C. 1990. *La increíble y triste historia de la sordera.* Caracas: Ceprosord.

———. 1993. La adquisición de la lengua escrita sin mediación de la lengua oral. (mimeo)

Soto, M. C. 1993. Jornadas XXVI Aniversario del Instituto Zuliano de Audición y Lenguaje. (mimeo)

Weinrich, U. 1974. *Lenguas en contacto.* Caracas: Universidad Central de Venezuela.

What's a Clock? "Suppose the Alarm Lights

Are Flashing . . .": Sociolinguistic and

Educational Implications of Comparing

ASL and English Word Definitions

Sara Schley

With the theoretical and applied attention being given to bilingual/
bicultural (hereafter, BiBi) education of Deaf students today, one must
consider how American Sign Language (ASL) and English are used in
sociolinguistic terms before determining how to implement bilingual curriculum materials. Any two languages display differences in how and
when they are used given different contexts of social interaction. In the
case of Deaf BiBi education, these differences are arguably a larger factor as the two languages involve separate modalities (i.e., written English
and signed ASL, which to date has no formal accessible written version).

This chapter addresses the issue of prerequisite abilities in acquiring
literacy skills; that is, developing communicative competence across a variety of interactional contexts. Moreover, the question of sociolinguistic
differences across both ASL and English are considered, using a context
of interaction frequently employed in classrooms–defining words.

Although many measures claim to assess language proficiency, much
current research supports a componential approach to defining and
assessing language proficiency (Snow 1987; Snow and Dolbear 1989).

This work could not have been completed without the help of Nancy Vincent,
Beth Baron, and Tina Neumann. The National Council of Teachers of English
and the U.S. Department of Education, Office of Special Education and Rehabilitative Services (#H023B20027) provided invaluable funding. Finally, I am
indebted to the community of a bilingual/bicultural school for Deaf children.

Under this view, different language tasks demand different types of skills. For example, compare the following two situations:

- A child is asked to define a word for someone sitting next to her at the kitchen table.
- She is asked to give a dictionary definition of a word by her classroom teacher.

The terms *contextualized* and *decontextualized* have been used (e.g., Snow 1983) to refer to language skills highlighting the distinction between these two interactional contexts. Decontextualized language tasks demand relatively little reliance on a present audience and instead rely on shared knowledge among speakers of the language but not shared knowledge of the physical or social context of the speaker. Examples of this could be giving an academic lecture, writing a paper, delivering a report, or giving a dictionary-like definition of a word. Contextualized tasks, on the other hand, require more reliance on the present context and shared knowledge of the current situation. For example, diary entries are contextualized productions, as are casual conversations, notes to oneself, dialogue journal writing, and on-line computer interactions. These terms are not meant to imply that a language sample can be entirely without context; they refer instead to the distinction between more planned forms of language and less planned forms of language.

Results presented here consider word definitions in both ASL and written English. In English, the task of giving word definitions can be interpreted in either a contextualized or a decontextualized manner. For instance, if a father asks his child to tell him what a clock is, she could simply point her finger at the wall (where there is a kitchen wall clock) and say "That's a clock." This response would be communicatively adequate but contextualized.

However, this response would perhaps not be appropriate if the question were asked at school by the child's teacher, in the context of a vocabulary test where the children had previously looked up the meaning of the word *clock* in a dictionary. In this latter situation, the teacher would be expecting a more decontextualized response, one that conformed more to a dictionary-like format, such as "a clock is a machine that tells time, but you don't wear it on your wrist."

A definitions task was used in a study of ASL and written English proficiency of Deaf children attending a program that is in the process of implementing a bilingual/bicultural curriculum. The purpose of this research is to evaluate Deaf children's productions of word definitions across contexts of interaction that may have quite different sociolinguistic influences depending on the language of production (ASL versus written English).[1] It is possible that the sociocultural contexts of language use are quite different for ASL discourse practices and for English. For example, some ASL narratives are a well-developed distanced form of discourse, but such a strong oral storytelling tradition does not exist among many users of English. On the other hand, ASL has rarely been used to explain highly technical fields of information, but such is commonly done in English. Sociolinguistic differences could influence whether these tasks are similar in form and function across both ASL and English.

PREVIOUS RESEARCH

The definitions task in particular has a fairly long history of use in the developmental literature (Snow 1990; Snow, Cancino, De Temple, and Schley 1991). Younger children tend to give functional definitions (Litowitz 1977), and they can also include anecdotal descriptions of the word. As children get older, superordinate categories begin to emerge, and the definitions become more complete and abstract (Watson 1985 provides a good review). Children's definitions also start conforming more frequently to distinct linguistic forms and look more like formal dictionary definitions.

Snow and her colleagues have tracked hearing children's skill at giving definitions in some detail. Several papers have been published that discuss cross-language and bilingual ties, ties to school performance, and communicative adequacy of both contextualized and decontextualized definitions (Davidson, Kline, and Snow 1986; Snow 1987, 1990; Snow, Cancino, De Temple, and Schley 1991; Snow, Cancino, Gonzales, and Shriberg 1989; Velasco 1989). This body of research suggests several things:

1. In Schley (1994), comparison is made between these Deaf subjects' performance in written English (their L2) and the performance of hearing nonnative English-speaking children. Although the hearing children and the Deaf children are not fully comparable as nonnative English speakers, the hearing sample provides a more appropriate comparison group than would a sample of native English-speaking children.

1. Giving formal dictionary-like definitions is a complex task, one not often mastered until fairly late (Snow 1983, 1987; Snow, Cancino, Gonzales, and Shriberg 1989).
2. Very informal contextualized definitions can be perfectly adequate in their communicative intent; consistently producing informal definitions is not associated with low communicative adequacy of the definitions (Snow 1987).
3. The ability to give formal definitions (and to use decontextualized language) is associated with school achievement and literacy. For example, children with a higher percentage of formal definitions (vs. informal definitions) also tend to do better on language subsections of the California Achievement Test (or C.A.T.), and children who have a lower percentage of formal definitions tend to score lower on the C.A.T. (Snow, Cancino, Gonzales, and Shriberg 1989). Similar results were found using the California Test of Basic Skills, or C.T.B.S. (Velasco 1989).
4. There are cross-language ties between skill at using decontextualized language and academic achievement; however, this holds true especially when the two languages are curricular languages. Simply having a high exposure to a language at home does not necessarily predict school success in that language. Instead, having school exposure to the second language predicts better performance on decontextualized language tasks and on literacy achievement (Davidson, Kline, and Snow 1986; Snow 1990; Snow, Cancino, De Temple, and Schley 1991). Malakoff (1988) also found higher performance in bilingual children on some tasks performed in the school language than on tasks performed in the home language.

The present research introduces yet another perspective on decontextualized and contextualized language skill in bilinguals. Here, the two curricular languages are ASL and English, a bimodal as well as bilingual case. Sociolinguistically, ASL and English are used in some different interactional contexts. Given that ties between componential skill and school achievement are fairly well documented in other groups of bilinguals, results of this study will inform the relatively new field of bilingual/bicultural Deaf education, where there is a paucity of research (Dragsow 1993).

Educationally, the request to define words "like in a dictionary" does not hold the same meaning in an ASL classroom context as it does in an English classroom. The definitions task was originally designed to assess how closely children can approximate a dictionary-like form; no such parallel exists in ASL. Although there are ASL dictionaries (e.g., Jamison 1983; Sternberg 1981, 1987; Stokoe, Casterline, and Croneberg 1976) in which lexical items are based on ASL formational parameters and also dictionaries for other sign languages (e.g., British Sign Language, or BSL [Brien 1992]), they are English-to-ASL translation dictionaries (or BSL, in one case). They are guides on "how to sign a word written in English." As such, they are organized in order of the spelling of the English words rather than on any distinct ASL formational parameter. Several multimedia versions of bilingual ASL/English dictionaries are currently in development (Cokely 1995; Hoffmeister 1994; Wilcox 1994). Some dictionaries are now being developed according to bilingual principles, rather than using an organization based purely in English (Brennan et al. 1993). Nonetheless, there are no ASL dictionaries in which the words are considered linguistically in the same language. Moreover, definitions in ASL discourse have not been studied previously.

What, then, constitutes an ASL definition? Four adult fluent ASL users were consulted in order to address this question. They responded that the norm was to give highly contextualized descriptions of meaning. For example, in the case of describing a concrete object, one would commonly point to an object, remind the audience of a situation in which the item was used, or give an example of what it does or how to use it. This chapter's title example is, in fact, such a definition; it is perfectly appropriate and expected in ASL discourse style.[2] All four, when pushed for more explicit descriptions of important components of an ASL definition, discussed the importance of mentioning functions or descriptive features of the word, and perhaps pointing to the object if one is present. When pushed even further, two of the four informants gave more and more English-like forms of definitions, explicitly switching into less ASL-like signing and giving syntactically correct English definitions.

2. Because this chapter has been written in English rather than ASL (which admittedly would be quite a feat), the title example has been translated into English.

The present study is interested in Deaf children's bilingual productions of word definitions. The following questions are asked in this study:

- Semantically, what do the children's ASL definitions and their English definitions look like?
- Syntactically, are there dictionary-like and contextualized definitions in their ASL productions? in their English productions?

The results are discussed in terms of sociolinguistic and educational implications.

Methods

This study's methodology followed that of previous work on contextualized and decontextualized language abilities, with adaptations made where appropriate to consider differences in working with Deaf children as well as with a nonwritten language.

Subjects

Twelve Deaf 9- to 11-year-olds were tested. All were students at one of the handful of schools that have started implementing a bilingual education curriculum for Deaf students. At this school, a commitment to the bilingual/bicultural approach began in the spring of 1989; it has involved in-service training for teachers and administrators, integrating ASL into the classroom as well as Deaf teachers and aides, no voicing of English while signing, using ASL or ASL-like signing, ASL training for nonfluent parents and teachers, and the appointment of a Deaf bilingual/ bicultural specialist. All subjects were severely to profoundly deaf (the average hearing level across both ears ranged from 85 dB to 117 dB). Only one child had Deaf parents, and an additional two children had Deaf siblings. Nine of the subjects were girls; three were boys. Three of the children had been registered at the school for two to three years, four had been there for six to seven years, and the remaining five children had been registered there for eight to ten years.

Nine of the subjects were tested in the spring of 1992; two years later, a second cohort of six children was tested, three of whom were included in this analysis (bringing the analytic sample size to a total of 12 Deaf children).[3] In part, the second cohort was included to increase the sample size, and in part, this dual-cohort approach helped verify that the analytic approach (detailed below) was valid.[4]

Task

Children were asked to give definitions of six nouns. This task was originally designed to determine the degree to which the children's definitions reflected an adult norm of dictionary-like definitions. Giving a dictionary definition of a word requires considerable syntactic and semantic skill, whereas salient and culturally specified information is given in a specific syntactic format. Doing this well in English demonstrates proficiency in using one kind of decontextualized language. For example, in English, instructions for the word knife were "can you tell me what the word *knife* means?" In ASL, comparable instructions were:

$$\overline{\text{KNIFE WHAT MEAN}}^{\text{t}}{}^{5}$$

3. Only the first three of the six children in the second cohort were included in this analysis. One of the three children not included was absent on two days in which the English productions were collected, and another attempt could not be scheduled. The other two children, although they completed the tasks in ASL, expressed extreme displeasure at having to do the tasks; in particular, they did not wish to be videotaped. Although their productions were collected, it is the opinion of this researcher that their wishes not to participate should have been respected. Also, the comparability of their productions to those of the remaining subjects is in question given their resistance.

4. In other words, analyses were initially run on the first cohort of nine children. When data from the second group of children were added, the means of all variables changed very little. This suggested that the means of the various measures were valid statistical summaries.

5. Transcription conventions are detailed in Appendix A. The *t* above the gloss of the signed production indicates that the utterance was topicalized. The horizontal line above the glossed signs indicates the duration of the topicalization.

The nouns were selected from the first (easiest) ten words of the WISC-R vocabulary subsection (Wechsler 1958). Most children were familiar with the words, and in cases in which they did not know a word, that definition was excluded from the analysis.

Procedures

Each child was tested individually in both ASL and English. In the ASL condition, a native signer elicited the language samples. She and each subject sat across from each other, and the experimenter videotaped the sessions. Language samples were transcribed in gloss form with some syntactic and nonmanual features encoded on the transcript (see Appendix A for transcription details). Many of the measures were coded directly from the transcripts, and a few measures were coded directly from the videotapes (the coding system is discussed in the following section).

For the English versions of the task, the experimenter sat at a desk in one cubicle of a central section of the school library; the child sat at a desk in a separate cubicle. Each cubicle contained a TTY so that both interlocutors "talked" (via typed interactions) back and forth to each other. Past research shows some precedent for using TTYs to look at Deaf children's language abilities (Johnson and Barton 1988; Schley 1991a, 1991b, 1994). This mode of communication was quite normal for most of these Deaf subjects, as natural as using a regular telephone is to a hearing 9- to 11-year-old. In addition, with a TTY the sessions are quite interactive: The language used was written English, but it was on-line and interactive English.

The experimenter's TTY recorded the testing session on a paper printout. Transcripts from the testing session were made by transferring the language productions to a computerized file using a modified version of the CHAT transcription system (MacWhinney 1991), a system developed to facilitate the sharing of databases of child talk (i.e., the Child Language Data Exchange System project, known as CHILDES).

Coding and Analytic Approach

A native English speaker fluent in ASL coded the English transcripts, and a highly proficient ASL user fluent in English coded the ASL language samples. The research coordinator verified each transcript and the coding. All disagreements about coding were resolved between the research coordinator and the research assistants before analysis of the data. The coding system for this task was designed to tap into the following areas:

1. A *semantic analysis* for both the ASL and English definitions included a detailed examination of their specific semantic components: definitional and descriptive features, synonyms, functions, examples, and comparisons. A measure of communicative adequacy is also included here. A coding manual is included in Appendix B, outlining these coding procedures in more detail. An overall semantic quality score was generated by summing the number of semantic features included in each definition (e.g., naming definitional or descriptive features, stating examples of use or functions, mentioning comparisons or synonyms).

2. A *syntactic analysis* was performed differently for ASL and English definitions. For ASL definitions, the analysis included a measure of ASL topic markers and restrictive relative clause constructions.[6] These features were chosen as units of analysis for two reasons. In a structural way, these linguistic features correspond most closely to English formal definitional syntax, in that the topicalized information is subsequently restricted, much like what occurs in a dictionary-like definition. Functionally, these features can serve to contextualize a description of a referent and might be expected to occur if children's definitions are highly contextualized (if they have mastered control of these linguistic features). So, although these features might occur if children were transferring knowledge about English definitional syntax, they might also occur if the child were producing adult-like ASL definitions (as adult native signers suggested that ASL definitions are contextualized).

Because the children were being tested at school (rather than in a more informal setting), they might have interpreted the task as one in which English-like forms of signing were more appropriate than ASL. If they did, this could result in either (a) using English-like signed forms in their

6. For an argument that these restrictive relative clause markers are actually topic markers, see Coulter (1983). The semantic function of such relative clauses is similar to that of English restrictive relative clauses. Syntactically, they are in some ways more similar to topic markers (Aarons 1994).

productions of definitions, or (b) using ASL constructions that are functionally similar to English decontextualized forms, such as topic-comment structure or restrictive relative clauses. The syntactic analysis was designed to answer the second possibility. To determine whether some children interpreted the task as one in which English-like forms were the target, each definition was analyzed with regard to how closely it followed distinct signed English dictionary format. Only one of the twelve children gave signed definitions that conformed to English dictionary conventions; this child consistently used a manual form of English and the syntactic structure "a _____ is something that _____." Since only one of the twelve children used this syntactic structure, a separate analytic approach was not used for her productions.

For English definitions, the syntactic analysis included the previously used "percent Formal Definition" (%FD) measure. This measures the frequency of dictionary-like definitions for any particular child out of the total number of definitions completed by that child. Children who give one dictionary-like definition out of six have a lower %FD score than children who give only dictionary-like word definitions. The formal definitional quality was also measured (see Appendix B).

RESULTS

Twelve children formed the subject pool for this study. All twelve Deaf subjects completed the task in ASL, and eight of them completed the task in English using a TTY. This represents one of the first attempts to analyze Deaf children's productions of word definitions and a chance to analyze the relative clause constructions within the definitions in ASL and English.

ASL Definitions

SEMANTIC ANALYSIS

A mean semantic quality score was derived for the six words the children were asked to define. This score included information about the definitional and descriptive features of the word, whether they used a synonym or not, whether they described the function of the word, whether they mentioned examples of the word, and whether they made

TABLE 1. *Means and Standard Deviations of Overall Quality Measures of ASL and English Definitions*

Quality	ASL (s.d.)	English (s.d.)
Semantic quality	2.41	2.08
	(.77)	(.78)
Communicative adequacy	1.55	2.07
	(.68)	(.76)

comparisons. As a group, the mean score for the children's word definitions was 2.41, the minimum score was 1.5, and the maximum was 3.67 (s.d.=.77). This was a measure of the semantic quality of each definition. Because this is the first analysis of signed definitions, there was no set target score.[7] Their mean communicative adequacy score was 1.55 (range: .33 to 2.67, s.d.=.68). Table 1 summarizes these results.

Table 2 summarizes semantic information across the ASL and English conditions. This information includes all of the components of the semantic quality scores. Across all words, they averaged 1.25 examples, .44 descriptions of function, .24 definitional features in each of their definitions, and .29 descriptive features (beyond criterial definitional features). The children did not use any synonyms in their ASL definitions, and used on average only .06 comparisons in each ASL definition.[8] Thus, semantically their definitions consisted mostly of giving examples of the target word, with fairly frequent use of descriptions of function. Definitional features and descriptive features were also used somewhat frequently, and synonyms and comparisons were rarely used. Examples of their definitions are included below. Although adult data were not considered in this study, recall that adult signers identified giving examples of use as well

7. Although not considered in this paper, hearing bilingual children had an overall semantic quality score of 3.22 (s.d.=.78) and overall communicative adequacy score of 3.28 (s.d.=.54).

8. For comparative purposes in giving definitions in English (their native language was French), hearing bilingual children also rarely use synonyms in their word definitions (Schley 1994, p. 57). They used an average of .92 (s.d.=.52) examples, .82 statements of function (s.d.=.30), .75 definitional features (s.d.=.30), .57 descriptive features (s.d.=.33), and very few synonyms and comparisons (mean synonyms=.05, s.d.=.11; mean comparisons=.1.5, s.d.=.15).

TABLE 2. *Means and Standard Deviations of Average Use of Semantic Information in Each ASL and English Definition*

Semantic Information	ASL (s.d.)	English (s.d.)
Examples	1.25	1.17
	(.49)	(.19)
Functions	0.44	0.59
	(.34)	(.42)
Definitional features	0.24	0.07
	(.38)	(.13)
Descriptive features	0.29	0.13
	(.18)	(.22)
Synonyms	0.00	0.08
	(0)	(.10)
Comparisons	0.06	0.05
	(.12)	(.08)

as functional descriptions as important components of defining an ASL word.

SYNTACTIC ANALYSIS

Syntactically, in ASL the Deaf children used an average of .15 topic markers in each definition and .19 restrictive relative clause constructions. Thus, each of these structures was used in fewer than one out of five word definitions. The average of their total number of topic markers and/or restrictive relative clause markers used in all six of their definitions was 2.72 (ranging from 0 to 11 across all 12 children, std=3.16). Clearly, children varied considerably in their use of these two syntactic structures. Some children did not use them at all, and at least one child used them consistently. From an analysis of these children's productions and from speaking to Deaf adult signers, it appears that syntactically there may be no distinction between dictionary-like and informal definitions in ASL.

EXAMPLES OF ASL DEFINITIONS

Several examples illustrate the children's ASL definitions. Subject #5, a child who started attending the bilingual program from a very young age (one year four months) through a parent-infant program gave the following definition of the word *umbrella:*

$$\overline{\qquad}^{\text{t}}$$
UMBRELLA

$$\overline{\qquad}^{\text{rc}}$$
KNOW OUTSIDE RAIN

CROUCH-UNDER-UMBRELLA[9]

NOT WET

"An umbrella? You know, it's raining outside, you crouch under something on top of a long handle, and stay dry." The overall semantic quality score of this definition was 3, reflecting the two examples of use ("it's raining outside" and "you crouch under . . .") as well as-the function ("stay dry"). Subject #8, in response to the same word, gave a less complete definition: The resulting overall semantic quality score was 1 (giving only an example of when you use an umbrella):

RAIN WET OPEN-UMBRELLA

"There's rain, it's wet, so you open an umbrella."

Both of these subjects included an example of how and/or when you use an umbrella ("it's raining outside . . ."). The first subject, however, also included a clear statement of the function of an umbrella, specifically "staying dry" by "crouching under something on top of a long thin handle."

English Definitions: Deaf Children Via TTY

SEMANTIC ANALYSIS

Eight of the twelve Deaf children completed the definitions task in English. Semantically, their definitional quality averaged 2.08 for each of their definitions (range: 1.00 to 3.17, s.d.=.78). Their mean communicative adequacy score was 2.07 (range= 1 to 2.83, s.d.=.76). These children used few synonyms in their English definitions, paralleling their ASL definitions. Their average number of synonyms in each definition was .08 (ranging from 0 to .2 across all words). In each definition, they used an average of .07 definitional features, .59 descriptions of function, .13

As noted in Appendix A, the ...umbrella form is distinct from the

$$\overline{\qquad}^{\text{t}}$$
UMBRELLA form.

descriptive features, 1.17 examples, and .05 comparisons. Semantically, their definitions in ASL and English were comparable (see Tables 1 and 2).[10] As with their ASL definitions, children used examples and descriptions of function most frequently in their English definitions.

SYNTACTIC ANALYSIS

Syntactically, English definitions were rated according to whether they were formal dictionary-like definitions or more informal definitions. Children averaged 2.8 formal definitions each, and 2.2 informal definitions. Overall, 37 percent of their English definitions were formal (rather than informal); this ranged from 0 to 100 percent (s.d.=.40) across the eight children. Their mean formal definitional quality score was 7.47 (range=5 to 10, s.d.=2.17). Their mean formal definitional supplement score (a measure of correct information about the word in addition to a formal definition) was .98 (range=0 to 1.5, s.d.=.59).[11] The formal definitional quality score was a measure of the syntactic structure, the adult-like quality of the superordinate (e.g., saying "a bicycle is a *vehicle*" is less vague than saying "a bicycle is a *thing*"), the complement and the number of correct definitional features (see Appendix 2 for more details about this coding system). What is most interesting about these results is the fact that some of the children did in fact give clear dictionary-like definitions, which in turn is a distinctly school-like task. The children did not give solely contextualized definitions.

EXAMPLES OF TTY DEFINITIONS

The Deaf children gave both dictionary-like and informal definitions. Subject #6 gave the following decontextualized definition of *umbrella,* which received an overall semantic quality score of 2: "Umbrella is a thing you use when it rains. . . you put it above your head." Another child (Subject #2) gave a contextualized definition for the same word, and the semantic quality of this definition was equal to 1, as she gave only an

10. Again, for comparative purposes, see footnotes 7 and 8 for a summary of results from a sample of hearing nonnative English-speaking children.

11. Hearing bilingual children (in their nonnative language) gave an average of 3.83 (s.d.=2.17) formal definitions each, and 1.16 (s.d.=1.34) informal definitions. They averaged 77 percent formal definitions out of all attempts. Their mean definitional quality score was 9.9 (s.d.=1.58), and their mean formal definitional supplement score was 1.44 (s.d.=.81).

example of use: "You use it when it rains." The same child (Subject #2) did give decontextualized definitions in response to other words. For the word *thief*, she replied: "who steal things that is not theirs." This definition received a semantic quality score of 2. This is an interesting example of either reduced English produced on a TTY or a veritable intrusion of ASL syntax when producing written English. This definition includes a perfect relative clause ("who steal things that is not theirs"), although the superordinate referent required in English was deleted. This could be an intrusion of topicalization, which is allowed in ASL, since the referent was mentioned in the previous utterance (by the adult asking the child to define the word).

Any cross-linguistic comparison at the moment is tentative, considering the relatively small sample size. The semantic quality of their definitions was similar across the two languages although it was slightly higher in ASL. This makes some sense as children are likely to possess similar conceptual knowledge about words in either language. The communicative adequacy of the definitions was somewhat higher in English, perhaps because the task of giving definitions was more likely to occur in an English setting for these children. Formal definition training in ASL does not seem to occur. Higher scores occur in the task's specific curricular language. This parallels previous research on hearing children's bilingual performance on the definitions task: The hearing bilingual children scored higher in their school language than they did in their native language (Davidson, Kline, and Snow 1986; Snow 1990; Snow, Cancino, De Temple, and Schley 1991).

CONCLUSIONS: DEFINITIONS TASK

The Deaf children produced definitions in ASL and English that were semantically quite similar. Consider subject #6's definitions for the word *knife:* in ASL–SOMETHING TO CUT WITH–and in English–"knife is sharp and you use it for cutting food." This child is the one child who consistently gave definitions in ASL that were structurally similar to English formal definitions. Her English definition was somewhat more complete, with the additional mention of "sharp," a defining feature of the word.

Subject #11 gave the following definitions for *knife* in ASL–CAN CUT LETTUCE HAMBURGER–and in English–"(t)hat mean if you cut (yo)ur meat and apples." Both of his definitions were structurally quite similar, with the inclusion of two examples of how and when a knife is used.

Subject #8 gave a typical ASL definition for the word *clock:*

SUPPOSE WANT KNOW TIME LOOK-AT TIME
#OR FLASH-LIGHT TIME LOOK-AT TIME FLASH-LIGHT

Translating this into English, it is clear that she described a few examples of when a clock is typically used: "Suppose you want to know what time it is, you look at a clock; or suppose the alarm-clock lights are flashing, you look at the clock, the alarm is going off." This is certainly a rather complete and communicative ASL definition and would be acceptable even from an adult signer to an unknown audience (a situation that might elicit fairly decontextualized use of language). What is striking is that this seems to be a distinctly contextualized definition: In the context of generating word definitions in ASL, there does not seem to be a distinction between contextualized and dictionary-like definitions.

From a theoretical perspective, it is striking that there seems to be no formal/informal definitional distinction in ASL discourse practice. The developmental literature in English and in other studies of bilingual performance has shown solid distinctions as well as developmental shifts and ties to literacy achievement. However, the literature has considered bilingual ties between only two spoken and written languages. Although there clearly is a distinction between contextualized and decontextualized language in ASL (Schley 1994, 1995; Zimmer 1990), it may be that specific differences in how and when ASL is used result in ASL-speakers not explicitly producing specific dictionary forms for defining words in their discourse.

From a sociocultural perspective, the lack of this definitional distinction is less striking. The structure of any language reflects the needs of its community of speakers. To date it seems that there is no clear parallel formal definition in ASL discourse practice and that giving dictionary-like definitions is not a common school task when ASL is the curricular language. This may change, of course, as the context of when, where, and how ASL is used changes. In English, all but one of the children do give dictionary-like definitions, clearly showing that they are able to give this kind of form.

It is not surprising to consider that some linguistic circumstances may not occur in ASL discourse practice and instead may be dealt with in more English-like contexts. This could explain what is happening with the definitions, in that giving dictionary definitions of words may be a task that explicitly happens only in more English-like situations. This does not suggest any sort of deficiency within ASL; it is, rather, a potentially distinct sociological phenomenon. Until ASL dictionaries are established and commonly used, it is credible to suggest that the distinction to date is not yet common in ASL discourse.

These children are in a bilingual/bicultural program that parallels in some ways various other models of bilingual education. For example, their educational program is similar to American "maintenance" programs, where English is taught as a second language and the native language is maintained, but the native language is perhaps not used in parallel sociocultural contexts. It is also similar to two-way bilingual schools, where both native and nonnative English-speaking children are taught in English and in a second language, as both ASL and English are curricular languages.

The fact that the task of defining words in both ASL and English may be qualitatively distinct (i.e., it means something quite different when comparing cross-usage in the two languages) makes it an interesting area of analysis.[12] Semantically, the children are producing similar definitions across the two languages. Syntactically, the formal definition syntax seems to occur only in English; such could not be identified in ASL. Given that there is currently no ASL-based dictionary, it is not surprising that Deaf children do not produce dictionary-like definitions in ASL.

Above and beyond the fact that there is currently no ASL-based dictionary, in all likelihood there is also a schooling effect. Comparing across

12. In some ways this is similar to work on the relation between language and thought (Whorf 1956), where cognitive categories are distinctly coded in different languages, but speakers of the individual languages are able to cognitively process distinctions not encoded in their language (e.g., lexical differences for color terms in Tarahumara, a language spoken by native people from Chihuahua, Mexico, and in English [Kay and Kempton 1984]; lexical and grammatical differences, such as counterfactuals in Chinese and in English [Wu 1993]). This work considers discourse events that may not be evenly distributed across ASL and English.

Deaf and hearing classrooms, there is arguably less of a reliance on using a dictionary in the former than in the latter. Using the dictionary for
vocabulary development (including alphabetizing, pronunciation keys and
syllable breaks, and learning unknown words) is commonly built into
the curriculum of hearing elementary school children (see Graves et al.
1994, p. 127, for an example from a chapter on classroom methods in
elementary reading). And for hearing children, skill at giving dictionary-
like definitions relates more strongly to school experience than it does
to home experience. Snow (1990) found that exposure to English at
school explained considerably more of the variance on English formal
definition scores than did exposure to English at home. The school
experience of Deaf children does not integrate frequent use of dictionaries into the classroom. Moreover, there is limited use of ASL as a
medium of instruction for English and for basic skills. In some ways it is
no surprise that, in ASL discourse practice, the definitions task does not
seem to tap into decontextualized use of language.

Sociolinguistically, these results are quite interesting. Little is yet known
about features of ASL when used in different interactional contexts (but
see Roy 1990 and Zimmer 1990). Much more needs to be known about
the types of features in ASL that vary as a function of nonindependent
situational factors. Consider various contexts of conversational interaction. The formality of an interactional situation, for instance, will influence conversational features. Different situations of conversational
interaction clearly invoke different conversational demands. If a child
were to interview a school principal and then his or her parent, the two
interviews would arguably look quite distinct. Although some work has
been done on this topic with hearing samples (for example, see Schley
and Snow 1992), little has been done with signed interactions.

Other factors (such as the following) will influence the shape of the
interaction: any perceived social distance (e.g., talking to a colleague vs.
a cultural icon), the functional nature of interactional context (e.g., compare cocktail party chitchat to the language used in an academic presentation), the place of interaction (compare school-like contexts to
interaction at a kitchen table), politeness factors, cultural boundaries (consider interactions with other Deaf people vs. with hearing individuals
[Lucas and Valli 1989, 1991, 1992], or interactions between Deaf persons of color and white Deaf Americans), and personal identity (e.g.,
group membership). Little is yet known about how ASL interactions can
vary given any of the above situational influences.

Studying word definitions represents one piece of this picture, in that the implications of performance on this task are so clearly tied to other areas (e.g., literacy, outcomes of schooling, and so on). Although not considered here, the semantic quality of the ASL definitions is positively associated with performance on standardized tests of English achievement (see Schley 1994). Whereas skill at informal definitions seems not to be related to academic achievement for hearing children, skill at dictionary-like formal definitions is so related. For Deaf children, an underlying proficiency in ASL (be it conversational proficiency or otherwise) may be a more important predictor of school achievement in English than is skill at decontextualized use of ASL.

This is hardly unexpected, given the case of bilingual hearing children, who have acquired whatever proficiency in English (their L 2) with an already established base in their native language. For Deaf children, having a strong underlying base of ASL (and therefore more proficiency in ASL before learning English) is most probably a crucial link to school achievement. Others have noted this in the literature (e.g., Moores 1987; Quigley and Paul 1984). This research represents one of the first attempts to analyze not children raised with ASL from birth at home, but children exposed to high quality input of ASL from a young age at school. These children are exposed to both informal and school-like versions of ASL, although they may or may not find this exposure at home. Many Deaf children are born to hearing parents, for whom ASL will usually not be a natively acquired language. With consistent exposure to both formal and informal ASL input at school, perhaps some of the cited disparities between educational achievement of Deaf children born to Deaf parents and Deaf children born to hearing parents (or those who became deaf sometime after birth) will diminish.

In sum, this chapter has provided an analysis of sociolinguistic differences in ASL and English word definitions. Although there is an identifiable way of defining words in English that is decontextualized, such a form may not exist in ASL. Educationally, differences such as this need to be considered in developing bilingual/bicultural curricula. Implications of these results go beyond identifying a sociolinguistic difference between ASL and English, since in other samples of subjects' skill, decontextualized forms of language seem to be related to school achievement (Cummins 1984). For Deaf children, a prerequisite step to success in school is of course obtaining proficiency in an accessible language, whereupon skills in that language across contexts of interaction can be transferred to English literacy.

REFERENCES

Aarons, D. 1994. Personal conversation with author.

Baker, C., and D. Cokely. 1980. *American Sign Language: A teacher's resource text on grammar and culture*. Silver Spring, Md.: T.J. Publishers.

Battison, R. 1978. *Lexical borrowing in American Sign Language*. Silver Spring, Md.: Linstok Press.

Brennan, M., D. Brien, J. Collins, F. Elton, and G. H. Turner. 1993. The dictionary of British Sign Language/English: A bilingual resource. Paper presented at LASER (Language of Sign as an Educational Resource) Conference, St. Albans, England.

Brien, D. 1992. *Dictionary of British Sign Language/English*. London: Faber and Faber.

Cokely, D. 1995. Telephone conversation with author.

Coulter, G. R. 1983. A conjoined analysis of American Sign Language relative clauses. *Discourse Processes* 6:305–318.

Cummins, J. 1984. *Bilingualism and special education: Issues in assessment and pedagogy*. Avon, England: Multilingual Matters, Ltd.

Davidson, R., S. Kline, and C. E. Snow. 1986. Definitions and definite noun phrases: Indicators of children's decontextualized language skills. *Journal of Research in Childhood Education* 1:1–37.

Drasgow, E. 1993. Bilingual/bicultural Deaf education: An overview. *Sign Language Studies* 80:243–266.

Graves, M. F., S. Watts, and B. Graves. 1994. *Essentials of classroom teaching: Elementary reading*. Boston: Allyn and Bacon.

Hoffmeister, B. 1990. ASL and its implications for education. In *Manual communication: Implications for education*, ed. H. Bornstein. Washington, D.C.: Gallaudet University Press.

Hoffmeister, R. 1994. Personal conversation with author.

Jamison, S. L. 1983. *Signs for computing terminology: A sign reference book for people in the computing field*. Silver Spring, Md.: National Association of the Deaf.

Johnson, H. A., and L. E. Barton. 1988. TDD conversations: A context for language sampling and analysis. *American Annals of the Deaf* 133:19–25.

Kay, P., and W. Kempton. 1984. What is the Sapir-Whorf hypothesis? *American Anthropologist* 86: 65–79.

Litowitz, B. 1977. Learning to make definitions. *Journal of Child Language* 4:289–304.

Lucas, C., and C. Valli. 1989. Language contact in the American Deaf community. In *The sociolinguistics of the Deaf community*, ed. C. Lucas. San Diego: Academic Press.

———. 1991. ASL or contact signing: Issues of judgment. *Language in Society* 20:201–216.

———. 1992. *Language contact in the American Deaf community.* San Diego: Academic Press.

MacWhinney, B. 1991. *The CHILDES project: Tools for analyzing talk.* Hillsdale, N.J.: Lawrence Erlbaum Associates.

Malakoff, M. 1988. The effect of language of instruction on reasoning in bilingual children. *Applied Psycholinguistics* 9:17–38.

Moores, D. 1987. *Educating the deaf: Psychology, principles, and practices.* Boston: Houghton Mifflin.

Quigley, S., and P. Paul. 1984. *Language and deafness.* San Diego: College Hill Press.

Roy, C. B. 1990. Features of discourse in an American Sign Language lecture. In *The sociolinguistics of the Deaf community*, ed. C. Lucas. San Diego: Academic Press.

Schley, S. 1991a. Language proficiency and bilingual education of Deaf children. Qualifying paper, Harvard University Graduate School of Education.

———. 1991b (March). Oral and written picture descriptions in ASL and English. Presentation given at Teachers of English to Speakers of Other Languages (TESOL) Convention, Vancouver, B.C.

———. 1994. Language proficiency and bilingual education of Deaf children. Ed.D. diss., Harvard University Graduate School of Education.

———. 1995 (March). Bilingual and bimodal proficiency of Deaf children. Presentation given at American Association of Applied Linguistics, Long Beach, California.

Schley, S., and C. E. Snow. 1992. The conversational skills of school-aged children. *Social Development* 1(1):18–35.

Snow, C. E. 1983. Literacy and language: Relationships during the preschool years. *Harvard Educational Review* 53(2):165–189.

———. 1987. Beyond conversation: Second language learners' acquisition of description and explanation. In *Research in second language learning: Focus on the classroom*, ed. J. Lantolf and A. Labarca. Norwood, N.J.: Ablex.

——— 1990. The development of definitional skill. *Journal of Child Language* 17(3):697–710.

Snow, C. E., H. Cancino, J. De Temple, and S. Schley. 1991. Giving formal definitions: A linguistic or metalinguistic skill? In *Language processing and language awareness by bilingual children*, ed. E. Bialystok. New York: Cambridge University Press.

Snow, C. E., H. Cancino, P. Gonzalez, and E. Shriberg. 1989. Giving formal definitions: An oral language correlate of school literacy. In *Classrooms and literacy*, ed. D. Bloome. Norwood, N.J.: Ablex.

Snow, C. E., and M. E. Dolbear. 1989. The relation of conversational skill to language proficiency in second language learners. Harvard University Graduate School of Education. Manuscript.

Sternberg, M. 1981. *American Sign Language: A comprehensive dictionary.* New York: Harper and Row.

————. 1987. *American Sign Language dictionary.* New York: Harper and Row.

Stokoe, W. C., D. C. Casterline, and C. G. Croneberg. 1976. *A dictionary of American Sign Language on linguistic principles.* Silver Spring, Md.: Linstok Press.

Supalla, T. 1986. The classifier system in ASL. In *Noun classification and categorization*, ed. C. Craig. Philadelphia: John Benjamins, North America.

Velasco, P. 1989. The relationship of oral decontextualized language and reading comprehension in bilingual children. Ed.D. diss., Harvard University Graduate School of Education.

Walworth, M., D. F. Moores, and T. J. O'Rourke. 1992. *A free hand: Enfranchising the education of Deaf children.* Silver Spring, Md.: T.J. Publishers.

Watson, R. 1985. Toward a theory of definition. *Journal of Child Language* 12:181–197.

Wechsler, D. 1958. *The measurement and appraisal of adult intelligence.* 4th edition. Baltimore: Williams and Wilkins.

Whorf, L. B. 1956. *Language, thought and reality.* Cambridge, Mass.: MIT Press.

Wilcox, S. 1994. Electronic mail communication.

Wu, H. F. 1993. "If triangles were circles. . . ," A study of counterfactuals in Chinese and in English. Ed.D. diss., Harvard University Graduate School of Education.

Zimmer, J. 1990. Toward a description of register variation in American Sign Language. In *The sociolinguistics of the Deaf community*, ed. C. Lucas. San Diego: Academic Press.

Transcription Details

Both English and ASL language productions were transcribed, keeping separate utterances on separate lines, and noting whether utterances were from the child or the adult. For English TTY productions, reduced spelling and grammatical mistakes were preserved in the transcripts (any level of error analysis was not considered here). Punctuation, however, was minimally added to the productions; in most cases, productions were transcribed as they appeared on the TTY paper printout. Any examples of children's TTY productions are presented as they were typed by the children; thus, any grammatical and spelling mistakes are real and not corrected.

In ASL, productions were transcribed in gloss form using small capital letters (Baker and Cokely 1980), where each produced sign was translated into English as accurately as possible and transcribed in the original syntactical order. Loose translations of the ASL productions are placed within double quotes beneath the production using traditional punctuation. In multimorphemic signs, in which one English word did not correspond to the signed form, a string of glossed English words was used, with the string conjoined using hyphens. "Plus" symbols (+) were used to indicate reduplication. Thus, the form UMBRELLA+ is used to gloss an ASL noun (with one reduplication, different from UMBRELLA, which is a verb form signed without repetition), and the form CROUCH-UNDER-UM-BRELLA is used to gloss a verb form of crouching under something on top of a pole held over one's head.

In addition, several nonmanual features were transcribed above the glossed line, using a horizontal line to indicate the length of production (i.e., across the appropriate sign glosses); featural codes were included above the horizontal line (e.g., a *t* for ASL topic-comment structure, an *rc* for relative clause markers. To distinguish between pronominal referents, the PRO1, PRO2 (and so on) convention was used, with the numerical reference consistently designating the same grammatical place marker within a discourse frame.

ASL fingerspelled loan signs (Battison 1978) were transcribed by using a # code before the gloss. Classifier predicates (morphemes that encode perceptual and semantic information about a referent [Supalla 1986]) were coded as *CL-* with a description of the classifier in noncapital letters concatenated with hyphens to the CL- code. To encode right- versus left-oriented body position, *lt* and *rt* were attached to the end of the sign's gloss. If a sign could be produced with either a one-handed or a two-handed form, an *1h* or a *2h* was enclosed in parentheses before the gloss. Any nonlinguistic gestures were described in noncapital letters between parentheses.

Coding of Definitions Task

Each definition provided by each subject was coded separately. The following variables were coded. The ASL and English coding schemes were different.

ASL CODING SYSTEM

Semantic Measures

The ASL definitions were scored to reflect how much semantic information was provided about the word being defined. Points were given for correct information about the following features; an overall measure of the definition's semantic quality was obtained by summing the individual components.

1. *Functions:* Score number of statements of function (abstract purpose or action) of noun. Be sure that the language is abstract. Note that applications (a specific instance of how or where something is used) do not count as function. They are coded as examples.

2. *Examples:* Score number that are correct. The emphasis here is on concrete noun phrases that present a specific situation. Application of a particular object, or instances of its use, are also counted as examples.

3. *Definitional Features:* Score number given that are on following list:

   BICYCLE–Two wheels, pedals, self-propelled (no motor)
   CLOCK–Number or hands, cyclical (not round), not worn on person, used in stationary position
   DONKEY–Mammalian, equine, horselike, herbivorous, long-eared
   KNIFE–Blade or point, handle, sharp, elongated
   THIEF–Criminal (adjective)
   UMBRELLA–Fabric, waterproof, dome or canopy, concave, handle/support, self-support, portable, collapsible

4. *Descriptive Features:* Score number of correct features given that do not appear on the list of definitional features.

5. *Comparisons:* Score number of comparisons present in definition.

6. *Synonyms:* Score number of synonyms present in definition.

Syntactic Measures

The ASL definitions were coded syntactically. The number of three restrictive relative clause markers (THAT, FOR-FOR, KNOW) was counted. Topic marker constructions were counted.

Communicative Adequacy (CA)

The entire definition is rated for how good a clue it is in terms of identifying the object or person in question. The levels of measure were as follows:

0   No chance
1   If both the child and the culture were familiar to the audience
2   Limited but not adequate definition
3   Probably adequate
4   Perfectly adequate and complete

ENGLISH CODING SYSTEM

Semantic Measures

The English definitions were also coded semantically. (See description of ASL semantic coding.)

Syntactic Coding

1. *Percent Formal Definitions (%FD):* Each definition is classified as either a "formal definition" or an "informal definition," and %FD reflects the proportion of formal definitions produced by each child. A formal definition includes at the very least a superordinate predicated by the word being defined.
2. *Formal Definitional Quality (FDQ):* The FDQ score is based on the sum of a variety of categories, such as ratings of each definition's syntax, the superordinate used, and the number of definitional features mentioned in the definition.

3. *Formal Definitional Supplement (FDS):* If nondefinitional but correct information about the meaning is provided in addition to a formal definition (e.g., examples of its use, descriptions, comparisons), instances were scored and summed for the "formal definitional supplement" (FDS) variable.

Communicative Adequacy (CA)

See the description for ASL coding.

Part 4 **Discourse Analysis**

Initiation in Visually Constructed Dialogue:

Reading Books with Three- to

Eight-Year-Old Students Who Are

Deaf and Hard of Hearing

Susan M. Mather

Simply reading a book aloud *to* a student is not enough–the story must be read *with* the student, including the student and adult in an interpersonal process that "involves not only an interaction between author and reader but also reader and listener" (Davidson, Lia, and Troyer 1988, 19). Strategies to create this interpersonal involvement have been documented for both spoken and written language modalities (Biber 1986, 1988; Chafe and Tannen 1987; Tannen 1985, 1988, 1989). Among the strategies are constructed dialogue, repetition, and use of imagery and details. When reading with students who are deaf and hard of hearing, adults must also create a sense of involvement–but in a visual mode because such children depend on visual stimuli. What nonlinguistic and linguistic forms of initiation in constructed dialogue in a visual language can and do teachers use to involve these students in reading activities?

This study is part of a three-year research grant from the Office of Special Education and Rehabilitative Services (OSERS) under the U.S. Department of Education. The purpose is to examine how teachers use initiation in constructed dialogue in a visual modality during their storyreading. These approaches are used by teachers of varying backgrounds and styles.

The author wishes to thank Ceil Lucas and Clayton Valli for their consultation and support; André Thibeault and Noni Warner for their assistance with this project; and Robert C. Johnson and Mary-Louise Giunta, whose perspectives and comments on my project and this chapter I value.

The study involved transcription and analysis of five videotaped reading activities by teachers. Five teachers (three hearing and two deaf) were asked to read a picture book (*Too Much Noise,* given to them one week beforehand to ensure familiarity with their classes). They were also told that the purpose of the study was to discover how to generate interpersonal involvement in storyreading, and they were encouraged to create as much involvement as they could.

This project has two goals. The initial goal is to analyze one of the interpersonal involvement strategies, that is, initiation in visually constructed dialogue used by teachers when reading with students. The second goal is to analyze factors that influence the quality and quantity of initiation in constructed dialogue, specifically the teacher's own dependence on visual and/or auditory stimuli and the instructional mode of communication (MCE or ASL) that the teacher uses.

LITERATURE REVIEW

This literature review covers involvement-focused and information-focused styles; intensity; constructed dialogue in spoken discourse; constructed dialogue and action in signed discourse; vocal initiation regulators; visual and tactile initiation regulators: visual and tactile regulators in deaf classrooms; and types of eye gaze.

Involvement-focused and Information-focused Styles

The literature reviewed in this section questions the generalization that spoken and written discourse are fundamentally different. It demonstrates that both modes share the textual dimension that focuses on involvement as opposed to information.

Tannen (1985, 1989) explains that in each kind of discourse, spoken and written, the speaker/writer has to decide how much emphasis to place on involvement as opposed to information. An involvement focus differs from an information focus in three ways. First, involvement-focused discourse relies highly on context; information-focused discourse relies less on immediate context. Second, involvement-focused discourse often supplies information for an audience that shares the same cultural and social backgrounds and assumptions about the world as the speaker/writer, permitting the audience to do the interpretive work; information-focused discourse provides optimal detailed information for an audience that may not share the same cultural background. Third, involvement-focused discourse depends upon paralinguistic and nonverbal channels to create cohesion; information-focused discourse establishes cohesion through lexicalization.

Despite marked differences in modes, Tannen (1988) finds that ordinary conversation and literary discourse share the same linguistic features used to create interpersonal involvement. She identifies certain features and divides them into two categories of language patterns. One category consists of features that sweep the audience along with their rhythm, sound, and shape. The other category includes those features that require audience participation in order to make sense, such as imagery, detail, and dialogue. Chafe (1982), Ochs (1979), Tannen (1982, 1985), and Schiffrin (1981) have observed that narration is more graphic when the narrator uses speech in the form of a first-person discourse–usually called "direct quotation" or "direct speech" but labeled "constructed dialogue" by Tannen (1986, 312)–instead of a third-person discourse ("indirect quotation" or "indirect speech").

In writing, the nonverbal and paralinguistic features are lost; they cannot be captured on paper. Writing, however, can create involvement by use of capitalization, underlining, italics, and exclamation points (Tannen 1988). Writing, although it relies on lexicalization (e.g., common dialogue introducers), can help create discourse as if it were face-to-face interaction by the addition of certain comments to written dialogue.

Intensity

Intensity is another way to create interpersonal involvement by revealing the speaker's social and emotional expression.

Labov (1984, 43-44) identifies intensity as a linguistic feature that conveys social and emotional information and defines it as "the emotional expression of social orientation toward the linguistic proposition." Labov finds that peripheral systems such as the use of prosody, vocal qualifiers, and gestures often serve as the primary means for expressing social and emotional information.

Labov explains that social and emotional information could be entirely verbalized through grammatical mechanisms (e.g., "I am moderately angry with you" or "I'm entirely committed to this line of action") (p. 43). Labov finds that the grammatical mechanism for conveying social and emotional information, however, has "lower chances of success" and that "listeners would not accept these words at their face value" (p. 43). Rather, the grammatical mechanism is "the primary means for conveying referential and cognitive information" (p. 43). Thus, social and emotional states, according to Labov, would be expressed through peripheral systems. He cautions that if we are to interpret the linguistic features of a discourse and we do not take into consideration social and emotional expression and their impact on the discourse, the analysis will be "incomplete" (p. 43).

Constructed Dialogue in Spoken Discourse

Tannen (1986, 1) argues that "the term *reported speech* is a misnomer. The examination of the lines of dialogue represented in storytelling or conversation, and the power of human memory, indicate that most of those lines were probably not actually spoken." She suggests that the term *reported speech* be replaced with another term, *constructed dialogue*, because her findings show that reported speech is not actually a verbatim report of words as they were spoken. She explains that speakers who are repeating their stories often reconstruct them as part of their creative process, and they are affected by their personal experience and hearsay. Tannen contends that this helps to create interpersonal involvement between speaker or writer and audience. In other words, as Tannen (1986, 1) argues,

> What is commonly referred to as reported speech or direct quotation in conversation is constructed dialogue, just as surely as is the dialogue created by fiction writers and playwrights. A difference is that in fiction and plays, the characters and actions are also constructed, whereas in personal narrative, they are based on actual characters and events. But even this difference is not absolute. Many works of fiction and drama are also based on real people and events, and many conversational storytellers—to the consternation of their children and spouses but the delight of their hearers—embellish and adjust characters and events.

Tannen (1989, 12) suggests that involvement is "an internal, even emotional connection individuals feel that binds them to the people as well as to places, things, activities, ideas, memories and words." She suggests that "it is a tenet of education that students understand information better, perhaps only, if they have discovered it for themselves rather than being told it."

One of the most powerful involvement strategies is constructed dialogue. Constructed dialogue helps to establish a bond between speaker and listener and create "a play peopled by characters who take on life and breath" (Tannen 1989, 103). The forms of constructed dialogue are direct quotation with common dialogue introducers (including such words and phrases as "say," "go," and "I'm like").

Constructed Dialogue and Action in Signed Discourse

Several studies state that constructed dialogue also exists in ASL. Take, for example, a deaf science teacher discussing the mating habits of stickleback fish with his students (Roy 1989). The teacher assumes the role of a stickleback fish and constructs the "comments" and "thoughts" of the fish via eye gaze and body movements.

Liddell (1980), Padden (1986, 1990), Meier (1990), Engberg-Pedersen (1992), Lillo-Martin (1992), Mather (1990), and Winston (1991, 1992) have referred to role playing or role shifting as conveying a character's thoughts, words, and actions. Lentz (1986) finds that a signer can assume two roles by shifting her body to indicate that she is changing from the first character to the second to form a dialogue between two imaginary characters.

Liddell (1995) notices that signers will associate with imaginary or surrogate people and engage them as though they are present. Signers even will associate with the imaginary person's height or position, looking down to a shorter individual or up to a taller one, or even carry on as though the person is lying on the bed.

Winston (1991, 1992) discusses constructed dialogue in ASL as being parallel to strategies found in spoken constructed dialogue, but she suggests that the science teacher's performance in the example from Roy (1989) is a form of constructed action. She suggests that constructed action is described as what is commonly thought of as role playing, as other researchers have indicated: "the signer assumes the posture and actions of a character, and imitates them either as mime, or while signing about the character" (cited in Metzger 1995, 3).

Vocal Initiation Regulators

Duncan (1972) observes that there are certain turn-taking regulators that participants employ to manage conversations. Referring to spoken English conversations, Duncan finds them to consist of body motion, sociocentric sequences ("but. . .umm" or "something" or "you know"), a drop in paralinguistic pitch or intensity, intonation, paralinguistic drawl, and other cues.

Wiener and Devoe (1974) identify four functional regulator types: initiation, continuation, shift, and termination. *Initiation* regulators are used by the speaker to start an exchange and by the addressee to evoke a response from the speaker. *Continuation* regulators are used by the speaker and indicate that the speaker's turn will continue despite a short pause. The addressee uses them to indicate that he or she is paying attention and that the speaker may continue. *Shift* regulators are used by the speaker who wishes to relinquish the turn or by the addressee who wishes to take a turn to speak. *Termination* regulators signal that either the speaker, the addressee, or both wish to terminate an exchange.

The words employed constitute only one component of vocal initiation regulators. As mentioned, Labov (1984, 43) argues that the full range of these regulators (e.g., use of prosody, vocal qualifiers, and body motion, or intensity and other cues) serve as the primary means for expressing social and emotional information; otherwise, listeners "would not accept these words at their face value."

Gumperz (1982, 1) observes that "once involved in a conversation, both speaker and hearer must actively respond to what transpires by signaling involvement, either directly through words or indirectly through gestures or similar nonverbal signals." Tannen (1989, 9) maintains that "conversational involvement, for Gumperz, is the basis of all linguistic understanding."

In interviews, I asked several hearing people to describe different situations in which they use initiation regulators to attract an addressee's attention (personal conversations with Robert Clover Johnson, Mary-Louise Giunta, and others). Some of the examples they gave are:

"Hey" in an excited voice (e.g., "Hey, let's go out for pizza!" or "Hey, I have something exciting to tell you!")

"Hey" in a loud voice (e.g., "Hey, don't do that!")

"Ma'am"(e.g., "Ma'am, can I talk with you for a minute?")

"Stop" or "Watch out" used to warn someone of danger (e.g., "Watch out, there is a car coming!")

"Excuse me" in a loud voice (e.g., "Excuse me, you parked in the wrong place" or "Excuse me, you can't sit there!")

"Excuse me" in a polite voice (e.g., "Excuse me, that is my chair.")

"What gives?" or "Yo" used to show concern; it can indicate that something is wrong or be used to find out what's happening. It often means that the speaker wants the addressee's immediate attention.

"What gives?" in a very angry tone (e.g., "What gives? I told you to show up one hour ago.")

"What gives?" in a less angry tone (e.g., "I told you to show up one hour ago. What gives?")

Visual and Tactile Initiation Regulators

Baker (1977) suggests that conversation among deaf people is different from that of their hearing peers because a deaf signer cannot initiate signing until the specified addressee is looking at the would-be signer. The signer cannot say something and be "heard" if the other is not watching. Baker finds that before one can initiate signing, the signer often summons the intended addressee's attention by employing one of several initiation regulators: waving a hand in front of or beside the addressee or visually creating sharp movements in body or hand motion.

I called these "visual initiation regulators" because the signer summons one's attention visually.

Baer (1991) discusses different types and uses of physical contact in the deaf community. Tapping (touching) is one. She explains that there are various kinds of tapping. The signer can tap *on the top* of an addressee's shoulder to signal that the signer wants the addressee's attention and has something to tell that person. If a person is standing (or sitting) and is blocking the view of another person behind him or her, the person in the back will tap gently *on the side* of the person's shoulder to signal that the view is blocked. The person being tapped will automatically move to the side without turning around and asking what the person in the back wants. Also, if the signer is furious and wants to talk with that addressee right away, the signer will *tap sharply* on the top of the addressee's shoulder. If the signer has something exciting, important, or urgent to tell, he or she will *continually and quickly tap* on the top of the shoulder.

I label these "tactile initiation regulators" because one must use physical contact to draw a person's attention when the addressee fails to respond or is not in the line of the signer's vision.

Visual and Tactile Regulators in Deaf Classrooms

In Mather (1987), similar regulators in deaf classrooms were found. Before a particular teacher initiated her signing, she employed either visual or tactile initiation regulators with her students, depending on whether the students were in or out of her line of vision. The teacher often double-checked to see if the students were ready to listen by nodding and signing, "READY?" (with nonmanual grammatical signals for yes-no questions). Students responded in acknowledgment by nodding. She did that every time she turned the page or averted her gaze from the students. Unfortunately, the study found that even though other teachers employed these visual or tactile initiation regulators with their students, they did not await the students' signal of nodding back to acknowledge their readiness to listen. As soon as the students started to gaze back at them, the teachers went on signing without securing their acknowledgment first. That explained the frequent disruptions in class; students cried out that they had missed something the teacher had just said.

In another study, I found similar patterns in interactions between an eighteen-month-old student and a teacher whenever the teacher would summon her student visually (Mather 1990). As soon as she noticed that her student had started to gaze at her, she initiated her signing. But the videotape of these encounters showed that he missed half of what the teacher had said because he gazed without full concentration and had not gotten a chance to "settle down" with his eye contact on his teacher. Unfortunately, analysis of classroom interaction showed that, throughout their interaction, the teacher did not give her student a chance to acknowledge that he was ready to listen. Thus, he missed the first critical information in the teacher's signing. It is arguable that the student was too young to acknowledge: The tape showed that a teacher-aide waited until the youngster "settled down" with his eye contact after she summoned him. The teacher-aide waited until eye contact was fully established eye contact before she initiated her signing, even though the youngster did not nod to acknowledge readiness.

Chen (1993) observed that in deaf homes, deaf adults employed the same initiation regulators with their young children.

These initiating regulators are important not only for deaf classrooms or homes; they have also affected CODA adults (hearing adults who grew up in deaf homes). Some of these adults have told me that they found it difficult to deal with school peers and teachers who did not use visual or tactile initiation regulators. Also, they found that they kept trying, without success, to establish eye contact with their teachers or peers before initiating conversation with them (personal conversations with Tom Bull and Pat Yates, whose son George is CODA). Preston (1994) related that some hearing peers in school made fun of the CODA students or called them weird. The hearing students complained that the CODA students seemed to gawk at their peers all the time and even liked to touch them. Some kids even rejected CODA children because they touched or looked at them too much. A hearing brother who grew up with two older deaf sisters often used tactile initiation regulators with his hearing friends after several attempts to get his friends' attention vocally or visually (personal communication with Peter Mozzer and his friends).

These studies demonstrate that in order to establish individual eye gaze between signer and addressee, the signer uses either visual or tactile initiation regulators.

In order to extend the examination and analysis of initiation regulators used by hearing and deaf people in the community, I conducted field observations in a variety of settings. My graduate assistant Noni Warner and I carried out separate surveys of initiation regulator use among hearing-hearing dyads, deaf-deaf dyads, and hearing-deaf dyads. Deaf storytellers and sign-language interpreters using initiation regulators were observed at various functions such as a meeting of the National Association of the Deaf, parties and social gatherings, and Gallaudet University lecture events.

The function of initiation regulators is not simply to summon someone's attention visually or physically; initiation regulators also convey social and emotional information via different types (degrees) of visual and tactile motions. This supports Labov's contentions cited earlier regarding hearing people.

Before one initiates signing, the following three items must be assessed, regardless of whether the addressee is paying attention:

1. Is the addressee in the signer's line of vision?
2. If not, is the addressee still within the line of peripheral vision?
3. Or is she completely out of the signer's line of vision?

This will determine the kind of initiation regulator the signer will use to elicit the addressee's attention.

If the answer is #1, the signer will use visual initiations by summoning or using sharp hand/body motion. If it is #2, the signer will move into the addressee's vision field and use eye-level gaze waving strategy, depending on what the addressee is doing (e.g., reading), and then will employ visual initiations within the addressee's gaze. If it is #3, the signer will use tactile initiation regulators.

There are different visual initiation regulators that the signer can also use to convey social and emotional information. If the signer simply wants to summon the addressee's attention, she will use a standard waving motion. For something important or exciting, she will wave continually and quickly. If upset or furious, she will wave sharply. However, the next two regulators employ different kinds of motion. For example, if the signer is very angry or upset, she might use a "stiff wave" only once. For something very important or urgent, she will continually "flap" like a bird.

The last two regulators can be considered equivalent to such vocal initiation regulators as "hey" and "excuse me" in a loud voice, or "what gives?"

Different tactile initiation regulators can be used by the signer to convey social and emotional information. If the signer merely wants to summon the addressee's attention, she will use a standard tap; to convey something important or exciting, she will tap continually and quickly; when upset or furious, she is likely to tap sharply.

For the first three regulators, the signer will use the bottom of the fingertips. However, for the next two, the signer will use different parts of the fingers. If the signer is very angry or upset, she will use the end of her fingertips to push the addressee's shoulder. With something very important or urgent to tell, she might continually "flap" the full finger length of her hand on the addressee's shoulder.

These examples indicate that there are various purposes for summoning someone's attention. Whether one is a speaker or signer, one still has a grammatical mechanism for conveying emotional status. However, speakers and signers employ different initiation regulators in getting an addressee's attention. The determining factor is whether the addressee can hear or not. To make a telephone call, the receiver will immediately know who is calling by the timbre of the voice; however, a person who makes a TTY call must identify her name first in typing so the receiver will know who is calling. There is no other way for the receiver to identify the caller merely by typing. In another situation, a speaker may call to the addressee regardless of whether she is in the speaker's line of vision. The addressee immediately knows who is calling by the quality of voice and then responds to acknowledge that she is ready to listen by employing one of several backchannel cues, "huh," "umm," or "yes."

Unlike speakers or hearing addressees, the signer must first ascertain whether the addressee is in the signer's direct or peripheral line of vision or completely out of the signer's line of vision before determining what kind of initiation regulators to use to capture the addressee's attention. Regardless of the addressee's hearing status, the signer can't initiate signing until eye contact is established.

In summary, first the signer summons the addressee, either physically or visually, and then secures the addressee's eye contact. After establishing eye contact with the signer, the addressee responds by nodding slightly to acknowledge her readiness to listen; the addressee may also use a nonmanual grammatical marker (Wh-q), with or without the sign "WHAT" (equivalent to signaling acknowledgment in spoken language by using backchannel cues such as "ummm"). Finally, the signer initiates signing.

Types of Eye Gaze

Two types of eye-gaze signals are used in deaf classrooms–individual eye gaze (I-GAZE) and group indicating eye gaze (G-GAZE) (Mather 1987). The first type, I-GAZE, requires mutual eye contact between the signer and an individual addressee. This gaze is held until the signer finishes or receives a reply from the addressee. The second, G-GAZE, is used in groups of as few as two addressees. Its purpose is to tell the group that the signer is talking to the group as a whole and not singling out an individual. It takes the form of a smooth arc-like gaze evenly directed at all members of the group and constantly moving across or around the group without pausing. Mather (1987) shows that teachers employ these gazes to regulate turn-taking during storyreading, to invite individual and group response, and to communicate with a particular student or with a group.

Teachers also use individual eye gaze to create a constructed dialogue between imaginary people during their storytelling. For example, one teacher told a story from the book, *Five Chinese Brothers,* as follows:

> One day, as he (the First Chinese Brother) was leaving the market-place, a little boy stopped him and asked him if he could go fishing with him. "No, it could not be done," said the First Chinese Brother.

During the narrative, she assumed the role of a little child asking an adult if he could go with him. In this role, she looked up to the imaginary Chinese brother as if he were tall and signed to him. Then she shifted her role from child to adult by shifting her head and eye gaze and then gazing down to the imaginary child and replying that he could not go with him.

The following is the transcription of the signed narrative:

*I-Chinese Brother		*I-little boy
head up, eye gaze up		head down, eye gaze down
Wh-q		head nod
CAN I GO WITH YOU	(Shifting)	NO, YOU CAN'T

Thus, teachers do use individual gaze for purposes other than to regulate turn-taking. They use it to create a visually constructed dialogue between two imaginary people and engage them as though they were in the environment of the signer.

I prefer the term *visually constructed dialogue* to *constructed action* because the former is found to be parallel to spoken constructed dialogue as a method of introducing a dialogue between the speaker (or signer) and addressee (listener). Instead of using the sign SAY, the teacher as a signer modified (re-created) a dialogue to introduce the speaker (signer) and vice versa in a visual modality by shifting her head up and gazing directly at the person or down to the person. This form helps create discourse as if it were signed in face-to-face interaction.

*Notes: I-Chinese Brother denotes that this is an individual gaze employed by a teacher who assumed the role of the child. The teacher employed an individual gaze to signal that she is talking with the Chinese brother and vice versa. Wh-q is a nonmanual grammatical marker to signal that a person is asking a question with or without signs. It consists of brow contraction and positive eye gaze.

Also, the term *constructed action* is too broad; the preliminary analysis showed that there are different forms of constructed dialogue repetition, and use of imagery and details that can be created visually. They are also found to be parallel to spoken ones.

STUDYING INITIATION IN STORYREADING

Book Selection

The following criteria were developed for selecting the book to be read in the study: (1) It must contain strategies (dialogue, repetition, imagery, and details) to encourage the production of imagery and detail involvement by teachers, and (2) it must be generally popular in order to encourage a successful book-reading event for everyone. *Too Much Noise,* by Ann McGovern, meets these criteria.

Teachers: Their Schools and Style of Bookreading

This study involved five teachers from three different types of school settings. A description of the teachers, by school setting, follows.

RESIDENTIAL SCHOOL

Two teachers (one hearing, one deaf) from a residential school for the deaf were chosen for the study. Both use American Sign Language with their students. The deaf teacher is also a noted storyteller. Her videotapes of telling stories are marketed and sold nationwide by a company that specializes in videotapes and books of signed stories in ASL. She had a group of six students who were six to eight years old. Her style of bookreading is to read the whole book first and then retell it in ASL.

The hearing teacher is well-known in the community for her involvement with people who are deaf and hard of hearing. She also is a certified sign language interpreter. She had a group of six students who were four to six years old. Her style of reading differs somewhat from that of the first teacher. She read each page first before retelling the story.

PUBLIC SCHOOL

Colleagues of the author recommended that a particular teacher from a public school be included in this project. This teacher, who is highly regarded and hearing, is a certified sign language interpreter. She switches from American Sign Language to Manually Coded English effectively and effortlessly. This teacher has a self-contained classroom (one of two in the school) of six 3- to 5-year-old deaf students. She uses both ASL and MCE with her students. This third teacher resembles the second teacher in that she reads each page first before retelling the story. On several occasions, the students interrupted her storytelling and forced her to reread the page or story line. This affected her style of storytelling, which is discussed in the results.

PRIVATE DAY SCHOOL

This school is interesting for two reasons: (1) Instruction is visually oriented, and (2) students with normal hearing are reversed-mainstreamed from public schools to that school for various reasons. Some students who have normal hearing are sent by their school district because they may benefit from visually centered activities. These include, for example, students who can hear but not talk, or students who cannot absorb information audiologically, necessitating their greater dependence on visual channels. Also, they include students with normal hearing whose parents are deaf and use sign language at home, as well as students who are siblings of deaf students. Both of the teachers from this school who participated in the study use Manually Coded English. One teacher, who is hard of hearing, had a group of twenty-two students (deaf, hard of hearing, and hearing). Their ages ranged from 5 to 7 years old. The other teacher, who is hearing, had a group of thirteen students (also deaf, hard of hearing, and hearing). They ranged in age from 3 to 5 years old. Both teachers used similar styles for storyreading. They read and signed almost each line instead of reading the whole passage and signing afterward. Both consulted their teacher-aide, who is fluent in ASL. Unlike these two, the first three teachers did not seek consultation for telling the story.

Table 1 summarizes each teacher's language use, auditory status, the age of her students, and the kind of school in which she teaches.

Data Analysis

TEACHER 1

The initiation data for this study show that Teacher 1 went through the first three of four processes (assess, summon, acknowledge) before she would initiate her signing (fourth process). As previous studies have

TABLE 1. *Background of Study Participants*

Teacher	Language Use	Auditory Status	Age of Students	Kind of School
1	ASL	Deaf	6 to 8	Residential
2	ASL	Hearing	4 to 6	Residential
3	ASL/MCE	Hearing	3 to 5	Public self-contained class
4	MCE	Deaf	5 to 7	Private mainstreamed
5	MCE	Hearing	3 to 5	Private mainstreamed

shown, a signer will determine the type of initiation (visual or tactile) regulator first and receive a signal from the addressee before she initiates her signing (Baker 1977; Mather 1987, 1990; Baer 1991; and Chen 1993).

In telling the story, *Too Much Noise,* Teacher 1 first described (assessed) what the wise man did, showed whether he was looking or not, before she began her constructed dialogue with him (see the example below); she did this regularly throughout the narrative (see Table 2). She used a visual initiation regulator three times (pages 10, 16, and 24) and used a tactile initiation regulator three times (pages 20, 28, and 32). These pages represent passages that require such initiations. Three examples (pages 10, 20, and 32) serve to illustrate how Teacher 1 used three different initiation regulators: wave, tap sharply, and push. She used them to show how Peter first was helpless with the noise in his house and asked the wise man for a suggestion. He ended up being angry with the wise man who made the same suggestion to Peter–to bring another animal to his house–five times.

The following passage from page 10 of *Too Much Noise* provided an opportunity for Teacher 1 to use a visual initiation regulator.

Peter went to see the wise man of the village. "What can I do?" Peter asked the wise man.

The teacher assumed the role of the wise man. In this role, she adjusted the wise man's pair of glasses and noticed Peter walking toward the old character (played by herself). Then the wise man uttered to himself, "WHAT?" when he saw Peter walking toward him. Teacher 1 then shifted her role from the wise man to Peter. In this role, she moved her body up and down as if Peter were walking briskly. As Peter, she signed, "CL:1" to illustrate that a person is walking toward the wise man. She then looked up at the wise man and summoned (waved) visually to get the wise man's attention.

I-Peter, Wh-q	I-Wise Man, head up
WHAT (Shifting)	CL:1 (a person walks) WAVE-summon

As Teacher 1 continued the role as Peter, she paused a bit to acknowledge the wise man's attention by raising her eyebrow to signal the nonmanual grammatical marker, Wh-q, before initiating her sign.

I-Wise Man, Wh-q
Pause. YOU KNOW THAT MY HOUSE...

For the parts on page 16, Teacher 1 used the same visual initiation regulator–WAVE-summon–twice (pp. 16 and 24); however, she used a different summon–the sign WELL–for another gloss on page 24.

In the following example (page 20), Teacher 1 used a tactile regulator to illustrate that she was upset with ever increasing noise (after bringing a cow and a donkey into the house)–she tapped sharply on the wise man's shoulder.

"Still too much noise," said Peter. And he went back to the wise man. "Get a sheep," said the wise man.

Teacher 1 assumed the role of Peter and complained that he was fed up with the growing noise and went back to the wise man. She signaled this by nodding her head and pursing her lips while she signed. And then she shifted her body from left to right to indicate that she had changed the role from Peter to the wise man. In this role, she was reading a book.

neutral gaze, head nod	O-G at book*, shift left to right
CL:1 (Shifting)	HOLD-A-BOOK

*Note: O-G at book stands for "Object gaze at the book"

Immediately she assumed the role of Peter by shifting back from right to left. In this role, she straightened her body up and sharply tapped the wise man's shoulder. Again she reassumed the role of the wise man, who reacted, startled by the sharp tap, and turned around and gazed at Peter while holding the pair of glasses in her right hand and the book in her left hand.

I-Wise Man, straightened body	neutral gaze, eye wide open
pursed lip	shoulder up and down
TAP-sharply (Shifting)	STARTLE

Slowly she turned around, put the book down, turned back to acknowledge Peter, and signed WHAT.

gaze down, body shift slightly	I-Peter, Wh-q
PUT-BOOK-ON-DESK	WHAT

In response to the wise man, Teacher 1 reassumed the role of Peter by clasping her hands and shifting her body from right to left, showing on her face an expression of despair, and then initiating her sign as follows:

I-Wise Man
(Shifting) WELL MY BED CREAK...

She used a different tactile initiation regulator–her fingertips–to show how angry she was while playing the role of Peter on p. 32.

Now Peter was angry.
He went to the wise man.
I told you my house was too noisy, he said.
My bed creaks . . .

When Teacher 1 assumed the role of Peter returning to the wise man, her signs became bigger and more tense because she was angry. Then she pushed the wise man, who was reading a book.

neutral gaze,	I-Wise Man,
signs bigger/tense	signs quick/tense
ANGRY	PUSH

Then she reassumed the role of the wise man by shifting from left to right. In this role, she gazed back to Peter and signed WHAT to signal an acknowledgment.

I-Peter, Wh-q
(Shifting) WHAT

Soon after the wise man acknowledged, Teacher 1 changed her role back to Peter by switching from right to the left and initiating dialogue.

I-Wise Man

(Shifting) MY HOUSE...

Results

The findings showed that Teacher 1 used four processes: assess-summon-acknowledge-initiate. In every passage, after she first assessed what the wise man was doing, she then summoned his attention and secured his acknowledgment before initiating her signing.

TEACHERS 2 THROUGH 5

Teacher 2 used the last three processes regularly (summon, acknowledge, and initiate) and used only visual initiation regulators. Unlike Teacher 1, she did not first establish what the wise man was doing, even though she secured the addressee's acknowledgment (individual gaze) by pausing a bit before initiating her signing. Teacher 2 skipped the last part of the story (page 32) due to students' restlessness (1994, personal interview with Teacher 2).

Teacher 3 did not use any of the four processes except the summon. She used a visual initiation regulator (wave) along with the individual gaze only twice (pages 10 and 16) when she told the story without reading the book aloud to her students. After the first, second, and fourth passages, she did not use the summons. Further analysis showed that every time a student interrupted her, she turned her gaze back to the book and "signed" (read) each line from the passage. Thus, reading the book possibly influenced her narrative style.

Teachers 4 and 5 did not use the four processes, except on page 10, where teacher 5 used a vocal initiation regulator. She vocalized the word *umm* and paused a bit before initiating her signing. This occurred when she first read the whole passage and then narrated in sign. For the rest of her narrative, she read and signed almost each line instead of reading the whole passage and signing afterwards. Teacher 4 employed the same strategy, reading and signing from each line.

Table 2 shows the type of initiation regulators that each teacher used during their narratives.

TABLE 2. *Visually Constructed Dialogue*

			Location of Initiation Regulators			
Teacher	Page 10	Page 16	Page 20	Page 24	Page 28	Page 32
1	Wave	Wave	Tap	Hand up	Tap sharply	Push
2	Wave	Wave	Wave	Wave	Wave	n/a
3	Wave	Wave	0	0	0	0
4	0	0	0	0	0	0
5	0	0	0	0	0	0

CONCLUSION

The two findings, regardless of the teacher's own dependence on visual and/or auditory stimuli and the instructional mode of communication (MCE or ASL), are as follows: First, when teachers read written-English stories aloud, as opposed to telling stories without English text, they did not re-create their story and, thus, did not establish visual, interpersonal involvement with their students. Second, when they did not read the book aloud, they would re-create the story and use visual and tactile initiation regulators, even though the characters were assumed to be hearing. As previous studies have shown, whether the addressee can hear or not, the signer (unlike a speaker) must first determine whether the addressee is in the signer's line of vision before selecting an initiation regulator to use to capture the addressee's attention. If the addressee is in the signer's line of vision, the signer must secure the addressee's eye contact (or acknowledgment) by employing individual gaze (I-Gaze) before initiating her signing.

These findings are supported by Tannen (1986), who argues that speakers who repeat their stories normally are re-creating them as part of the creative process and are affected by their personal experience. She contends that this process has the benefit of creating interpersonal involvement between speaker or writer and audience. She notes that many storytellers embellish and modify characters and events in re-creating works of fiction and drama, frequently basing their re-creations on real people and events. The narrative styles of teachers 3, 4, and 5, therefore, will inevitably differ if I ask them to read the book first and retell the story without reading and signing each line.

The data showed that either interrupting a teacher's storyreading or reading line by line apparently affected their narrative style.

This study showed that interpersonal involvement can be created visually, through initiation in constructed dialogue. Thus, the teachers used a visual dialogue introducer to open a constructed dialogue. Instead of using one of the common dialogue introducers, "say," the first three teachers used one of the visual initiation regulators (e.g., wave) along with individual gaze (I-Gaze) as a form of visual dialogue introducers. This approach helped create the constructed dialogue as if it were a signed face-to-face interaction between the signer and addressee. This does not mean that the last two teachers did not use visual interpersonal involvement; the preliminary analysis showed that they did use visual means (e.g., body movements, eye gaze, role shifting, and other visual cues) when they told different parts of the story (e.g., repetition, imagery, details, and other parts as well).

In short, the study incorporating observations by members of the deaf community showed that a signer can't initiate signing until she assesses whether the addressee is in or out of her line of vision, chooses the proper initiation regulator to elicit the addressee's attention, and then receives a form of acknowledgment (e.g., headnod) from the addressee. Then the dialogue can begin. Further, the study finds that one can employ individual gaze to create the effect of imaginary face-to-face dialogue, as well as to regulate turn-taking, as other studies have shown (Mather 1987, 1990; Chen 1993).

REFERENCES

Baer, A. 1991. Tactility in the deaf community. Paper presented at the Gallaudet University Department of Sign Communication Lecture Series, February, Washington, D.C.

Baker, C. 1977. Regulators and turn-taking in American Sign Language discourse. In *On the other hand*, ed. L. Friedman. New York: Academic Press.

Biber, D. 1986. Spoken and written textual dimensions in English: Resolving the contradictory findings. *Language* 62:384–414.

———. 1988. *Variation across speech and writing*. Cambridge: Cambridge University Press.

Chafe, W. 1982. Integration and involvement in speaking, writing, and oral literature. In *Spoken and written language: Exploring orality and literacy,* ed. D. Tannen. Advances in Discourse Processes, vol. 9. Norwood, N.J.: Ablex.

Chafe, W., and D. Tannen. 1987. The relation between written and spoken language. *Annual Review in Anthropology* 16:383–407.

Chen, C. M. 1993. Attention-getting strategies used by a deaf adult with deaf children. In *Communication forum 1993,* ed. E. A. Winston. Washington, D.C.: Gallaudet University School of Communication.

Davidson, J. L., D. Lia, and C. R. Troyer. 1988. Emerging literacy: What we know should determine what we do. Counterpoint and beyond: A response to *Becoming a nation of readers,* ed. J. L. Davidson. Urbana, Ill.: National Council of Teachers of English.

Duncan, S. 1972. Some signals and rules for taking speaking turns in conversations. *Journal of Personal and Social Psychology,* 23:283–292.

Engberg-Pedersen, E. 1992. Speech reports, reported thoughts, and other kinds of reports. Paper presented at Theoretical Issues in Sign Language Research IV, San Diego, California.

Gumperz, J. J. 1982. *Discourse strategies.* Cambridge: Cambridge University Press.

Labov, W. 1984. Intensity. In *Meaning, form, and use in context: Linguistic applications,* ed. D. Schiffrin. Washington, D.C.: Georgetown University Press.

Lentz, E. M. 1986. Strategies for teaching verbs and role shifting. In *Proceedings of the fourth national symposium on sign language research and teaching,* ed. C. Padden. Silver Spring, Md.: National Association of the Deaf.

Liddell, S. 1980. *American Sign Language syntax.* The Hague: Mouton.

———. 1995. Real, surrogate, and token space: Grammatical consequences in ASL. In *Language, gesture, and space,* ed. K. Emmorey and J. Reilly. Hillsdale, N.J.: Lawrence Erlbaum Associates.

Lillo-Martin, D. 1992. The point of view predicate in American Sign Language. Paper presented at Theoretical Issues in Sign Language Research IV, San Diego, California.

Mather, S. M. 1987. Eye gaze and communication in a deaf classroom. *Sign Language Studies* 54:11–30.

———. 1990. Home and classroom communication. In *Educational and developmental aspects of deafness,* ed. D. Moores and K. P. Meadow-Orlans. Washington, D.C.: Gallaudet University Press.

———. 1994. Adult/deaf-toddler discourse. In *Post Milan–ASL and English literacy: Issue, trends, and research,* ed. B. D. Snider. Washington, D.C.: Gallaudet University College for Continuing Education.

Meier, R. 1990. Person deixis in American Sign Language. In *Theoretical issues in sign language research*. Vol. 1, Linguistics, ed. S. Fischer and P. Siple. Chicago: University of Chicago Press.

Metzger, M. 1995. Constructed dialogue and constructed action in American Sign Language. In *Sociolinguistics in Deaf communities*, ed. C. Lucas. Washington, D.C.: Gallaudet University Press.

Ochs, E. 1979. Planned and unplanned discourse. In *Discourse and syntax*, ed. T. Givon. New York: Academic Press.

Padden, C. 1986. Verbs and role-shifting in American Sign Language. In *Proceedings of the fourth national symposium on sign language research and teaching*, ed. C. Padden. Silver Spring, Md.: National Association of the Deaf.

———, ed. 1986. *Proceedings of the fourth national symposium on sign language research and teaching*. Silver Spring, Md.: National Association of the Deaf.

———. 1990. The relation between space and grammar in ASL verb morphology. In *Sign language research: Theoretical issues*, ed. C. Lucas. Washington, D.C.: Gallaudet University Press.

Preston, P. 1994. *Mother father deaf: Living between sound and silence*. Cambridge, Mass.: Harvard University Press.

Roy, C. 1989. Features of discourse in an American Sign Language lecture. In *The sociolinguistics of the Deaf community*, ed. C. Lucas. New York: Academic Press.

Schiffrin, D. 1981. Tense variation in narrative. *Language* 57:45–62.

Tannen, D. 1982. Oral and literate strategies in spoken and written narratives. *Language* 58:1–21.

———. 1985. Relative focus on involvement in oral and written discourse. In *Literacy, language, and learning: The nature and consequences of reading and writing*, ed. D. R. Olson, N. Torrance, and A. Hildyard. Cambridge: Cambridge University Press.

———. 1986. Introducing constructed dialogue in Greek and American conversational and literary narrative. In *Direct and indirect speech*, ed. F. Coulmas. Berlin: Mouton de Gruyter.

———. 1988. Hearing voices in conversation, fiction, and mixed genres. In *Linguistics in context: Connecting observation and understanding*, ed. D. Tannen. Norwood, N.J.: Ablex.

———. 1989. *Talking voices: Repetition, dialogue, and imagery in conversational discourse*. Studies in interactional sociolinguistics, Vol. 6. Cambridge: Cambridge University Press.

Wiener, M., and S. Devoe. 1974. Regulators, channels, and communication disruption. Research proposal, Clark University.

Winston, E. A. 1991. Spatial referencing and cohesion in an American Sign Language text. *Sign Language Studies* 73:397–410.

————. 1992. Space and involvement in an American Sign Language lecture. In *Expanding horizons: Proceedings of the twelfth national convention of the registry of interpreters for the deaf*, ed. J. Plant-Moeller. Silver Spring, Md.: RID Publications.

Linguistic and Pragmatic Aspects

of the Interrogative Form in

Italian Sign Language

Pietro Celo

This research focuses on observing aspects of the interrogative form in Italian Sign Language (LIS) and its pragmatic features in particular.

Because this research is based on observation, it is important to define an observer's qualifications. The observer does not simply observe; he must also "be able to give sense and meaning to what he sees, learns and proves; he is someone who, beyond observing, also possesses the skills of interpreting" (Fabbri 1990, 30; Morin 1993, 76).

My own observations are somewhat colored by my personal experiences—my parents are deaf, and I have been bilingual from birth. As a consequence, I have been intensely involved with deaf people and conscious of the meaning of learning and using a language different from the usual one, with all its technical and affective aspects.

Starting from this privileged viewpoint, I examined theoretical contributions dealing with pragmatics.[1]

One of the most important results of this research was the complete consciousness of a language I had used since childhood in a natural and

---

1. I reviewed Bateson's (1972) and Watzlawick's (1967) studies as well as those of some of the protagonists of psycholinguistic research and philosophical reflections about language: Austin (1962), Fillmore (1968), Searle (1969), Parisi-Antinucci (1973), and Green (1990) as far as performatives, linguistic acts, and pragmatics are concerned. With regard to sign language, I made use of Volterra (1981, 1985, 1987, 1991) and the Institute of Psychology, of the Italian National Research Council's studies, and the works of Klima and Bellugi (1979), Attili and Ricci-Bitti (1983), Bickel (1979, 1980, 1989), and Radutzky (1989, 1990, 1992).

spontaneous way; the fact of pondering on "signs" allowed me to comprehend the "sense" of what I "meant" and, specifically, the analysis of the interrogative form brought me a bit closer to the understanding of how I know what I believe I know.

PRAGMATICS

My working hypothesis and my reflections in general concern the field of pragmatics—the study of those relationships between language and context that are codified by the structure of the language itself (Anolli and Scurati 1989, 40), or, as Georgia M. Green asserts (1990), the comprehension of human intentional action, the interpretation of those acts that are supposed to have been undertaken in order to reach a goal.

The most important studies, after Fillmore's (1968) contributions on presupposition, derive from the encounter between the Semantics School and Austin's philosophy of language (1962). Austin's theory on linguistic acts draws attention to the need to analyze the concrete uses of language in order to understand its very nature. The main concepts of pragmatics include shared belief, speaker intention, mental project, and communicative act. Assuming that means and ends imply communication, pragmatics considers all sorts of communication, including nonverbal, nonconventional, and nonsymbolic (Green 1990, p. 4). But the pragmatic aspects fundamental to this research are those that deal with the performative, that is, the underlying intention in our sentences.

Bateson (1972, 79) postulated two different levels of analysis and abstraction in communication: the same communication act can take place in a "frame" or reference scheme tied to a context in which a real linguistic "action" is contained. The distinction between frame and action may provide the archetype of the differentiation between "action" and "intention" in communication that has been studied by psycholinguists in recent years.

Using these concepts, Watzlawick asserts that every communication act contains a piece of information (report) and an order (command). The report represents its content, and the command refers to the kind of message expressed and must be brought back to the relationship between those who are communicating (Watzlawick et al. 1967).

According to the cybernetic approach, then, report conveys the "data" of communication, whereas command expresses the way communication must be considered; "every communication act is made up by an aspect of content and an aspect of relation in such a way as the latter is metacommunication" (ibid.).

If we believe that the concept of intention may be even partly tied to the notion of command and considered as the frame of a communication act, then, from a strictly linguistic point of view, we must address the studies of "performatives," which are the basis for communicative intention. It is important to consider Searle's distinction between "illocutionary act" and "sentence": In a given sentence there may be different illocutionary acts according to the speaker's intention. For example:

Vieni a cena con me? (Would you come to dinner with me?)
Vieni a cena con me. (Come and have dinner with me.)
Vieni a cena con me! (Come and have dinner with me!)

These sentences have a similar structure (the example is much more obvious in Italian because the sentence structure is exactly the same), but they have different duties in accordance with the speaker's illocutionary acts and intentions.

The illocutionary act is signaled by intonation, often by verb moods, by the presence of an explicit performative verb, by pauses, and by the context (Volterra and Taeschner 1986, 28).

Ross (1970) claims that there are real performative structures underlying human communication; it is as if, while speaking, we unconsciously imply sentences such as "I tell you," "I ask you," and "I order you." In support of this, Parisi-Antinucci's semantic generative model (1973) asserts that the analysis of the sentence structure cannot be considered complete if the speaker's intention is not taken into consideration. The representation of a sentence is then composed of two parts: The first conveys the speaker's intention, the second expresses the content over which the intention is exerted. The representation of the intention is called "performative," and the representation of the content is defined as "sentence." As Searle and Ross pointed out, the speaker's intention is a "linguistic act" carried out in such a way as to make the interlocutor understand, by the use of nonverbal communication and tone of voice, that what one is saying implies an order rather than a question or an affirmation (Anolli and Scurati 1989, 99). The authors assert that every sentence implies an intention and, as a consequence, a performative.

As far as the Italian language is concerned, in the previous example ("come and have dinner with me"), the performative is perceived in the tone of voice (order, request, information) or can be characterized by the use of performative sentences such as to ask, to order, or to inform (ibid.).

The semantic generative model of Parisi-Antinucci is an extremely useful and complete instrument for analyzing the semantic structure of the sentence and for considering its pragmatic aspects of intention and context.

Another fundamental contribution deals with the previously mentioned subject of an "action taking place in a frame" (Bruner 1966). Bruner is particularly concerned with the mother-son relationship, but it is also true that every kind of dialogue implies an effort to understand the speaker's intention and therefore the performatives. According to Bruner, this communication takes place within organized contexts (format) whose features are shared by all those who take part in the communication; it is a set of procedures that organize reciprocal relations as if they were a plan of action (script) agreed on by everybody.

The specification of the scheme (script) as a communication signal that allows the framing of the content of a communication act is similar to the performative structure and the already mentioned concept of "command."

The last subject connected with pragmatics is represented by those "elements of indication" whose reference functionally depends on the context of their assertion (Green 1990, 23); among them we find pronouns, adverbs, verb moods, demonstratives, and interrogatives, and the listener—to understand the speaker's intention–has to interpret them pragmatically, by accessing elements of the nonlinguistic context. These signals reveal the existence of pragmatic structures of communication, expression, and decoding; when accepted, they allow communication among persons.

Because of my interest in the pragmatic aspects of the interrogative form in Italian Sign Language, I took into account research and debate concerning pragmatics and performatives. As a matter of fact, the interrogative form in general is a strictly pragmatic subject whose signal, in spoken languages at least, is the tone of voice that underlines the interrogative intention and, therefore, the interrogative performative. The tone of voice is surely not the only device by which an interrogative intention is emphasized; either the verb tense or the interrogative pronoun makes it clear to the listener that the speaker's utterance is a question. This is the difference between Wh-questions ("Wh" translates into Italian as "K," since the initial sound of almost all wh-words in Italian [*cosa, chi, come, quando,* and so on] is phonetically /k/) and yes-no questions, which can be answered by a simple yes or no, without any "signal of interrogation" except possibly a change in the tone of voice (Bickel 1980, 557).

Interrogative communication, then, possesses all the pragmatic features we have been outlining: tone of voice, nonmanual features, and interrogative pronouns all work as elements of indication; they can be considered as interrogative performatives that imply an interrogative intention.

In LIS we face the same problems and pragmatic features in a different communication modality: a visual-manual mode that substitutes for the acoustic-vocal one and in which ways of decoding and expressing the interrogation are different and original.

ASPECTS OF SIGN LANGUAGE

A fundamental part of this research is represented by the attention given to Italian Sign Language as a meaningful code of communication. LIS possesses all the morphosyntactic features necessary to be considered a real language: It grows old and renews itself, it favors simpler structures and tends toward standardization, and it develops technical vocabulary and can be compared with the sign languages of other countries.

A certain knowledge of nonverbal communication is necessary in order to understand better the meaning of sign language; in fact, the importance given to the verbal system is a peculiar feature of those who, being able to hear, live in a world of words, syllables, and letters. On the other hand, it is also clear that speaking does not only imply the use of words; as a consequence, the verbal system does not correspond only to those aspects that are conventionally contained in written language (Attili and Ricci-Bitti 1983, 13). Comprehension of speech relies in large part on other systems that are called nonverbal: intonation system, paralinguistic system, kinesics. During communicative interaction, all these systems are simultaneously at work and allow the listener to formulate a precise idea of the intention and the content of what is being said, but nonverbal communication is specifically important in that it enables the listener to evaluate the coherence or incoherence of the different systems. Nonverbal communication, therefore, has the metacommunicative function of providing elements with which to interpret the meaning of verbal utterances. As it will be shown later, in the case of Deaf people, the attention of those who are "seeing" language is focused on nonverbal components that could be defined as "nonmanual." The particular attention devoted to the aspects of metacommunication of the nonmanual systems is one of the distinctive features of LIS.

Like other natural sign languages, LIS is morphologically constituted, in fact, also by a nonmanual component that, in comparison to spoken language, does not simply represent nonverbal communication, but is fundamental to understanding most of the single signs and more complex sentence structures (Volterra 1987, 159).

Torso position, eye gaze, head and shoulder movement, mouth opening, and facial expression represent all those elements that take part in the performance of signs and sentences in LIS and, as Liddell asserts (1980), "are significant in forming signals which carry linguistic information necessary for an understanding of the structure of ASL utterances."

Franchi provides an exhaustive description of the nonmanual components of LIS (Volterra 1987, 160) asserting that, in sign languages, every sign possesses its own nonmanual component. Particular facial expressions go with single signs especially if the latter represent feelings or emotions, and oral components such as the opening of the mouth or the emission of one or more puffs often accompany the performance of some other signs.

Nonmanual components may have a morphosyntactic function with regard to the superlative form of adjectives or those verbs that imply repetition or a sudden action. As far as sentence and speech are concerned, nonmanual components are fundamental in order to express the speaker's intention.

Going back to the subject of intentions, which concerns interrogative, negative and relative forms, imperative and conditional, every form is obviously characterized by some specific nonmanual features: head inclination or shoulder movement, eyebrow movement or mouth opening (Poggi 1987, 326).

One of the last and most important aspects of LIS is the so-called personification (Pizzuto 1987, 207). This element is particularly meaningful with regard to personal pronouns that are signaled by eye gaze shifting from right to left or by postural changes giving the idea of role shift, a personification of the one who is performing communicative actions with and among more interlocutors (e.g., in telling a story).

As mentioned before, this research is based on my everyday relationship with this phenomenon: a familiarity due to my double condition of "signer" and hearing person. I judged it important to offer a theoretical framework of pragmatics in general and sign language to provide scientific and experimental support to my work. I have stressed those performative components that, in LIS, are expressed by nonmanual manifestations in such a way as to give an exhaustive picture of the speaker's intentions, whatever the linguistic code might be (sign language or verbal language).

Hypothesis and Aims

One could postulate that LIS has specific mechanisms for the interrogative form comparable to those of verbal languages; therefore, the aim of this research is the observation and identification of pragmatic aspects in Italian Sign Language.

Methodology

The study was conducted within the Deaf community of Verbania (northwest Italy), which leads a rather provincial and not particularly stimulating social life. Sign language there receives the influence of the Lombardy and Piedmont regions (Attili and Ricci-Bitti 1983, 154).

Groups of Deaf people were observed in spontaneous conversations at parties or meetings. All the data were collected by putting down in writing everything considered meaningful to the aim of the study. I transcribed from the sign language into written Italian language. After this preliminary stage, I chose a random sample of six subjects—all Deaf from birth—out of a community of sixty Deaf people different in age, sex, and level of education. The sample was asked to answer questions from an information form.

I videotaped two thirty-minute free conversations of the representative sample on January 27 and 28, 1993; the setting was domestic (the home of one of the subjects) and the tone was informal. Subjects spoke in a natural way, constantly changing topics of discussion. Uneasiness was not detected during the conversations, probably due to practice recordings made previously. While transcribing into the Italian written lan-

TABLE I. *Data Concerning the Six-Subject Sample*

Subject	Sex	Age	Occupation	Married	Children	LIS	Lipreading	School
1	F	59	retired	yes, to a deaf man	yes	yes	yes	Prinotti (Turin)
2	M	60	retired	yes, to a deaf woman	yes	yes	yes	Pavoni (Brescia)
3	F	42	worker	yes, to a deaf man	yes	yes	yes	Via Prinetti (Milan)
4	M	38	clerk	yes, to a deaf woman	yes	yes	yes	Via Settembrini (Milan)
5	M	38	worker	yes, to a deaf woman	no	yes	yes	Pianezza (Turin)
6	F	28	housewife	yes, to a deaf man	no	yes	yes	Piazza Arduino (Milan)

guage, I also made some remarks about particular signs using a notational system for Italian Sign Language. The notational system includes the transcription of the sign in a citational form emphasizing the location, the handshape, the movement, and the orientation of the sign. I identified twenty interrogative sentences in the first conversation and twenty-nine in the second one.

In some respects the data collection was very unusual: The observer was bilingual, deeply involved in the dynamics of the phenomenon, and he himself videotaped the conversations. Furthermore, everything took place in a most natural way since I knew all the subjects (Camaioni and Simion 1990, 49-50).

Data Interpretation and Elaboration

Given the enormous difficulty of writing down sentences in LIS, I made a qualitative analysis of the collected data. Focusing on the pragmatic aspects of the interrogative form, I considered the distinction between Wh-questions and yes-no questions, pointed out by several linguistic theorists as being one of interrogative form. The results were gathered and discussed in two separate parts, each of which discusses the distinction between syntactic and pragmatic aspects of the interrogative form. In conclusion, the nonmanual parameters of communication that represent the most important evidence of an interrogative intention in progress were carefully observed.

Results

WH-QUESTIONS

Wh-questions are always introduced by interrogative formulas such as *who? what? where? when?* and *why?*

Chi sei? (Who are you?)

Cosa vuoi? (What do you want?)

Dove siamo? (Where are we?)

Quando parti? (When will you leave?)

Perché mangi? (Why are you eating?)

Syntactic Aspects

The six-subject sample showed the usage of specific manual signs that automatically decoded the meaning of interrogative formulas of Wh-questions. Handshape, location, palm movement, and orientation were different according to the meaning of the introducing form of the question. (See Figure 4.)

Wh-questions should be easily recognized by the interlocutor because of the existence of this specific interrogative introduction; nevertheless, they are accompanied by nonmanual components that underline the interrogative intention; they are syntactic markers of the interrogative form. Observation and videorecordings support Franchi's assertion that a particular facial expression was attached to every sign. As has been found in other sign languages (e.g., ASL, Danish Sign Language, Swedish Sign Language), squinted eyebrows, a forward inclination of the head, and a prolonged final hold are nonmanual indicators for Wh-questions in LIS. For instance, the interrogative sign "chi?"("who?"), performed with the G handshape on the chin, is accompanied by a horizontal stretching of lips (as in a forced smile), an accentuation of the cheeks as a consequence of lip movements, a slight squinting, and eyebrows down.

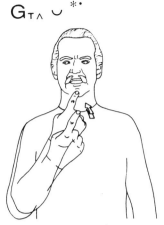

FIGURE I. CHI ("Who")

(Note: The pictures are taken with permission from Radutzky 1992, and the notation system is based on the one devised by Stokoe et al. 1965.)

(See Figure 1.) In this case, the role of spoken Italian as the majority language is clear.

YES/NO QUESTIONS

I found nonpragmatic markers accompanying yes-no questions in LIS. All of the markers I found are of a syntactic nature.

Pragmatic Aspects

In spoken language, yes-no questions are easily recognized due to voice intonation. This kind of question is not difficult to understand within a conversation between speakers.

Whereas intonation points out the presence of an interrogative form in spoken languages, facial expressions are the key to overcoming the possible ambiguity of yes-no questions in sign languages.

Syntactic Aspects

Yes-no questions are characterized by a degree of ambiguity because they can sometimes be confused with expressions that imply assertion or imperative intention.

It is again a syntactic marker, a nonmanual component of LIS, that allows the signer to understand the interrogative intention of a sentence. This nonmanual component is associated with the whole of the expression. In the sentence "Vieni a cena con me?" (Would you come to dinner with me?), we can find head bent and eyebrows raised.

My observations confirm other researchers' results over the last few years on interrogation performed by nonmanual components (Volterra 1987, 168). There is a bending forward of head and torso, a raising of the eyebrows, and consequent accentuation of the aperture of the eyes and wrinkling of the brow every time the signer poses a question.

Pragmatic Aspects

Being aware that it is impossible to resolve the ambiguity of certain sentences without the help of a specific performative, I found out that, with regard to performatives, LIS includes at least two that do not exist in verbal language. Observation suggests that there is a particular sign that introduces interrogative intention. This sign does not appear very frequently, but its existence is certain. I would define it as a pragmatic and performative sign: the hand is a flat O handshape in the signing space in front of the signer (or on the back of the other hand with down-oriented palm) and executes a movement that is repeated at least twice, as in Figure 2.

Unlike introductory signs of Wh-questions, this sign cannot be translated literally in the spoken language; it merely conveys the idea of the

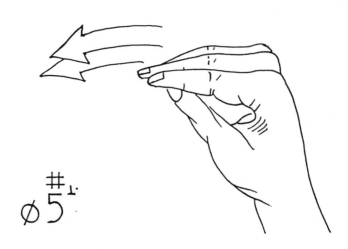

FIGURE 2. *A pragmatic and performative sign that introduces interrogative intent.*

signer's interrogative intention. We can find it both at the beginning of the interrogative sentence and at the end, with a function similar to the orthographic interrogative symbol used in written Spanish. In the first tape, the sign occurs four times: three times preceding the interrogative sentence and one time following it. In the second tape, it occurs twice, only preceding the interrogative sentence. If the sign is produced before the question, the eyebrows are down, and the torso is slightly pulled back. However, if it is produced after the question, it has nonmanual features of a yes-no question (i.e., eyebrows up, head forward).

Eye gaze:	no contact		contact
Eyebrows:	down		up
Body:	back		forward
Signs:	CHIEDERE (pause)	VEDERE AMERICA NUOVO PRESIDENTE	
Translation:	*Io ti chiedo. Hai visto in America il nuovo presidente?*		
	(I ask you. Did you see the new president in America?)		

Eyebrows:		up
Body:		forward
Signs:	NUMERO UGUALE GERMANIA (pause)	CHIEDERE
Translation:	*Ci sarà un numero come in Germania? Io ti chiedo.*	
	(Will there be the same number as in Germany? I ask you.)	

It is interesting to note that, at least twice, this sign is accompanied by a shifting of the eye gaze by the signer away from the co-interlocutor, as if to get a conversational turn.

Another sign that has the same features and is seldom used is the one performed by reproducing a question mark in the signing space in front of the signer, with the hand in a G handshape and palm oriented toward the interlocutor. (See Figure 3.)

This sign appeared three times in the first tape, always after the interrogative sentence, with the torso slightly pulled back and with the nonmanual feature of a yes-no question.

Eyebrows:		up
Body:	forward	back
Signs:	SEMPRE (pause)	PUNTO INTERROGATIVO
Translation:	*Sarà per sempre? Io chiedo.*	
	(Will it be forever? I ask.)	

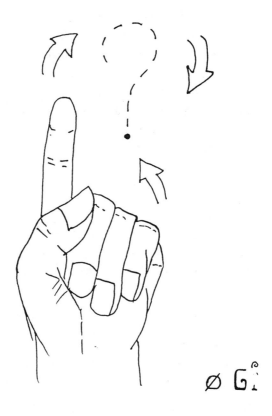

FIGURE 3. *A pragmatic and performative sign used to convey doubt and uncertainty.*

This sign always has a meaning of doubt and expresses the uncertainty and sometimes the skepticism regarding the issue addressed by the question. The meaning of "I don't know," "I'm not sure," or "I don't believe it" is understood.

The same considerations about two different signs with the same meaning appeared in Liddell's research (1978) on nonmanual signals in ASL. Those signs are used to express doubt or disagreement.

Analysis of the Results

My research reveals the existence of two different but combined kinds of aspect in the interrogative form of LIS: syntactic aspect and pragmatic performatives. Both of them represent the interrogative intention implied in the signed sentence.

Syntactic aspects are expressed by nonmanual components of LIS: facial expressions, head and torso position, and so on (see Figure 4); the most interesting element that emerged from the observation was the difference in sign execution according to the kind of question, Wh-question or yes-no question. In the first case, there are specific nonmanual components limited to Wh-signals (who?, what?, why?, where?, when?), whereas, in the second case, there is a standard attitude that accompanies yes-no questions expressing their interrogative intention.

Pragmatic performatives are shown with specific signs in the yes-no questions; there are at least two pragmatic and performative signs— "metasigns"——that have the specific function of signaling the interrogative form that will be used before or after we have signed. These signs are lexical signals of pragmatic intentions.

When these signs are produced after the interrogative sentence, the nonmanual components that accompany them are similar to those described for yes-no questions. It seems that the nonmanual component of the interrogative sentence is being projected on the pragmatic markers. In fact, if the flat O pragmatic marker occurs before the question, it has its own nonmanual marker with eyebrows down that flags the interrogative, in effect topicalizing it. And if the pragmatic meaning of the marker is doubt or skepticism (which is the case with the G handshape marker), the torso is pulled back slightly as if to establish a distance from the question. To be noted also is the shift in the eye gaze of the signer that accompanies the flat O version, interpretable possibly as a request for a turn.

The two signs previously described are not frequently used in LIS and, outside the context of the sentence, signify "question" and "question mark."

Finally, these pragmatic signs concern only the category of yes-no questions and exclude, with regards to my observations, all other kinds of interrogation (such as rhetorical or ironic interrogation).

CONCLUSION

I conclude this chapter with some considerations of the opening hypothesis, that is, the observation of pragmatic aspects of the interrogative form in LIS.

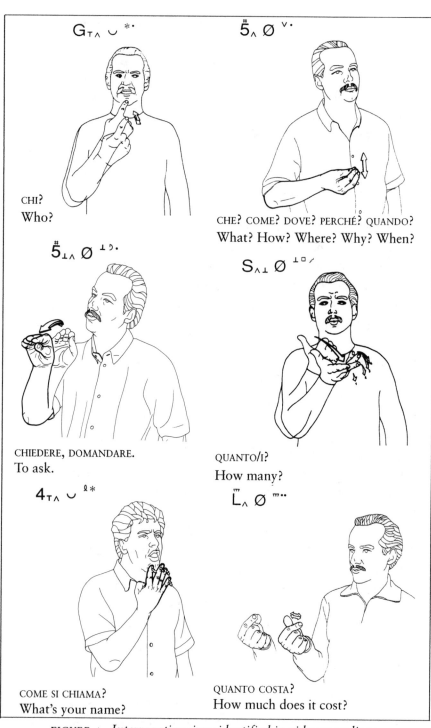

FIGURE 4. *Interrogative signs identified in videorecordings*

Deaf people pay particular attention to the nonverbal frame of what is expressed, independent of the linguistic code used, and, therefore, to all components of nonverbal communication. Sight, in a Deaf person, may serve as a channel for transmitting all information expressed in this way (Volterra 1991, 207). It must be considered that a Deaf person always perceives a question via the visual channel and that LIS possesses performative aspects capable of revealing the pragmatic intentions of the interlocutor (Poggi 1987, 326).

At least one issue is strictly connected with my observation, data gathering, and conclusions: Can we consider the possibility of teaching and the use of self-awareness of pragmatic signs employed by LIS signers as a valid educational intervention? This research involved adults who were Deaf from birth because their knowledge of LIS was richer and more complete, but the presence of performative signs and aspects can be seen in both Deaf adults and Deaf children. As far as the latter are concerned, we wonder whether it is sufficient to teach a correct morphosyntactic system to guarantee fluent use of the language or whether it is only the usage itself that can ensure the formal correctness of the language (Bickel 1980, 550). The answer seems connected with a constant use, in the linguistic education of a Deaf child, of performatives such as interrogation, exclamation, and command, which address the use of the language toward more abstract and complex realities (Bickel 1980, 557).

As Bickel suggests, it is appropriate to start children on the performative use of language, to make them capable of comprehending and posing questions (Bickel 1979, 129). Perhaps the teaching of the pragmatic elements of the interrogative form in LIS could present a solution to this problem and favor a spontaneous development of metalinguistic skills in Deaf children (Bickel 1989, 239).

However, children have a global perception of sonorous elements (in the case of hearing children) or visual elements (in the case of Deaf children) that constitute language; just as the hearing child grasps all those aspects that are not apparent in speech, so the Deaf child is fascinated by all nonmanual components of LIS (Bickel 1979, 125) that represent the intention implied in communication (Liddell 1980).

Italian Sign Language is the language Deaf people learn spontaneously. It is part of their life and condition; it is the code Deaf persons tend to prefer over the vocal one, and the use of both of them develops more complete communicative skills (Battacchi and Montanini-Manfredi 1991, 27). With regard to this, I support the prospect of bilingualism of Deaf people—a prospect personified in the most recent studies on sign languages of other countries.

The conclusion of this research is open to various solutions since, given the existence of pragmatic aspects in LIS, the discussion of their contribution remains a matter of study and research.

REFERENCES

Angelini, N., R. Borgioli, A. Folchi, and M. Mastromatteo. 1991. *I primi 400 segni. Piccolo dizionario della lingua italiana dei segni per comunicare con I sordi*. Firenze: La Nuova Italia.

Anolli, L., and C. Scurati, eds. 1989. *Il bambino, segno, simbolo, parola*. Milano: Franco Angeli.

Antinucci, F., and D. Parisi. 1976. Lo sviluppo semantico nel primo linguaggio del bambino. In *Psicolinguistica*, ed. F. Antinucci and C. Castelfranchi. Bologna: Il Mulino.

Argyle, M. 1977. *Bodily communication*. London: Methuen and Co.

Attili, G., and A. Ricci-Bitti, eds. 1983. *I gesti e I segni*. Roma: Bulzoni.

Austin, J. L. 1962. *How to do things with words*. Cambridge, Mass.: Harvard University Press.

Baker, C., and C. Padden. 1978. Focusing on the nonmanual components of American Sign Language. In *Understanding language through sign language research*, ed. P. Siple. New York: Academic Press.

Baker-Shenk, C. 1985. Nonmanual behaviors in sign language: Methodological concerns and recent findings. In *Sign language research 1983*, ed. W. Stokoe and V. Volterra. Silver Spring, Md.: Linstok Press. Roma: Istituto di Psicologia C.N.R.

Barbieri, M.S. 1977. *Gli inizi del linguaggio: Aspetti cognitivi e comunicativi*. Firenze: La Nuova Italia.

Bateson, G. 1972. *Steps to an ecology of mind*. New York: Chandler.

———. 1979. *Mind and nature: A necessary unity*. New York: Dutton.

Battacchi, M., and M. Montanini-Manfredi. 1991. *Pensiero e comunicazione nei bambini sordi*. Bologna: Clued.

Bergman, B. 1984. Nonmanual components in signed language: Some sentence types in Swedish Sign Language. In *Recent research on European sign languages*, ed. F. Loncke, P. Boyes-Braem, and Y. Lebrun. Lisse: Swets and Zeitlinger B.V.

Bickel, J. 1979. Competenza linguistica e competenza comunicativa nelle sordità infantili. In *Metodi e tecniche nel campo dell'educazione, riabilitazione, istruzione dei bambini sordi*. Milano: C.R.S. Amplifon Edizioni Tecniche.

————. 1980. Il modello pragmatico come guida per l'acquisizione del linguaggio nel bambino sordo. *Neuropsichiatria infantile.* Fasc. 227.

————. 1989. Sordità infantili. In *Il bambino con problemi di linguaggio.* Lovorno: Belforte Editore Libraio.

Bigi, A. 1991. La lingua segnica tra Lingua Italiana dei Segni (LIS) e Linguaggio Mimico Gestuale Italiano. *Effetta* 10.

Boyes-Braem, P., M. L. Fournier, F. Rickli, S. Corazza, M. L. Franchi, and V. Volterra. 1990. A comparison of techniques for expressing semantic roles and locative relations in two different languages. In *SLR 1987. Papers from the fourth international symposium on sign language research,* ed. W. H. Edmonson and F. Karlsson. Hamburg: Signum Press.

Brackett, D. 1985. Strategie di comunicazione di gruppo per i bambini sordi. *The Volta Review* (January). Milano: C.R.S. Amplifon Edizioni Tecniche.

Brown, G., and G. Yule. 1986. Il ruolo del contesto nell'interpretazione. In *Analisi del discorso.* Bologna: Il Mulino.

Bruner, J. S., R. Olver, and R. Greenfield. 1966. *Studies in cognitive growth.* New York: Wiley.

Camaioni, L., and F. Simion. 1990. *Metodi di ricerca in psicologia dello sviluppo.* Bologna: Il Mulino.

Camaioni, L., V. Volterra, and E. Bates. 1986. *La comunicazione nel primo anno di vita.* Torino: Boringhieri.

Chomsky, N. 1969. *Language and mind.* New York: Harcourt, Brace, and World.

Corazza, S. 1990, The morphology of classifier handshape in Italian Sign Language (LIS). In *Sign language research,* ed. C. Lucas. Washington, D.C.: Gallaudet University Press.

Corazza, S., E. Radutzky, A. Santarelli, M. L. Verdirossi, V. Volterra, and A. Zingarini. 1985. Italian Sign Language: A general summary of research. In *Sign language research 1983,* ed. W. Stokoe and V. Volterra. Silver Spring, Md.: Linstok Press. Roma: Istituto di Psicologia C.N.R.

Demetrio, D. 1991. *Educatori di professione.* Firenze: La Nuova Italia.

Engberg-Pedersen, E. 1990. Pragmatics of nonmanual behavior in Danish Sign Language. In *SLR 1987. Papers from the fourth international symposium on sign language research,* ed. W. H. Edmonson and F. Karlsson. Hamburg: Signum Press.

Fabbri, D. 1990. *La memoria della regina.* Milano: Guerrini e Associati.

Fabbri, D., and L. Formenti. 1991. *Carte d'identità.* Milano: Franco Angeli.

Fillmore, C. 1968. La grammatica dei casi. In *La linguistica: Aspetti e problemi,* ed. L. Heilmann and E. Rigotti. Bologna: Il Mulino.

Furth, H.G. 1971. *Pensiero senza linguaggio.* Padova: Armando.

Green, G.M. 1990. *Pragmatica.* Padova: Franco Muzzio.

Hinde, R. 1972 . *Nonverbal communication.* Cambridge: Cambridge University Press.

Klima, E., and U. Bellugi. 1979. *The signs of language.* Cambridge, Mass.: Harvard University Press.

Lentin, L. 1973. *Il bambino e la lingua parlata.* Roma: Armando.

Liddell, S. R. 1978. Nonmanual signals and relative clauses in American Sign Language. In *Understanding language through sign language research,* ed. P. Siple. New York: Academic Press.

———. 1980. *American Sign Language syntax.* The Hague/Paris/New York: Mouton.

———. 1985. Segments and syllables in ASL: Evidence from compound formation. In *Sign language research 1983,* ed. W. Stokoe and V. Volterra. Silver Spring, Md.: Linstok Press. Roma: Istituto di Psicologia C.N.R.

Lumbelli, L. 1978. *Pedagogia della comunicazione verbale.* Milano: Franco Angeli.

Magarotto, C., ed. 1983. Deafness today and tomorrow, reality and utopia. In *Proceedings of the ninth congress of the World Federation of the Deaf.* Roma: Magarotto.

Maragna, S., and L. Pagliarini Rampelli. 1985. A preliminary study of Italian Sign Language conducted in a school for the deaf in Rome. In *Sign language research 1983,* ed. W. Stokoe and V. Volterra. Silver Spring, Md.: Linstok Press. Roma: Istituto di Psicologia C.N.R.

Montanini-Manfredi, M., M. Facchini, and L. Fruggeri. 1979. *Da gesto al gesto: Il bambino sordo tra gesto e parola.* Bologna: Cappelli.

Morin, E. 1993. *Introduzione al pensiero complesso.* Milano: Sperling and Kupfer.

Oleron, P. 1978. *Le langage gestuel des sordes: Syntax et communication.* Paris: Edition du CNRS.

Parisi, D., and F. Antinucci. 1973. *Elementi di grammatica.* Torino: Boringhieri.

Paulus, J. 1971. *Linguaggio e funzione simbolica.* Roma: Armando.

Pigliacampo, R. 1991. *Sociopsicopedagogia del bambino sordo.* Quattroventi edicion. Urbino.

Pizzuto, E. 1987. Aspetti morfo-sintattici. In *La Lingua Italiana dei Segni,* ed. V. Volterra. Bologna: Il Mulino.

Pizzuto, E., E. Giuranna, and G. Gambino. 1990. Manual and nonmanual morphology in Italian Sign Language: Grammatical constraints and discourse processes. In *Sign language research,* ed. C. Lucas. Washington, D.C.: Gallaudet University Press.

Poggi, I., ed. 1987. Lessico e grammatica nei gesti e nelle parole. In *Le parole nella testa: Guida a una educazione linguistica positivista.* Bologna: Il Mulino.

Radutzky, E. J. 1989. La Lingua Italiana dei Segni: Historical change in the sign language of Deaf people in Italy. Ph.D. diss.

———. 1990. The changing handshape in Italian Sign Language. In *SLR 1987. Papers from the fourth international symposium on sign language research,* ed. W. H. Edmonson and F. Karlsson. Hamburg: Signum Press.

Radutzky, E. J., et al., eds. 1992. *Dizionario bilingue elementare della Lingua Italiana dei Segni*. Roma: Edizioni Rappa.

Riva-Crugnola, C. 1988. *Nascita del simbolo e costituzione dell 'oggetto nella prima infanzia*. Milano: Franco Angeli.

Romeo, O. 1991. *Dizionario dei segni: La lingua dei segni in 1400 immagini*. Bologna: Zanichelli.

Ross, J. 1970. On declarative sentences. In *Readings in English transformational grammar*, ed. R. J. Jacobs and P. S. Rosenbaum. Waltham, Mass: Ginn and Co.

Sacks, O. 1989. *Seeing voices: A journey into the world of the deaf*. Berkeley and Los Angeles: University of California Press.

Schaffer, H.R., ed. 1977. *Studies in mother-infant interaction*. London: Academic Press.

Searle, J. 1969. *Speech acts*. Cambridge: Cambridge University Press.

Stokoe, W. 1978. *Sign language structure*. Silver Spring, Md.: Linstok Press.

Stokoe, W., D. Casterline, and C. Croneberg. 1965. *Dictionary of America Sign Language on linguistic principles*. Silver Spring, Md.: Linstok Press.

Stokoe, W., and V. Volterra, eds. 1985. *Sign language research 1983*. Silver Spring, Md.: Linstok Press. Roma: Istituto di Psicologia C.N.R.

Valli, C., and C. Lucas. 1992. *Linguistics of American Sign Language: A resource text for ASL users*. Washington, D.C.: Gallaudet University Press.

Volterra, V., ed. 1981. *I segni come parole: La comunicazione dei sordi*. Torino: Boringhieri.

———, ed. 1985. Educazione bimodale e bilingue del bambino sordo. In *Età evolutiva*. Firenze: Giunti-Barbera.

———, ed. 1987. *La Lingua Italiana dei Segni: La comunicazione visivo-gestuale dei sordi*. Bologna: Il Mulino.

———. 1991. La competenza linguistica del bambino sordo. In *Apprendimento e patologia neuropsichica nei primi anni di vita*, ed. G. Masi and G. Ferretti. Roma: Bola.

Volterra, V., S. Corazza, A. Laudanna, E. Radutzky, and F. Natale. 1984. Italian Sign Language: The order of elements in the declarative sentence. In *Recent research on European sign languages,* ed. F. Loncke, P. Boyes-Braem, and Y. Lebrun. Lisse: Swets and Zeitlinger B.V.

Volterra, V., and T. Taeschner. 1986. *Strumenti di analisi per la prima valutazione del linguaggio infantile*. Roma: Bulzoni.

Vygotskii, L.S. 1964. *Thought and language*. Cambridge, Mass.: MIT Press.

Watzlawick, P., J. Bavelas, and D. Jackson. 1967. *Pragmatics of human communication: A study of interactional patterns, pathologies, and paradoxes*. New York: Norton.

Werner, H., and B. Kaplan. 1963. *Symbol formation: An organismic developmental approach to language and expression of thought*. New York: Wiley.

The Tobacco Story: Narrative Structure

in an American Sign Language Story

Julie Wilson

This chapter presents an in-depth analysis of the structure of an ASL narrative, the "Tobacco Story." In this paper, we focus on two leading methods by which narratives have been analyzed: Labov's (1972) narrative sections of abstract, orientation, complicating action, and evaluation, and Gee's (1986) analysis of narrative structure in oral cultures, involving an underlying poetic structure consisting of lines, stanzas, and strophes. The tobacco story has many characteristics of the highly developed narratives that arise in a largely oral culture.

The structure of narratives in spoken language has been analyzed a great deal, resulting in many different ways of describing narrative structure, including "work on story grammars, schemas and scripts, macrostructures, text grammars, and several sorts of conversational analysis" (Gee 1986, 391). Researchers have investigated narratives seeking their basic definition and structure. However, to what extent are the models they have developed applicable across cultures and languages, and to what extent are they specific to particular languages and cultures? Narratives in spoken languages have been categorized according to prosodic features (Gee 1986); many of these criteria cannot apply to language in a different modality (e.g., signed languages, which do not have intonation contours or pitch). Labov was able to differentiate what he calls the evaluation and the complicating action sections in English narratives on the basis of syntactic complexity (Labov 1972); can the same distinction apply to signed languages? ASL morphology in particular is very different from that of English. To what extent does morphology play a role in delineating narrative sections in ASL? This chapter attempts to develop a preliminary description of the structure of an ASL narrative and to identify characteristics of different elements of the narrative.

The first theory of narrative structure was that of Labov (1972). Labov defined a minimal narrative as sequence of at least two clauses that are temporally ordered. Narrative clauses (complicating action) have "temporal juncture": if the clauses were rearranged, the result would be a different narrative. Therefore, a sentence such as "I was running down the street when suddenly I met Jones" could not satisfy this minimal definition because rearranging the clauses would not produce a different narrative: "I met Jones when I was running down the street." However, in a sentence such as "The guy jumped into the car and pointed a gun at me," reversing the two clauses would create a different story.

Most narratives are much longer than Labov's basic definition. Though two "event" clauses with temporal juncture are the minimal requirements, what Labov terms a "fully-formed" narrative contains other kinds of clauses. The event clauses are part of the complicating action section of the narrative. The sections of narrative that may appear are, in order:

1. Abstract: A sentence at the beginning that summarizes the story
2. Orientation: Clauses near the beginning that provide a setting
3. Complicating action: The events of the narrative; what happened
4. Evaluation: The point of the story
5. Coda: The narrative is brought back to present time

Labov categorized narrative elements mainly by their function. Empirically, these narrative sections, particularly the evaluation and complicating action, could be distinguished by their syntax. The syntax of complicating action clauses is simple: verbs are in the simple past or historical present tense; evaluation clauses are signaled by departures from this basic syntax and tense, including the presence of modals, negatives, repetition, and expressive phonology.

Since Labov, other researchers have developed different ways to describe the structure of a narrative. One of these was Gee (1986), who analyzed the narratives of a young African-American girl and compared them to those of a white school teacher. Unlike Labov, he did not seek functional sections of narrative; rather, he examined pauses and prosodic features such as intonation contours to segment the narratives. Based on these features, he was able to divide the narrative into smaller units (lines) and larger units (stanzas). A line, which may or may not be a clause, is the basic "idea unit," containing only one piece of new information. In the stories Gee analyzed, lines are marked by a continuous intonation contour, ending on a nonfalling pitch glide. Often lines end with a short pause or hesitation, or other boundary markers. The lines are grouped into stanzas, usually of four lines each, also marked by intonation and a larger pause. Further, narratives contain even larger units, called strophes and sections. Gee, comparing the stories of the young African-American girl with the elderly white schoolteacher, concluded that both had the same underlying structure; however, the schoolteacher did not mark stanzas as overtly as did the young girl.

CROSS-LINGUISTIC DIFFERENCES IN NARRATIVE STRUCTURE

Although Labov and Gee sometimes write as if narrative structure were universal, they acknowledge that their analysis of one speaker's narratives would "at best, tell us directly only about the units that appear to be operative in the language of (part of) one particular cultural group" (Gee 1986, 393). Several researchers have studied narratives in languages other than English and found differences from the earlier descriptions. Hymes (1981) examined the narratives of Native-American speakers and found that they are, as in Gee's analysis of American-English speakers, patterned into verses and lines. The patterning was seen in the initial linguistic elements that are the "regulatory principle itself. . .they are the aspects of the measuring that makes the material verse"(318).

In their 1991 article, Minami and McCabe examined short oral narratives by Japanese children. They based their analysis on both Gee's technique of stanza analysis and the Labovian technique of categorizing clauses according to function. Their results showed that Japanese narratives tended to be succinct and in a set format of three stanzas of three lines each. In the typical stanza, the first line serves as an orientation, the second describes an act, and the third, an outcome. They argue that the haiku, with its brief stanzas and set number of lines, has penetrated so deeply into Japanese culture that it serves as a discourse regulator for stories told in everyday life by schoolchildren.

These three descriptions (Gee, Hymes, and Minami and McCabe) of poetic narrative structures all seem to fit the general description of narrative as consisting of lines and stanzas (and sometimes verses or strophes), and all three appear to match these sections with a rhetorical pattern (such as Labov's model or Minami and McCabe's orientation-act-outcome). The area in which they differ, however, is in what regulates the lines and stanzas. Minami and McCabe find that Japanese narratives are patterned episodically, with strict regulation on how many lines make up a stanza and how many stanzas can be contained in the entire narrative (Minami and McCabe 1991). Chinookian stanzas do not have a tight structure or a fixed length, but the first linguistic element in each line follows a pattern, typically a parallel structure (Hymes 1981, 318). Gee finds that American English narratives have an event structure: Events and the syntactic form of their telling are parallel within the lines of a stanza (Gee 1986).

NARRATIVE IN AMERICAN SIGN LANGUAGE

Do narratives in American Sign Language (ASL) organize themselves into lines, stanzas, and verses as do the spoken languages mentioned? The researchers in the previous section suggest that narratives tend to pattern themselves in that way, particularly in oral cultures (Hymes 1981; Gee 1986). ASL—as an unwritten language—could easily qualify as a language with a rich "oral" tradition. If ASL does follow the patterns mentioned above, how does it regulate its stanzas and lines? What rhetorical pattern does an ASL narrative follow?

Preliminary research into the stanza organization of an ASL narrative has been undertaken by Gee and Kegl (1983). They identified episodes on the basis of length of pauses in the narrative. They found that the episodes that the pauses identified were strongly correlated with their intuitive division of the narrative into episodes based on rhetorical function, sections with labels such as *setting, catalyst, failure,* and *success* (Gee and Kegl 1983). Pauses seem to provide additional empirical evidence for the existence of sectioning in ASL narratives; however, they do not necessarily provide evidence for what regulates this sectioning.

More recent research was conducted by Bahan and Supalla, who used Gee's (1986) framework of narrative structure. Within this framework, they identified the role of eye gaze as one of the nonmanual behaviors that define lines in an ASL narrative. A change in eye gaze, as well as the presence of a pause, a blink, or a head nod, are phenomena that most often occur at the end of a line in ASL (Bahan and Supalla 1995).

Aside from these two articles, there has been little work that deals specifically with the structure of narrative in ASL. However, there has been some work in the area of discourse features in ASL lectures (Roy 1989; Winston 1991, 1993). Lectures, like narratives, take the form of a single long turn by one signer and thus may have some features in common with them.

Roy identified episodes in the ASL lecture. The signals that distinguish episodes are lexical items that are used as discourse markers: the signs NOW and NOW-THAT appear at the boundaries between episodes (Roy 1989). Winston also studied a lecture in ASL, focussing on the use of space to contrast different ideas. She concluded that space can have evaluative force in ASL that it cannot have in spoken languages (1993); placement of entities in space also serves to create cohesion in a text (1991). Winston's and Roy's studies raise the possibility that space or the parallel use of discourse markers throughout sections may serve as discourse regulators much as the length of a stanza does in Japanese children's narratives.

THE PRESENT RESEARCH: METHODOLOGY

The data in this analysis were collected as part of a three-year project on sociolinguistic variation in ASL sponsored by the National Science Foundation. The story included in the data is an ASL narrative collected from an adult Deaf signer. The narrative was told by an older Deaf man whom I will call John; the story he tells is about three minutes long. The narrative occurs during an informal group interaction involving six older ASL users. The story is about a boy in school who begins chewing tobacco during class and spitting it out the window. The teacher can't figure out what's happening, and neither can the principal in his first appearance. The punchline of the story occurs when the principal returns and reveals that he has discovered the tobacco-chewing because, sitting in his office directly below the class, he noticed brown stains all over the flagpole outside his window.

I selected this from several narratives because it has the advantage of being both locally situated in an informal context and because it is a story of personal rather than vicarious experience. Labov claims that the latter is crucial for the study of evaluation in narrative (1972, 366-368).

The following is the text of John's narrative, the tobacco story. It includes glossing conventions from ASL, from the discourse analysis of spoken languages, and my own additions. The English translation of the story is in Appendix 1.

Glossing Conventions and Symbols

{ = two utterances at the same time
[= the utterance begins with no pause after the previous speaker
" " = reported speech
numbers in bold = pause time
underlined utterance = comments by interlocutor
GLOSS (p) = the sign is a pantomime, not a lexical sign
GLOSS (g) = the sign is a gesture, not a lexical sign
[GLOSS GLOSS]t = the preceding sign(s) are topicalized
CL: = classifier predicate
loc: = nonlocative sign with a locative function (i.e., it occurs in a location other than its unmarked one)

Nonmanual signals, including nonlinguistic facial expressions, are glossed with brackets indicating what part of the discourse they accompany. If a marked facial expression persists without being accompanied by signs, the pause time is noted in bold.

TOBACCO STORY

1   USED-TO ME CLASS ON THERE
2   AND THERE
3   REMEMBER...[39] MRS GILL
4   FORGET THAT TEACHER?
5   MY TEACHER
6   S-H-E WRITE BLACK B-R-D ("board")
7   WRITE (loc: blackboard)
8   ME, J-A-C-K, S-A-N-D-Y (SANDY (name sign))
9   ME, JACK CL: BE-SEATED-SIDE-BY-SIDE...[20]
10 WELL (g) JACK TOBACCO (IN CLASS, REMEMBER ILLEGAL)...[20] PUT-IN-MOUTH
11 BE-CHEWING (p)
12 TEACH WRITE (loc: board)

13 WINDOW RAISE (p) DURING WEATHER COLD

14 WINTER TIME

15 RAISE-WINDOW (p) ABOUT-THIS-MUCH (cl)

16 BE-CHEWING (p)

17 LOOK-AROUND (p)

18 SPIT (p)

19 CL: GO-THROUGH-OPENING

20 BE-EXTREMELY-SKILLED CL: GO-THROUGH-OPENING...[40]

21 TEACHER LOOK-AROUND

22 "WHAT THAT SOUND?"

23 [innocent expression [60]] LOOK-AT-EACH-OTHER "NOTHING MUCH"

24 WRITE (on board)

25 BE-CHEWING SPIT (pant)

26 WINDOW SPIT (iterative)

27 BE-EXTREMELY-SKILLED-AT CL: GO-THROUGH OPENING (iterative)

28 NOT CL : HIT-THE-EDGE-OF-OPENING [CL: SPLATTER-OVER-OPENING
shaking head slightly [24]]

29 CL: GO-THROUGH-OPENING (iterative) BE-EXTREMELY-SKILLED-AT...[18]

30 D-R B-R-I-L-L, KNOW PRO-3 (to audience)

31   {B-R-I-L-L

32   {SIGN USED-TO #W-H-T D-R...

33 neg-sign   {b-by-mouth ("Brill") (nodding)

34   {b-by-mouth b-by-mouth

35 [D-R B-R-I-L-L (facial expression: stern) ENTER (emph.)] WITHOUT KNOCK

36 [ENTER LOOK-AROUND (continued stern expression)]

37 [innocent expression [70] LOOK-AT-EACH-OTHER]

38 COME-WALKING-OVER (p)...[31]

39 PRO-3 STICK-OUT-AND-WIGGLE-TONGUE (p) (pointing to tongue)...[29]

40 S SANDY (S-A-N-D-Y) STICK-OUT-AND-WIGGLE-TONGUE (pant.)...[27]

41 LOOK...[60]

42 STICK-OUT-AND-WIGGLE-TONGUE (p) simultaneously with WHAT?

43 ME...[24] [STICK-OUT-AND-WIGGLE-TONGUE (p) f.e.: negative, innocent]

44 GO-AWAY (g)...[46]

45 TURN-TO-SIDE (p) "HEY (g) HAPPEN MOUTH?"

46 (body shift) "LEAVE SWALLOW (emph) TOBACCO FINISH SWALLOW

47 BRILL LOOK

48 FINISH NONE

49 LEAVE...[18]

50 FEW MINUTE

51 FEW MINUTE...[75]

52 JACK FEEL

53 NO-NO (g) (in response to an interlocutor who is out of sight)

54 JACK FEEL GREEN FACE

55 SICK

56 [puffs out cheeks — as if holding in vomit]

57 HAVE-TO GO INFIRMARY HAVE-TO...[20]

58 LEAVE

59 LATER DOOR-OPEN

60 [expression: look up in astonishment [61]]

61 BRILL AGAIN LOOK...[36]

62 "I (Eng. sign) THINK ("thought") S-O" ...[39]

63 "HOW KNOW PRO-3 ("BRILL")?

64 PRO-I NONE, PRO-3

65 JACK HAVE

66 "HOW KNOW PRO-3?"...[10]

67 "LOOK-THERE WINDOW"...

68 [lean forward, expression of astonishment [40]]

69 F-L-A-G CL: LARGE-CYLINDRICAL-OBJECT

70 CL: TREE-SHAPED CL: SUBSTANCE-BE-SPREAD-ON ('th')

71 [BRILL O-F-F-I-C-E] (t) BELOW ('cs')

72 OUR CLASS ABOVE ('cs')...

73 (unintelligible conversational repair) BRILL MUST LOOK WINDOW

74 [expression of astonishment] CL: FLAT-SUBSTANCE-SPREAD-ON

75 LOOK

76 GO-UP

77 "CLASS, OH-I-SEE"

78 THAT CATCH

79 THAT SEE THAT HOW BRILL FIND O-U-T...[54]

80 GOOD

81 {GOOD OLD D-A-Y-S

82 {HI

83 B-R-I-L-L, BRILL FROM CALIFORNIA KNOW ....

The tobacco story does include many of the narrative sections that Labov described. However, the first element—the abstract—is not present: although John introduces the topic of school, he does not summarize the story. Lines 3-9 compose an orientation, although, as Labov said, orientation can be included at various points throughout the narrative as well as in the beginning (there are further orientation clauses after line 10). The orientation identifies the teacher and the three students and tells the audience what they were doing. (Note that the orientation clauses could be reversed without changing the meaning of the section: The narrator could have signed "me, Jack, and Sandy were sitting side by side" before signing "the teacher was writing on the board.") As Labov has noted, orientations in English clauses are often in the progressive aspect (1972, 364); in my translation, these clauses are also in the progressive aspect. The question of what devices ASL uses to mark various sections of narratives is important. In this narrative, the orientation clauses, in contrast to the complicating action and evaluation clauses, contain no constructed dialogue, pantomime, or marked facial expression.

Complicating Action and Evaluation Clauses

Most of the narrative is composed of complicating action interwoven with evaluation. The complicating action clauses, those that relate what happened, are in lines such as 21-24:

21   TEACHER LOOK-AROUND
22   "WHAT THAT SOUND?"
23   [innocent expression [60]] LOOK-AT-EACH-OTHER "NOTHING MUCH"
24   WRITE (on board)

These clauses could not be reversed and still compose the same story. The students' reply in 23, for instance, must follow the teacher's question in 22.

More difficult to identify are evaluation clauses. Evaluation explains why the events (in the complicating action) are important (or exciting, terrifying, or amusing): Evaluation in narrative gives hearers an idea of why the story is being told. Labov writes that storytelling is designed primarily to ward off one potential question from the audience: "So what?"

(1972, 366). Evaluation is the element that conveys the point of the narrative. Accomplishing evaluation in narrative is not often as simple as establishing a separate clause that says, "It was really exciting" or "I felt scared"; in fact, these more overt strategies are those that Labov termed "external evaluation." Narrators that use these strategies are usually judged less skilled and are often those who come from less oral cultures (Labov 1972). The more developed, powerful narratives are those that have evaluation embedded and interwoven with event clauses.

Labov's 1972 work, "The Transformation of Experience in Narrative Syntax," deals mainly with embedded (internal) evaluation and the syntactic clues that can help the analyst find the evaluation in a story. Briefly, he claims that the syntax of complicating action clauses (without evaluation) is relatively simple. Clauses with modals, negatives, quantifiers such as "all," which are repeated, or any comparisons of the present state of affairs with a conditional one, have an evaluative force.

Several lexical signs and clauses in the tobacco story supply external evaluation. In lines 27–29, the narrator supplies an evaluation of Jack's skill in spitting tobacco:

27   BE-EXTREMELY-SKILLED-AT CL: GO-THROUGH OPENING (iterative)
28   NOT CL : HIT-THE-EDGE-OF-OPENING [CL: SPLATTER-OVER-OPENING SHAK-
        ING HEAD SLIGHTLY [24]]
29   CL: GO-THROUGH-OPENING (ITERATIVE) BE-EXTREMELY-SKILLED-AT...[18]

The sign glossed as "BE-EXTREMELY-SKILLED-AT" ("F" at the chin) is an external evaluation in which the narrator steps back and comments on the events of the narrative. However, this section contains another element, a sign that has undergone a morphological process: "CL: GO-THROUGH-OPENING (iterative)." Klima and Bellugi (1979) identify a number of inflections that reduplicate or change the movement of a verb. The inflection in lines 27 and 29 consists of a fast reduplication of the movement of the sign. This aspectual inflection itself is evaluative of Jack's skill in getting the tobacco through the window. The inflection functions as a quantifier (it might be translated into English with the quantifier *every*: "He got it through *every* time"). The sentence with the inflection, therefore, does not identify the kind of unitary event of the complicating action; rather, the repetitive nature of the inflection serves to emphasize Jack's skill. Also evaluative in this section is the repetition of the sign GO-THROUGH-OPENING itself, in lines 18 and 19 (without the inflection) and lines 27 and 29 (with the inflection).

Another use of complex morphology to indicate evaluation occurs in line 35:

35 [D-R B-R-I-L-L (facial expression: stern) ENTER (intense)] WITHOUT KNOCK

In this example, the sign ENTER is articulated once with a long hold at the beginning and a rapid and tense movement. This change in the sign's movement indicates that Dr. Brill's entrance into the room was particularly sudden and dramatic. This inflection also occurs in line 45, in which Jack swallows the tobacco: In both instances, the change in aspect illustrates the surprising nature of the accompanying verb and contributes to the drama of the story.

Chafe (1990) claims that stories are built around unexpected, marked events. These events are naturally the most evaluated. In lines 35 and 45, aspectual inflections accompany verbs referring to events that are evaluated by the narrator as surprising or dramatic. These two events seem to be boundaries in the narrative. Line 35 marks the introduction of a new character into the narrative, and line 45 is the beginning of a serious change in state: Jack, who previously has fooled the teacher and Dr. Brill, now begins to feel the consequences of his actions, and the balance of knowledge shifts. In the rest of the story, Dr. Brill is able to act against the boys by discovering their secret.

These data indicate that ASL signers use aspectual inflections to evaluate the content of a story. However, a more prevalent form of evaluation than either syntactic or morphological devices in this story is the use of expressive phonology, which in spoken language can consist of suprasegmental changes in the articulation of words ("And we were fightin' for a l-o-ong ti-ime, buddy" [Labov 1972, 179]) or the punctuation of a narrative with onomatopoeic sounds (e.g., hitting sounds in a narrative about a fight).

This latter technique of imitating the sounds that actually occurred is used much more extensively in the ASL story than in the narratives Labov studied. Of course, the phonology of ASL is based on gesture rather than sound; therefore, expressive phonology in ASL consists of gesture and pantomime, which are iconically constructed to imitate actual events. These devices are completely distinct from ASL signs, which contain morphemes with regular forms and meanings. Metzger (1995) analyzes ASL narratives and identifies the phenomenon of "constructed action," which seems to be identical to the pantomime and other nonmanual behaviors discussed here. Metzger finds several different levels of constructed action; however, those will not be discussed in detail here.

Although ASL signs themselves are not pantomime, some signs are so iconic that it is difficult to distinguish the two; therefore, the notations of constructed action (pantomime) in the tobacco story are somewhat rough. Nevertheless, a clear example of pantomime is the following section in the tobacco story:

16   BE-CHEWING (p)
17   LOOK-AROUND (p)
18   SPIT (p)
19   CL: GO-THROUGH-OPENING
20   BE-EXTREMELY-SKILLED CL: GO-THROUGH-OPENING...[40]

ASL has lexical signs for the actions of looking around and spitting, yet the narrator chooses to mime these two actions or, in other words, to construct the action instead of narrating it. The location of these clauses in the narrative is important. Here they are found in a section that introduces a new action to the story: It is the first time that Jack has spit the tobacco. In fact, Jack's spitting is the unexpected event that motivates the story. The narrator chooses to set this off from other complicating action clauses by using "expressive phonology" instead of lexical signs. This is evaluation: Rather than just relating a sequence of events, it departs from unmarked ASL structure to increase the dramatic force of events. As the earlier examples of aspectual inflections were used to highlight and evaluate crucial events, constructed action here occurs at an important boundary in the narrative.

Another related device used to evaluate the narrative occurs in roleshifting, or constructed dialogue. Tannen (1989) first applied this term to what had previously been called "reported speech," referring simply to a direct rather than an indirect representation of someone's speech (or signing). More recently, Metzger (1995) has analyzed constructed dialogue in ASL narratives as part of constructed action. She finds that constructed dialogue in ASL operates similarly to that in spoken languages.

In one of the spoken language narratives Tannen analyzed, constructed dialogue was shown to be accompanied often by changes in suprasegmental features: Narrators changed their voice quality to reveal something about the character of the person who is "speaking." These nonlinguistic features are a way of evaluating the story. They express the narrator's opinion or judgments about participants in events and give each participant a more individualistic quality. Tannen also notes, through her cross-linguistic comparison of constructed dialogue, that in some cultures this device is used more frequently than others. A brief look at this narrative and some familiarity with other narratives in ASL will convince the reader that ASL users make frequent use of this device, certainly more so than English speakers do.

The suprasegmental feature in ASL equivalent to that discussed above is facial expression. Liddell (1980) discusses a facial expression that he terms "surprise": This facial expression, unlike many in ASL, is neither a grammatical marker nor associated with ASL lexical items. Rather, it indicates surprise on the part of the speaker. This device is used often in the tobacco narrative. The narrator produces different marked facial expressions and associates them both with different speakers (constructed signers) with signers' reactions to events. I have indicated these facial expressions in parentheses.

A:

21 TEACHER LOOK-AROUND

22 "WHAT THAT SOUND?"

23 [innocent expression [60]] LOOK-AT-EACH-OTHER "NOTHING MUCH"

B:

73 (unintelligible conversational repair) BRILL MUST LOOK WINDOW

74 [expression of astonishment] CL: FLAT-SUBSTANCE-SPREAD-ON

In A and B above, facial expressions indicate signers' reactions to events. In 23, the "innocent expression" consists of a widening of the eyes, tightening of the mouth, and a slight raising of the eyebrow. In line 74, John expresses astonishment by leaning forward, widening his eyes, and, most markedly, dropping his jaw. However, unlike in Liddell's examples, these facial expressions do not accompany signing. Rather, the signer pauses (in 23 he pauses for 60 frames) while he makes the facial expression, then resumes a less marked facial expression and continues signing. Interestingly, throughout the narrative, John never signs anything like "I was shocked" or "We looked at each other innocently." Instead, the lexical signs stop completely to allow for a pause and a marked facial expression, held for a second or two. This strategy evaluates narrative events, providing information without actually "saying" anything. It is also a kind of constructed action, showing what was actually happening in the situation.

Another type of facial expression occurs in the following:

35 [D-R B-R-I-L-L (facial expression: stern) ENTER (emph.)] WITHOUT KNOCK
36 [ENTER LOOK-AROUND (continued stern expression)]
37 [innocent expression [70] LOOK-AT-EACH-OTHER]

Throughout lines 35 and 36, there is a stern facial expression produced, which accompanies the animation of Dr. Brill; during the parenthetical expression in 35, WITHOUT KNOCK, the stern expression disappears. Unlike the expressions discussed above, this expression is accompanied by signing. It also obviously serves an evaluative purpose, helping the audience to understand more about Brill than would a description of his actions.

Throughout the narrative, John chooses nonlexical means for evaluation as much as possible. Those he chooses–inflectional morphology, pantomime, and facial expressions to evaluate characters and events–are usually not part of the ASL lexicon. These, especially the latter two, are departures from standard ASL syntax and morphology. Of course, it is not true that all ASL narratives use similar devices for evaluation. In another narrative, a woman relates an encounter with the police:

4 TWO-OF-THEM SAY WON'T SLEEP
5 NERVOUS
6 G-R-A-N-D-S-O-N WON'T S-O TO-HECK-WITH-IT

15 RUN (left to right)
16 "HEY KNOCK-ON-DOOR THERE (fwd) OPEN-THE-DOOR"
17 BARBARA SCARED
18 NERVOUS

This narrative, the police story, is included as Appendix B. From these two excerpts from the data, we can see that, rather than using nonlexical means to show Barbara's reaction to events, the narrator comments on it: BARBARA SCARED (17) and NERVOUS (5 and 18). It seems that ASL's devices for embedded evaluation—pantomime and facial expression—are not equally used by all narrators.

Analyzing Pauses

We have seen how the tobacco story can be divided into clauses or parts of clauses that have different functions within the narrative, such as for orientation, complicating action, and evaluation. However, it has also been suggested that narratives can be segmented into larger units of varying sizes that have been termed stanzas, strophes, verses, and sections.

In Gee and Kegl's (1983) analysis of pause data in two ASL narratives, longer pauses in narratives showed a strong correspondence to intuitive notions about narrative/story structure. They found the longest pause in the story and bisected the story there; then they continued to bisect the sections based on the largest pauses. The result was a "tree" structure of larger and smaller narrative units. I first use the same method with the tobacco story.

An initial question is how to define a pause in ASL. Gee and Kegl's definition of a pause included long holds where the hands are unmoving and transitions from one sign to the next. However, under this definition, some long holds that are part of an inflection or simply part of the nature of the sign would be counted as pauses. (For instance, when the sign GOOD is inflected for emphasis, it will have a long hold at the beginning; the sign BE-SITTING is one whose movement simply consists of a long hold without any movement segment at all.) A claim about signed languages that is accepted here is that they consist of movements and holds; holds are therefore parts of signs, not pauses (Liddell and Johnson 1989).

With the goal of measuring pauses between signs, pauses are defined differently here. A pause is an interval in which the handshape of the previous sign is no longer held, but the handshape of the next sign has not begun to be formed; hands may or may not be in the signer's lap. In addition, during this interval the signer has no marked facial expression or nonmanual signal.

I measured pauses in the tobacco story using the "slow advance" button of a VCR. Each number represents one frame that advanced on the machine. The results can be seen in the earlier transcription of the narrative, where pauses are shown by bolded numbers in brackets. Most utterances did not contain pauses between the end of one sign and the articulation of the next sign; this was the case between clauses as well as within them.

Most of the pauses in the story are between twenty and thirty frames.

There are two longer pauses near the beginning and end of the story; in line 3 there is a 39-frame pause, and in line 78 there is a 54-frame pause. These seem to mark the beginning and end of the narrative. Other long pauses occur in line 40 (a 60-frame pause) and line 51 (a 75-frame pause).

Following Gee and Kegl, the text is bisected at the largest pause—in this case, at line 51. This division of the narrative into two basic segments seems to fit well with our intuitive understanding of how the narrative is structured: The story up to that point is about the boys misbehaving and not getting caught (first by the teacher and then by Dr. Brill), and the section following line 51 relates the consequences. However, in further divisions, Gee and Kegl's method does not succeed. The next largest breaks in the text are lines 41 (a 60-frame pause) and 62 (a 39-frame pause). Line 62 could be said to be another episode boundary in the text, coming after the revelation that Brill knows what the students are doing; however, the pause at the end of line 41 occurs in the middle of an episode that tells of Brill looking at the boys' tongues. There does not seem to be a natural boundary between episodes there.

Aside from the three large pauses (at the beginning, middle, and end), most of the pauses in the narrative are not as strongly traceable to structural entities such as theme/rheme, act/result, and so on as they are to shifts in speaker. In this narrative, there is extensive use of signing and actions attributed to participants in the situation. Many long pauses in the narrative are not associated with the division of the narrative into sections; rather, in accordance with Bahan and Supalla's work on pauses associated with what they called reference shifting, pauses are often associated with a shift in constructed signer. Many examples of pauses occurring with constructed dialogue are in the tobacco narrative. For instance, lines 39–43 relate the examination of the children's tongues by Dr. Brill. This seems clearly to be one episode in the narrative; however, there are pauses after every line in this section:

39   PRO-3 STICK-OUT-AND-WIGGLE-TONGUE (p) (pointing to tongue)...[29]
40   S SANDY (S-A-N-D-Y) STICK-OUT-AND-WIGGLE-TONGUE (pant.)...[27]
41   LOOK...[60]
42   STICK-OUT-AND-WIGGLE-TONGUE (p) simultaneously with WHAT?
43   ME...[24] [STICK-OUT-AND-WIGGLE-TONGUE (p) f.e.: negative, innocent]

The pauses in this section correspond to changes in the actor. In line 39, it is Brill who says "you—stick out your tongue!". Line 40 switches to Sandy, who complies. In line 41, Brill looks at Sandy's tongue; in line 42 it is another of the boys (probably Jack) who must stick out his tongue next. Line 43 is interesting because it is one of only two lines in the narrative in which a pause occurs in the middle of a clause. (The other is line 9, which includes a pause after a parenthetical clause.) In line 43, the narrator specifies to the signer that the following constructed dialogue belongs to (himself), pauses, and then reconstructs what he did in the actual situation. However, in line 39 there seems to be no such pause between the name of the next signer and his constructed dialogue: "Sandy stuck out and wiggled his tongue."

The association of pauses with a shift in the constructed signer becomes even stronger if we analyze any interval without movement of the hands as a pause. There are several occasions in the narrative when the narrator's hands are unmoving and in his lap for a long time. For example, in line 23, the narrator pauses for sixty frames with a marked facial expression.

21 TEACHER LOOK-AROUND

22 "WHAT THAT SOUND?"

23 [innocent expression [60]] LOOK-AT-EACH-OTHER "NOTHING MUCH"

24 WRITE (on board)

The facial expression in line 23 serves to separate the dialogue of the teacher in 22 from that of the students in line 23. In line 60, another marked facial expression encompasses an entire line in the narrative:

58 LEAVE

59 LATER DOOR-OPEN

60 [expression: look up in astonishment [61]]

61 BRILL AGAIN LOOK...[36]

62 "I (Eng. sign) THINK ("thought") S-O" ...[39]

The interpretation of pauses in the narrative as accompanying shifts in the constructed signer explains many pauses. Reexamining Gee and Kegl's (1983) data, it can be seen that in the two stories they analyzed, only one involved any transition point between the reported signers, and that one story had only one such transition.

Another pause that is unrelated to either constructed signing or sectioning the narrative is that between lines 28 and 29:

27 BE-EXTREMELY-SKILLED-AT CL: GO-THROUGH OPENING (iterative)

28   NOT CL : HIT-THE-EDGE-OF-OPENING [CL: SPLATTER-OVER-OPENING shaking head slightly [24]]

29   CL: GO-THROUGH-OPENING (iterative) BE-EXTREMELY-SKILLED-AT...[18]

Between lines 28 and 29, there is a 24-frame pause in which the narrator shakes his head and purses his lips slightly, a negative facial expression. This pause seems impossible to attribute to sectioning of the narrative, as line 29, rather than containing a new idea unit, is a repetition of line 27. Instead, this pause seems to contribute to the evaluation of the narrative. As discussed above, facial expressions that accompany signing or pauses can be evaluative in nature; in this section of the narrative, the pause seems to provide an evaluation of Jack's skill.

However, the largest pause in the narrative, in line 50, does seem to be a marker between major sections. If we exclude those pauses associated with shifts in reference and with evaluation, the pause data prove useful for sectioning the story. The pauses that remain are those in lines 9, 20, 29, 38, 43, 51, 56, and 68. (I have excluded the pauses near the beginning and end of the narrative as marking the boundaries of the story.) The following is my tentative division of the story into sections based on pauses as boundary markers and other boundary markers to be discussed below.

TOBACCO STORY

Entry into Storyworld

1   USED-TO ME CLASS ON THERE

2   AND THERE

3   REMEMBER...[39]

(Boundary of narrative)

Section One

Strophe One

STANZA ONE

This stanza is composed of orientation clauses; the beginning is marked by interaction with an interlocutor.

MRS GILL

4   FORGET THAT TEACHER?
5   MY TEACHER
6   S-H-E WRITE BLACK B-R-D ("board")
7   WRITE (loc: blackboard)
8   ME, J-A-C-K, S-A-N-D-Y (SANDY (name sign))
9   ME, JACK CL: BE-SEATED-SIDE-BY-SIDE...[20]

STANZA TWO

Pauses occur in line 8 and line 9, and the first sign in line 10 is the discourse marker WELL. This marks the end of the orientation and the beginning of complicating action.

10   WELL (g) JACK TOBACCO (IN CLASS, REMEMBER ILLEGAL)...[20] PUT-IN-MOUTH
11   BE-CHEWING (p)
12   TEACH WRITE (loc: board)
13   WINDOW RAISE (p) DURING WEATHER COLD
14   WINTER TIME
15   RAISE-WINDOW (p) ABOUT-THIS-MUCH (cl)
16   BE-CHEWING (p)
17   LOOK-AROUND (p)
18   SPIT (p)
19   CL: GO-THROUGH-OPENING
20   BE-EXTREMELY-SKILLED CL: GO-THROUGH-OPENING...[40]

STANZA THREE

A pause occurs in line 20, and there is a change of referent and theme.

21   TEACHER LOOK-AROUND
22   "WHAT THAT SOUND?"
23   [innocent expression [60]] LOOK-AT-EACH-OTHER "NOTHING MUCH"
24   WRITE (on board)
25   BE-CHEWING SPIT (pant)
26   WINDOW SPIT (iterative)
27   BE-EXTREMELY-SKILLED-AT CL: GO-THROUGH OPENING (iterative)
28   NOT CL : HIT-THE-EDGE-OF-OPENING [CL: SPLATTER-OVER-OPENING shaking head slightly [24]]
29   CL: GO-THROUGH-OPENING (iterative) BE-EXTREMELY-SKILLED-AT...[18]

Strophe Two

STANZA FOUR

This stanza is marked by a pause in line 28 and by interaction with interlocutor. It also introduces a new character to the story who initiates an episode of investigation.

30   D-R B-R-I-L-L, KNOW PRO-3 (to audience)

31   {B-R-I-L-L

32   {SIGN USED-TO #W-H-T D-R...

33   neg-sign   {b-by-mouth ("Brill") (nodding)

34   {b-by-mouth b-by-mouth

35   [D-R B-R-I-L-L (facial expression: stern) ENTER (emph.)] WITHOUT KNOCK

36   [ENTER LOOK-AROUND (continued stern expression)]

37   [innocent expression [70] LOOK-AT-EACH-OTHER]

38   COME-WALKING-OVER (p)...[31]

STANZA FIVE

There is a pause in line 38 to mark this boundary.

39   PRO-3 STICK-OUT-AND-WIGGLE-TONGUE (p) (pointing to tongue)...[29]

40   S SANDY (S-A-N-D-Y) STICK-OUT-AND-WIGGLE-TONGUE (pant.)...[27]

41   LOOK...[60]

42   STICK-OUT-AND-WIGGLE-TONGUE (p) simultaneously with WHAT?

43   ME...[24] [STICK-OUT-AND-WIGGLE-TONGUE (p) f.e.: negative, innocent]

44   GO-AWAY (g)...[46]

STANZA SIX

This is also separated from the previous stanza by a pause. Also, at this point there is a major change in scene as Brill leaves.

45   TURN-TO-SIDE (p) "HEY (g) HAPPEN MOUTH?"

46   (body shift) "LEAVE SWALLOW (emph) TOBACCO FINISH SWALLOW"

47   BRILL LOOK

48   FINISH NONE

49   LEAVE...[18]

50   FEW MINUTE

51   FEW MINUTE...[75]

Strophe Three

STANZA SEVEN

The narrator pauses here and interacts with a member of the audience.

52 JACK FEEL

53 NO-NO (g) (in response to an interlocutor who is out of sight)

54 JACK FEEL GREEN FACE

55 SICK

56 [puffs out cheeks — as if holding in vomit]

57 HAVE-TO GO INFIRMARY HAVE-TO...[20]

STANZA EIGHT

58 LEAVE

59 LATER DOOR-OPEN

60 [expression: look up in astonishment [61]]

61 BRILL AGAIN LOOK...[36]

62 "I (Eng. sign) THINK ("thought") S-O" ...[39]

63 "HOW KNOW PRO-3 ("BRILL")?"

64 PRO-I NONE, PRO-3

65 JACK HAVE

66 "HOW KNOW PRO-3?"...[10]

67 "LOOK-THERE WINDOW"...

68 [lean forward, expression of astonishment [40]]

Strophe Four

STANZA NINE

69 F-L-A-G CL: LARGE-CYLINDRICAL-OBJECT

70 CL: TREE-SHAPED CL: SUBSTANCE-BE-SPREAD-ON ('th')

71 [BRILL O-F-F-I-C-E] (t) BELOW ('cs')

72 OUR CLASS ABOVE ('cs')...

STANZA TEN

73 (unintelligible conversational repair) BRILL MUST LOOK WINDOW

74 [expression of astonishment] CL: FLAT-SUBSTANCE-SPREAD-ON

75 LOOK

76 GO-UP
77 "CLASS, OH-I-SEE"
78 THAT CATCH
79 THAT SEE THAT HOW BRILL FIND O-U-T...[54]

CODA

80 GOOD
81 {GOOD OLD D-A-Y-S
82 {HI
83 B-R-I-L-L, BRILL FROM CALIFORNIA KNOW....

Gee (1986), analyzing spoken language data, defined several other boundary markers used to separate sections in a narrative. These include repairs, false starts, and "nonclausal idea units." Gee defines a "line" in narrative as an element that contains one idea unit, one piece of new information. Although in the unmarked cases, idea units are clauses, the marked nonclausal idea unit may mark a boundary between sections or episodes. One example of this in the data marks what has been identified as the major division of the story (i.e., lines 50-51). The FEW MINUTE, which is repeated there, is nonclausal but is, by Gee's definition, an idea unit.

Another possible boundary marker in the ASL narrative is that of interaction with an interlocutor. This occurs in line 4, which marks the beginning of the narrative; in lines 30-31, the introduction of Dr. Brill; in lines 52-53, when Jack becomes sick; and at the end of the story, after the coda of "Those were the good old days." Interestingly, the interaction in lines 52-53 coincides with the FEW MINUTE nonclausal idea unit and the longest pause in the narrative. On the basis of this evidence, the narrative can clearly be divided at lines 52-53 into two sections. This conclusion also seems to match a more intuitive feeling of what happens in the story: Until lines 52-53, the boys successfully fool the teacher and Dr. Brill; at line 54, the situation changes, and Jack begins to feel the consequences of his actions, leading to the discovery of the tobacco-chewing. Thus, the axis on which the story turns is the knowledge-states of characters in the story.

In section one, the longest pause occurs in line 47, and a pause of nearly equivalent length occurs in line 20. However, there are no other identified boundary markers in these two lines. Other lines that include smaller pauses, or no pauses at all, do contain other boundary markers. What seems to be the most important transition point within this section occurs between lines 29 and 30. Though the pause here is only twenty frames, the narrator significantly breaks the narrative pattern by interacting with his audience. In addition, at this point he introduces a new character in the narrative (Dr. Brill), and the following section (strophe) is separate from the previous section in its theme: It moves from the boys' deception of the teacher to an investigation and further deception of the new character.

Section one is now divided into two strophes. The second section poses more problems for clear division into sections. Intuitively, it seems to be divisible into four episodes: Jack becomes sick, Dr. Brill suddenly enters, the students find out that he knows about the tobacco, and then it is explained how he knows. The division of what follows line 68 into another strophe is based purely on the content of the two sections because the realization of how Dr. Brill discovered the tobacco chewing seems like an important, and separate, strophe.

Further sectioning the narrative are stanzas, smaller units of discourse, several of which are contained in one strophe. The divisions of these stanzas are mainly based on the pause data, though it also includes evidence such as the presence of the discourse marker WELL in line 10 and a repair in line 73. In addition, changes in scene and theme were considered to mark boundaries between stanzas.

DISCUSSION

Although the methods for dividing the narrative need further development, clearly the analysis has shown that this ASL narrative is not a unitary whole: It has an internal structure that includes subsections of a certain length. The stanzas identified earlier are between six and ten lines in length. The data that evidence the existence of stanzas are consistent with a functional analysis of the clauses in each stanza. That is, each stanza is held together by a certain function or pattern, which may be the stanza's function as an orientation to the narrative, a section of constructed dialogue between two or more signers, or the revelation of a character's own perspective and knowledge.

The first stanza in the tobacco story contains no action at all; it is composed entirely of orientation clauses and is also the shortest stanza in the narrative.

Stanzas are often composed of an interchange between two or more signers, as is the case with stanzas five, six, and eight. In these stanzas, a constructed conversation is coterminous with the stanza's boundaries. This reveals again the importance of constructed dialogue for this ASL narrative. As discussed previously in relation to a Labovian analysis, constructed dialogue and the nonmanual signals that accompany it often serve an important evaluative function in ASL narrative. The device of constructed dialogue is extensively used in ASL. It seems that, in relation to a stanza analysis, constructed dialogue can actually regulate the stanzas, controlling the length of stanzas and thus the rhythm of the story.

When not marking a continuous segment of constructed dialogue, stanzas in the narrative tend to relate to one knowledge state. Knowledge state refers to the portion of the world seen through one character's perspective. This character's perspective is constructed in much the same way that a conversation is constructed by the narrator. The narrator himself knows the facts of the events (he knows how Brill found out about the tobacco spitting), and he conveys the knowledge through an animation of the characters' knowledge at the time. Stanzas eight and nine are examples of this. Stanza eight is Brill's second entrance; the knowledge state that is animated is the student's lack of knowledge and surprise that Brill found out about the tobacco. Stanza nine moves to a different knowledge state, which animates Brill's actions and thoughts at an earlier time. The disjunct between the two stanzas thus corresponds to a disjunct in the knowledge being animated. These stanzas are not entirely composed of dialogue; however, in their revelations of a single perspective (or character's thoughts), they function like a constructed monologue. Once again, constructed dialogue (including thoughts and perspective) and action regulate the structure of the narrative. Constructed dialogue, then, may prove to be the factor that controls the form and length of sections in ASL narratives.

CONCLUSION

The structure of this ASL narrative has been analyzed in two ways: a Labovian method that involved finding the function of various clauses or parts of clauses in the narrative, and the method developed by Gee that attempts to divide the narrative into sections. Both of these models, derived from spoken language data, have been shown to apply equally well to data from a signed language. In both of these analyses, constructed dialogue was an important strategy used by the narrator. In one, constructed dialogue functioned to evaluate the narrative; in another, it regulated the length and form of the stanzas in the narrative. Within ASL, the use of constructed dialogue is an important strategy that may be a key to understanding the structure of narrative.

REFERENCES

Bahan, B., and S. Supalla. 1995. Line segmentation and narrative structure: A study of eye gaze behavior in ASL. In *Language, gesture, and space*, ed. K. Emmorey and J. Reilly. Hillsdale, N.J.: Lawrence Erlbaum Associates.

Brown, G., and G. Yule. 1983. *Discourse analysis*. Cambridge: Cambridge University Press.

Chafe, W. 1990. Some things narratives tell us about the mind. In *Narrative thought and narrative language*, ed. B. Britton and A. Pellegrini. Hillsdale, N.J.: Lawrence Erlbaum Associates.

Gee, J. 1986. Units in the production of narrative discourse. *Discourse Processes* 9:391–422.

Gee, J., and J. Kegl. 1983. Narrative/story structure, pausing, and American Sign Language. *Discourse Processes* 6:243–258.

Hymes, D. 1981. *"In vain I tried to tell you"*: Essays in Native American ethnopoetics. Philadelphia: University of Pennsylvania Press.

Klima, E., and U. Bellugi. 1979. *The signs of language*. Cambridge, Mass.: Harvard University Press.

Labov, W. 1972. The transformation of experience in narrative syntax. In *Language in the inner city: Studies in the Black English vernacular*. Philadelphia: University of Pennsylvania Press.

Liddell, S. 1980. *American Sign Language syntax*. The Hague: Mouton.

Liddell, S., and R. Johnson. 1989. American Sign Language: The phonological base. *Sign Language Studies* 64:195–277.

Metzger, M. 1995. Constructed dialogue and constructed action. In *Sociolinguistics in Deaf communities*, ed. C. Lucas. Washington, D.C.: Gallaudet University Press.

Minami, M., and A. McCabe. 1991. Haiku as a discourse regulation device. *Language in Society* 4:577–599.

Roy, C. 1989. Features of discourse in an American Sign Language lecture. In

The Sociolinguistics of the Deaf community, ed. C. Lucas. San Diego: Academic Press.

Schiffrin, D. 1987. *Discourse markers*. New York: Cambridge University Press.

Tannen, D. 1989. "Oh talking voice that is so sweet": Constructing dialogue in conversation. In *Talking voices: Repetition, dialogue, and imagery in conversational discourse*. Studies in Interactional Sociolinguistics, Vol. 6. Cambridge: Cambridge University Press.

Winston, E. 1991. Spatial referencing and cohesion in an American Sign Language text. *Sign Language Studies* 73:397–409.

———. 1993. Spatial mapping in comparative discourse frames in an American Sign Language lecture. Ph.D. diss., Georgetown University.

The Tobacco Story

And you remember . . . Mrs. Gill? Have you forgotten that teacher? She was my teacher. She was writing on the blackboard, just writing and writing. Me, Jack, and Sandy were there. Jack and I were sitting side by side. Well . . . Jack had some tobacco (remember that's not allowed in class) and he put it in his mouth and was chewing it. He opened the window — the weather was cold, it was winter time — he raised the window a few inches. He chewed the tobacco, looked around, and then spit the tobacco through the window. He was very good at getting it to go through the window.

Then the teacher turned around and looked. "What's that sound?" she said. We looked at each other innocently and said, "Nothing." So she started writing, and Jack kept chewing the tobacco and spitting it out the window. He was very good at getting it to go through the window, again and again. It never hit the edge of the window and splattered over the opening.

Do you know Dr. Brill? What did we call him? Oh, [gives sign name]. Dr. Brill suddenly entered the room — without knocking! He came in and looked around sternly. We looked at each other innocently. He came walking over and said, "You — stick your tongue out!" Sandy stuck his tongue out. He looked. Another boy stuck his tongue out, wondering what was going on. I stuck out my tongue. Then he went away. I turned to Jack and said "Hey, what happened to the tobacco?" "I swallowed it! I swallowed the tobacco! Brill looked, he didn't see any, then he left."

A few minutes later, Jack started to . . . no, no [responding to audience] . . . Jack started to turn green. He was sick. He had to go to the infirmary. He left. Later, we were astonished to see the door open again. Brill came in again and looked around. "I thought so!" he said. "How did you know? I didn't have any, he didn't . . . Jack had it. How did you know?" "Look out the window!"

We looked and were astonished at what we saw. There was a flagpole outside the window that was just plastered with tobacco stains. Brill's office was right below. Our class was immediately above. Brill must have looked out and seen that stuff all over the flagpole and gone upstairs. "Oh, there's a class there, I see." That's what got us caught. That's how Brill found out. Those were the good old days.

Police Story

1 TIME^TEN

2 PRO-3 ABOUT I I

3 BARBARA (rapid nods during production) BE-SITTING

4 TWO-OF THEM SAY WON'T SLEEP

5 NERVOUS

6 G-R-A-N-D-S-O-N WON'T S-O TO-HECK-WITH-IT

7 SIT TURN-LT-OFF T-V

8 TURN-LT-OFF (2 hd). after this, big hn and pause.

9 NOTICE SIRENS OPPOSITE OTHER D-I-R-E-C-T-I-O-N

10 LOOK (head recoil)

11 SON G-R-A-N-D-S-O-N NOT THERE (rt)

12 GO PRO-3(poss) ROOM THERE (lft)

13 LOOK

14 WONDER

15 RUN (lft to rt)

16 "HEY KNOCK-ON-DOOR THERE (fwd) OPEN-THE-DOOR"

17 BARBARA SCARED

18 NERVOUS

19 GO-THERE (from ctr to fwd)

20 OPEN-DOOR

21 PEER-OUT (pantomime)

22 POLICE (gesture — all set???) "IT WAS THE POLICE."

23 SEE G-R-A-N-D-S-O-N MOVE-ASIDE (rt—gesture)

24 BARBARA MOVE-ASIDE (lft-gesture)

25 PRO-3 WRITE SAY B-O-Y-S AROUND ESCAPE FROM PRISON

26 BARBARA SCARED

27 NOTICE THREE THEMSELVES THREE POLICE THERE ENTER

28 BIG LIGHT WITH POWER LIGHT

29 SHINE-LIGHT-ALL-OVER (cl-locative)

30 GO-AROUND

31 LOOK-AROUND (leans forward and looks at the area where hands go)

32 "O-K FINE"

33 "SEE (cond) INFORM KNOW"

34 O-K CLOSE-DOOR

35 WINDOW (topic) DECIDE MUST TELL G-R-A-N-D-S-O-N

36 CLOSE-WINDOW (exhaustive)

37 PUT A-C-O-N

38 FINISH SCARED

39 TRAVEL-ALL-OVER (on a higher level, with pas hd below in b hs)

40 A-C-O-N

41 ONE WINDOW BELOW G-R-A-N-D-S-O-N STILL U-N-L-O-C-K

42 WON'T GO-DOWNSTAIRS

43 SCARED

44 ALERT-3

45 HUSBAND BE-PATIENT

46 GET-UP

47 GO-THERE2 (ctr to down)

48 LOCK (gesture) FINISH

49 GO-THERE2 (down to up and ctr)

50 ALL-NIGHT, MORNING, NEWSPAPER EXPLAIN CLEAR

Part 5 Second Language Learning

Just How Hard Is It to Learn ASL?

The Case for ASL as a

Truly Foreign Language

Rhonda Jacobs

The question of how difficult it is to learn ASL (American Sign Language) is asked of D/deaf[1] people, interpreters, and hearing signers on an almost daily basis. The standard response, at least since ASL began to receive recognition as a formal language in the 1960s and 1970s,[2] has been along the lines of "Oh, about the same as any other language. It depends on your facility with languages, but about as hard as Spanish or French or any other language you might take." The point is to note that "Yes, ASL really is a language, contrary to much popular misconception, and yes, people do study it, both language learners and linguists, and it does take time and effort." However, responses vary. One deaf friend, who learned to sign as an adult, when asked how long it takes to learn to sign, responded "Oh, it's easy—took me two weeks." I stopped breathing for a moment as I reached to pick my heart up off the floor. If learning ASL is "about the same as learning any other language," is it

I would like to thank Terry Berkeley, Helen Chang, Betty Colonomos, Val Dively, Carol Padden, Theresa Smith, Galal Walker, Ron Walton, and James Woodward for their valuable insights and support on this project.

1. The capitalized "D" Deaf is a convention established by researchers and members of the Deaf community to refer to those who are culturally and linguistically Deaf (i.e., users of American Sign Language), whereas the small "d" deaf refers to those who cannot hear but do not regard themselves as culturally Deaf (Woodward 1972).

2. In 1960, William C. Stokoe published the first linguistic study of ASL (*Sign Language Structure: An Outline of the Visual Communication Systems of the American Deaf.* Baker and Battison 1980).

then "about like learning Spanish" or "about like learning Greek" or "about like learning Swahili" or "about like learning Chinese"? The focus of this chapter is on the concept of "degree of foreignness." If ASL is to be considered a foreign language, just how foreign is it from English? And what are the implications of its degree of foreignness on its placement within academic programs, the length and structure of those programs, the instructors who teach ASL, and the training of interpreters who work between ASL and spoken English?

For the reader who is unfamiliar with ASL and signed languages, I will point out that there is a great difference between knowing how to sign or learning signs—and learning/knowing ASL. Many people, particularly those who have learned to sign as adults, both hearing and deaf, learn the vocabulary, the signs of American Sign Language, and restructure the syntax so the signs follow English word order. This type of signing, known by such terms as English-based signing[3] or, by some linguists, as contact signing,[4] is quite common and often accomplishes the intended purpose, that is, some type of communication or information sharing, but it is not American Sign Language. This description is a simplistic mention of a very complex subject, and many people use this type of signing as their primary means of communication. However, for our purposes, I refer to American Sign Language, a natural language that is structurally and grammatically very different from English, and to American Deaf culture (ADC), the culture of the American community of users of ASL.

So, then, how hard is it to learn ASL? As one who has been studying the language formally as a second language learner as well as acquiring

3. In addition to naturally occurring language mixing (code-switching and contact signing) and signing in English word order, there are also several artificially invented sign systems or codes intended to represent English manually. In all, there is quite a wide variety of terms used to convey a wide variety of things people do with their hands. Many of these systems or codes attempt to represent English, but they are not languages, and although these various types of signing may incorporate different features of ASL, they are not ASL. I refer to "things people do with their hands" because one of the predominant features of ASL that is generally missing from these coded systems is nonmanual grammar—the facial expressions that are actually the grammar of ASL.

4. Lucas and Valli (1992). Contact signing refers to the type of signing that ensues when two language communities (in this case users of English and users of ASL) come into contact. This situation, an accommodation by both parties, was previously referred to as PSE (Pidgin Sign English) (Woodward 1972, 1973).

it informally for more than ten years, using it professionally for more than eight years, and still encountering many situations in which I struggle, the question is very prescient to me. In fact, the degree of language learning difficulty is important for any foreign language instruction, signed or spoken. Thus far, the only groups who have attempted to study this notion have focused on spoken languages. Although one cannot apply all research on spoken languages to signed languages, one can use this as a starting point since there is no comparable research on signed languages.

Prominent among the groups focusing on the difficulty of foreign language learning are the Foreign Service Institute (FSI) and the Defense Language Institute (DLI). FSI and DLI group languages into four categories based on how difficult they are to learn for speakers of English. Category 1 languages, which include Spanish, French, and German,[5] are the easiest for speakers of English to learn. Categories 2, 3, and 4 languages are, by degree, harder or take more time in which to become proficient for speakers of English; category 4, the hardest, includes Arabic, Chinese, Japanese, and Korean (Walker 1989; Walton 1992). (See appendix A.)

Walton notes,

> Difficulty is measured by the number of instructional contact hours required to reach prescribed levels of proficiency as determined by standardized proficiency tests. Proficiency is rated on a scale of 0 (no functional proficiency) to 5 (the proficiency of an educated native speaker). . . . For a student with average language learning aptitude the FSI experience indicates that to reach a proficiency level of 2 requires 480 contact hours for a Category 1 language such as French, German or Spanish, but 1,320 contact hours for a Category 4 language such as Chinese or Japanese. Assuming an academic Chinese program that allotted ten contact hours per week at the elementary level, five hours per week at the intermediate level (many programs do not provide nearly so many contact hours at these two levels), and three hours per week at all subsequent levels, 1,320 contact hours would roughly correspond to eight years of academic study in order to reach the 2 proficiency rating. Based on the same contact hour scheme it would require roughly one and a half years to reach this same level in French. (pp. 2-3)

5. German is a category 1 language for FSI and a category 2 for DLI.

Another way that foreign language educators in the United States separate languages is to refer to the traditionally taught languages, French, German, and Spanish as one group, and to all the other languages as the Less Commonly Taught Languages, or LCTLs (often abbreviated as LCTs) (Walker 1989). These languages are further broken down into three subgroups:

(1) less commonly taught European languages such as Russian, Italian, Portuguese, and Swedish; (2) higher-enrollment non-Indo-European languages, such as Arabic, Chinese, and Japanese; and (3) lower-enrollment non-Indo-European languages such as Burmese, Indonesian, and Swahili. (Walton 1992, p. 1)

Group 2 and 3 languages "are sometimes termed 'Truly Foreign Languages' (TFLs) to distinguish them from languages that are cognate to English"[6] (ibid). These languages often are radically different from one another, and grouping them together at all may seem pointless. As Walker (1989) says, "thinking of LCTs as a category of language is like thinking of 'nonelephants' as a category of animals . . . ." (p. 111) However, the distinction is not only linguistic, it is also political. According to Walker,

"however disparate the languages or their pedagogical situations may be, the power of institutions is sufficient to imbue the term LCTs with meaning . . . .The concept is wielded, sometimes arbitrarily, either to allocate resources (Why, yes. Not enough students are studying LCTs) or to deny them (Why, no. Not enough students are studying LCTs)" (ibid p. 112).

My purpose is to discuss ASL's position in this schema, argue for its inclusion in the category of Truly Foreign Languages, and show that in terms of difficulty for speakers of English, ASL should be thought of as a category 4 language according to the FSI/DLI classification. Once ASL is thought of as a category 4 language, there begin to be profound implications for the structure and length of ASL programs, expected achievement levels of students in these programs, and for entrance requirements into ASL–English interpreting programs, the underlying impetus being a "deep concern about whether or not language pedagogy [and by extension, interpreting pedagogy] is adequately fulfilling its responsibilities to

6. This term was first presented by Jorden and Walton (1987).

our society" (ibid). In fact, if these implications are taken to their logical conclusion, it becomes clear that the majority of ASL–English interpreting programs are based on faulty assumptions. Therefore, the expectations are unrealistic, and ASL–English interpreters do not graduate with the same level of proficiency as professionally trained spoken language interpreters.

My main motivation for viewing ASL in the light of Truly Foreign Languages is to change how we look at language proficiency requirements for entrance into ASL-English interpreting programs. Many programs currently require "passing grades" in ASL I–IV. This generally equals four semesters of three-credit-hour (three hours per week) classes. Based on a 15-week semester, this equals 180 hours of classroom instruction. Even if ASL is seen as a category 1 language (on a par with Spanish or French), the findings of the FSI show that "to reach a proficiency level 2 requires 480 contact hours." This could be done in a year and a half assuming ten hours per week at the elementary level and five hours per week at the intermediate level (Walton p. 3). With the present state of affairs, this would mean that in the "good" interpreting programs (those that require students to pass ASL IV before entering), students are entering *300 hours short* of a level 2 proficiency. If ASL is seen as a category 4 language, however, that would put the beginning interpreting student in their first interpreting class *1140 hours short* of a level 2 proficiency. Moreover, of those programs that do require passing grades in ASL I–IV before students are allowed to begin their interpreting coursework, most are baccalaureate level programs.[7] The majority of interpreting programs, however, are housed in community colleges and, by law, must have open-door admissions policies.

There are three spoken language interpreting programs in the world (Georgetown University, Monterey, and the Sorbonne). Currently, students entering these programs are required to have native or near-native proficiency levels in their native and second languages and often a working knowledge of a third language. At Monterey, "to qualify for admission, students must have native or near-native proficiency in English and at least one of the following languages. . . ."[8] At Georgetown University, the entrance exam is more holistic, and, therefore, a standardized profi-

7. Based upon a telephone survey.
8. Monterey Institute of International Studies, Graduate School Brochure, 1992-1994.

ciency exam would be insufficient; however, the faculty look at several factors when evaluating students for admission:

Comprehension of content and purpose of discourse: what is being stated and why, to whom, and by whom. Grammatical structure, idiomatic expressions, and a wide range of vocabulary and cultural background all come into play.

Expression in the target language, written and oral test: correct grammatical usage, range and appropriateness of vocabulary, ease and clarity of style. For the oral part of the examination, the candidate's voice quality, poise, and appropriate accent are important, as is spelling for the written part.

Speed of work: Oral presentations should be made at the normal rate of spontaneous speech–about 120-150 words per minute . . . (Bowen and Bowen 1985)

If compared with the FSI language proficiency rankings, these requirements seem roughly to correspond to at least a level 3 proficiency:

Speaking 3 (General Professional Proficiency)

Able to speak the language with sufficient structural accuracy and vocabulary to participate effectively in most formal and informal conversations on practical, social, and professional topics. (See Appendix B, Proficiency Rankings)

In other words, students entering these programs are expected to be fluent bilinguals. This hardly seems an excessive demand to ask of people planning on making interpreting their career. The faculty of the interpreting program at Gallaudet University, the only master's level program in ASL–English interpreting, requires their entering students to have a proficiency level of 2.5 (on their own internally developed scale) and a 3.5 on exiting. Aside from the Gallaudet program, there are currently ten programs nationally at the bachelor's level and approximately ninety-three programs altogether in the United States.[9] Since, as noted above,

9. From the booklet "Interpreter Training Programs: United States and Canada," 1993. Waubonsee Community College. The numbers and programs listed have been amended by the author based on a phone survey. This booklet lists one other program at the master's level that is not included in the body of this paper due to insufficient data.

most of these programs operate out of community colleges that, by law, must maintain an open enrollment policy, many students enter interpreting programs with no prior knowledge of ASL.

What does this say about expectations for teachers of ASL–English interpretation? Essentially, the impossible is being expected of them. And what is this telling the beginning student of interpretation? It is saying, "We know you are barely conversant in the language, but we are going to teach you to interpret anyway, and in two to four years you will graduate and start working as a language/culture expert and mediator. We know you have some weaknesses in your second language, so we will provide some extra 'remedial/tutorial' training–maybe 100 hours over the next two years–so by the time you graduate and start calling yourself an interpreter, you will be at proficiency level 5 (it is hoped, although this is not always the case) in your native language, and somewhere between a level 1 and 2 in your second language. Good luck." Good luck indeed. Many of those people who call themselves "sign language interpreters"[10] are often not looked upon very favorably by many members of the Deaf community. Is it any wonder? Often they earn quite good salaries while needing approximately 2000 more hours to be fully bilingual–the prerequisite for entering a spoken language interpreting program (based on 2400-2760 hours to achieve a proficiency level 3 in a category 4 language at FSI; Walker 1989, p. 18).

If bilingualism were the prerequisite for admittance to an ASL–English interpreting program, and both the faculty and administration had a comprehensive understanding of what is required to become a proficient bilingual, and if this understanding were communicated to prospective students of interpretation, the system might become one that graduates

10. The term "sign language interpreter," although in common usage, is technically a misnomer. Sign language (or signed language) per se refers to the modality being used: a signed language as opposed to a spoken language. To say "we need to hire a sign language interpreter for this event" is akin to saying "we need to hire a spoken language interpreter for this event." Hence, this chapter refers to ASL-English interpreters and interpreting programs since interpretation, by definition, is an event that takes place between users of two languages. The reality of situations in which interpreters find themselves may be more complex, involving a variety of modalities and language varieties, but, for the purpose of this chapter, I refer to the standard situation of interpreting between a user of spoken English and a user of American Sign Language.

interpreters worthy of the name. As a result, those who are considering a career in interpretation would have a more realistic picture of what they are getting into before they start, and of the time, effort, and proficiency levels expected of them.[11] In gathering information for this paper, I called the staff at one interpreting program located in a community college and inquired about the entrance requirements for the program. The instructor's assistant said, "Entrance requirements?" I said, "Yes, in terms of ASL proficiency levels or ASL courses passed?" The person thought for a moment and replied, "No, anyone can come in."

A second implication of looking at ASL as a Truly Foreign Language is the impact it could have on the structure and length of ASL programs. Although the study of ASL is becoming increasingly popular, the most one usually sees in terms of academic course offerings is ASL I–IV, with some programs offering up to ASL VI and/or additional courses in fingerspelling, structure of ASL, and American Deaf culture. If, however, it was realized that ASL is not only worthy of study but also exponentially harder to learn than Spanish or French, it may be possible to see more ASL programs expand to include such topics as grammar, culture, register, number systems, and sociolinguistics, as well as allowing for enough classroom contact hours (in addition to informal contact hours) for students to gain a desired level of proficiency. Indeed, "two years of language study, a typical requirement for Category 1 cognate languages, is merely an introduction to a language in Category 4"(Walton, p. 8). Thus, students of ASL who aspire to become interpreters or use ASL as part of their professional life would know that taking two years of ASL

11. "Just yesterday I answered a call in my office only to hear an innocent voice inquire, 'Do you offer classes in Portuguese at your school?' to which I answered, 'I'm sorry, sir, you've made a mistake. A school of interpretation is not a language teaching institution. What we teach is the technique of interpretation, and only those persons who are perfectly fluent in two foreign languages and who can handle their native tongue with eloquence and precision are admitted to the program. These aspiring interpreters must also be versatile and they must be fast thinkers. Furthermore, they must have an inborn curiosity and must have the ability to take an interest in each and every area of human activity. Finally, interpretation requires that one have nerves of steel, great self-control and acute and sustained powers of concentration.'

My unseen caller had nothing further to say, and I hung up the phone." (Maurice Gravier, Professor, University of Paris–Sorbonne, in the preface to *In*

is a good first step on the path, not the end goal. If those responsible for the establishment and content of programs became aware of the complexity of ASL and the length of time necessary to attain advanced proficiency, and that this proficiency is a prerequisite to becoming an interpreter, this could lead to degree programs in ASL at the graduate as well as undergraduate levels. At present, although there is one program that offers a B.A. in Sign Language Studies with a choice of concentrations, and four universities with degree programs in Deaf Studies (including Gallaudet University's recently established program), there are no programs that offer full degrees in American Sign Language.

An even more important concern than the length of ASL programs or the awarding of degrees in ASL is the recognition of the pedagogical challenges implicit in teaching ASL, particularly because ASL classes are popping up all over the country at every level of instruction from kindergarten to graduate school. As Gary Olsen has noted, "a groundswell can be devastating if proper precautions are not taken. Without proper standardization of curriculum, instructor qualifications, and certification, this sudden spontaneity of acceptance of ASL can be devastating. ASL, as we know it today, could be drastically altered or lost" (Olsen 1988, p. 100, in Wilcox and Wilcox 1991, p. 79).

These pedagogical challenges, as will be pointed out subsequently, are the same challenges faced by instructors of the TFLs. It is hoped that by seeing the similarities between ASL and the TFLs, the case can be made to include ASL as a Truly Foreign Language. With regard to placing ASL into a "difficulty" category, there is no database from which to draw, nor rigorously structured language school and population such as that found at DLI from which to collect a database. And there is no standardized proficiency test with which to measure students' skills. Consequently, it is impossible statistically to say that it takes the average student "X" number of years to reach proficiency level "Y." However, in my discussions with instructors of ASL and interpretation, the anecdotal evidence suggests that it takes the average student between six and fifteen years to become comfortably "proficient." Therefore, although the specific correlation between length of time and proficiency cannot be drawn at this point, it is hoped that the degree of difference between English and ASL, linguistically and culturally, can be shown to be sufficient to regard ASL as a Category 4 language.

For languages, particularly signed languages that are vying for their rightful place among spoken languages in fields such as linguistics and language pedagogy, it is important to be wary of the "me too" attitude (Wilcox 1993). However, the issues that make up TFL pedagogy are analogous to those that make up ASL pedagogy. If ASL is seen within the framework of a TFL, the benefits that could be gained in terms of mindset, academic requirements and expectations, recognition of pedagogical challenges, educational policy and planning, and funding issues would greatly outweigh any benefits derived from a more existential coexistence. With this note in mind, I examine those factors common to TFLs that seem also to apply to ASL and also factors unique to ASL, but that serve to differentiate ASL pedagogy from that of the more commonly taught languages.

These factors divide roughly into three areas: linguistics, culture, and pedagogy, with pedagogy broadly defined as not only the teaching of a language but also student motivation, the history and values behind and surrounding particular pedagogical traditions, the situation of the field and its approach to pedagogy, and issues regarding the teachers themselves.

LINGUISTIC FACTORS

In the area of language and linguistics, the very fact that ASL is not Spanish, French, or German automatically qualifies it as an LCT. The further fact that it is not part of the IndoEuropean family of languages seems to make it, by definition, a TFL. One could stop right there. However, there are myriad characteristics that define the TFLs (or LCTs) that provide rationale for their coming together as a group and for explaining the nature of the difficulty of learning each language. Furthermore, these characteristics address the criteria that serve to place each language in its requisite FSI/DLI difficulty grouping.

The most important difference between a cognate language (one from the same language family) and a TFL is the linguistic code, which includes such features as the morphology, grammar, and discourse structure of a language (Walton 1992, p. 3). It can be difficult enough to explain just how different two radically different spoken languages are from each other. To add to this difficulty the further task of explaining how different a signed language is from a spoken language seems almost akin to comparing apples and oranges. As Wilcox and Wilcox (1991) claim, "It is as difficult to explain how ASL is different from English as it is to explain how a non-IndoEuropean language such as Navajo is different from English" (p. 20). Linguistic features aside, the most obvious difference between spoken English and ASL is that of modality, or channel: spoken English being aural-oral and ASL being visual-gestural. For most second language learners, the simple fact of modality difference requires them to enter a world to which they have been hitherto unexposed: the world of vision. This may seem an odd statement since everyone, barring those who do not have any usable vision, sees. However, receiving a language visually is completely different from enjoying a painting or looking both ways before crossing a street.

As with spoken languages, the signs/words of ASL are mostly arbitrary: There is no obvious relation between a sign and its referent. However, ASL does have a certain amount of iconicity; that is, there are certain signs that to some extent visually represent their referents. Although in some cases, this element of iconicity may lead to greater vocabulary transparency to second language learners than the opaque tones of Chinese, the visual discrimination necessary to comprehend a signed language is as unfamiliar to a spoken-language-based native as the phonetic systems of many Category 3 and 4 spoken languages are to a Category 1-based native. For example, it would seem that fingerspelling, where one handshape (sign) represents each letter of the English alphabet, would be the easiest aspect of ASL for an English speaker to master (the logic being if one can read English one merely has to memorize a new set of symbols and apply them to reading the same words). In fact, the reception of fingerspelling is one of the hardest aspects of ASL for an English speaking second language learner to master. Even those who are proficient in receptive American fingerspelling face an incredible struggle trying to learn British fingerspelling as it requires a whole new set of visual discrimination patterns. The fact that the shapes of either signed language are representative of the same (English) alphabetic system is almost irrelevant when one considers the number of years it takes to become proficient at receiving a fingerspelled word at normal conversational speed.

Another element of ASL that proves exceedingly difficult for hearing second language learners to master is that of nonmanual grammar. Both expressively and receptively, aspects such as nonmanual (facial) markers (including eyebrow movement, head tilting and nodding to show topic/comment structure, yes-no vs. Wh-questions, relative clauses, and so on), modifiers (ASL mouthing, tongue movement, and so forth, to show adjectives and adverbs), and eye-gaze functions (e.g., pronominalization and turn-taking) are some of the most elusive features of the language. Not only do many second language learners not master these features; often they are not even aware that they exist. This nonawareness of the existence of linguistic categories is a particular problem for learners of Category 4 languages. As with a student of Chinese, one "must first establish the existence of tones as real categories" (Walker 1989) before the student can proceed to learn vocabulary items in Chinese. Nonmanual grammar in ASL and tones in Chinese, although radically different in function, present comparable levels of difficulty for the second language learner.

Students of ASL often think they are in for an easier time when they learn that ASL has no copulas, articles, or passives. Similarly with Chinese, "the total lack of inflection . . . at first delights learners and then confuses them as they realize they must discover another way to deal with the information that inflection conveys in other languages" (ibid). Also with time, "Chinese [read: ASL] has no grammatical tense, so the learner is spared the rather straightforward task of matching a Chinese linguistic element to a familiar grammatical concept; rather they are presented with the task of discovering an entirely new concept of linguistic time" (ibid).

Without going in depth into ASL phonology or morphology, I shall mention two additional aspects of morphology not already mentioned, for "on this level especially, ASL differs radically from English" (Wilcox and Wilcox 1991). The first aspect of morphology is that ASL is a polysynthetic language (Johnson and Liddell 1984). It differs considerably from synthetic languages such as English and even more so from isolating languages such as Chinese. For example, Chinese depends heavily on syntax and has almost no morphological inflections, whereas English, a synthetic language, uses a combination of syntax and morphological inflections. ASL, in contrast, as a polysynthetic language, depends heavily upon morphological inflections. In fact, multimorphemic signs in ASL often have a number of bound morphemes, and one multimorphemic sign can actually be a whole sentence. What is important here is that "the way morphemes are combined in ASL is often quite different from the way they are combined in English" (Wilcox and

Wilcox). In English, free and bound morphemes are combined sequentially (for example, prefixes, then roots, then suffixes). In ASL, many morphemes, such as subject and object agreement on directional verbs are simultaneously expressed. For example, in the ASL translation of the English sentence "He gives it to me," there is technically only one sign; however, it comprises three bound morphemes that are simultaneously expressed. Similarly with aspectual inflections such as durational aspect, the concept of duration cannot be separated from the root sign.

The second aspect of ASL morphology that is exceedingly difficult for second language learners to master is the concept of classifier predicates.[12] Since English does not have anything analogous to classifier predicates and the use of classifier predicates is a hallmark of ASL, it points to the degree of difference between English and ASL. As with English-speaking students struggling to learn the tones of Chinese, there is nothing to fall back on in the students' native language base. Wilcox and Wilcox explain that,

> Classifiers in ASL are combinations of two or more root morphemes (Padden 1987). One morpheme, the handshape, indicates the class of nouns to which the words belong, such as all people; upright objects, such as a boulder, a book, or a cup; surface vehicles, such as cars, bicycles, trucks, motorcycles, boats; round, thin objects, such as a coin or a cookie; long, thin objects, such as a pencil or pole; and many more. The second morpheme consists of a root movement that indicates the location and/or movement of the object. Examples are the following: a surface vehicle traveling up a long winding road, and several upright objects in a row on a long, flat object (perhaps a row of books on a bookshelf).

> American Sign Language makes extensive use of classifier morphology not only in everyday conversations but also in ASL poetry and storytelling. It is in the area of classifiers that native English speakers have the most difficulty in ASL. Classifiers are not used in the English language, and this may be why English structures interfere in the second language student's utterances in ASL. Fluency in the use and comprehension of classifiers is one mark of ASL competence (p. 36).

12. Editor's note: These predicates have traditionally been referred to in the literature simply as classifiers. However, they function as predicates, and only the handshape portion of the predicate is a classifier. Hence the use in this chapter of the term *classifier predicates*.

Culture plays an important role in pragmatics, or "the way that language is used within social contexts" (Walton, p. 3). One difficulty here is that most non-IndoEuropean languages and cultures are half a world away, whereas ASL and American Deaf culture (ADC) developed and exist within the United States. To state that ADC is as different from mainstream American (hearing) culture as is Chinese culture, is a view to which many people are quite resistant. After all, American Deaf people eat the same food and wear the same clothing as American hearing people.

A notion that is even more resisted by many people is that of children having a culture different from that of their parents. However culture is described, one worldwide constant is that culture is passed down from parents to children (at least for that category of culture that is acquired naturally by children). Imagine telling a set of new (Anglo-American) parents in the delivery ward, "Congratulations, you have just given birth to a beautiful baby girl. By the way, your baby is Japanese. For the rest of her life, her first language will be Japanese, her culture and those with whom she associates also will be Japanese." As you can imagine, this would not be well received. Although approximately ten percent of Deaf children are born to Deaf parents and naturally acquire ASL as their native language, the other ninety percent are born to hearing parents; thus, the foregoing situation is analogous to what many parents eventually come to realize. Therefore, recognizing that a culture exists among an autonomous group of adults is only one half of the difficulty. The other half is recognizing the rights of children to become enculturated into something their parents cannot give them.

The point here is neither to explain Deaf culture nor compare it with hearing culture. Others have already done that. However, if we are using culture as one criterion for placing a language in a specific difficulty grouping, one problem that we have in trying to determine how different one culture is from another is that we lack the metalanguage with which to talk about culture (Walker 1989, 1991, p. 9). But if we look at culture as "what you need to know to play the game" and look at language as subsumed under culture—as one of the tools necessary to play the game (ibid)—then a language that is radically different from the (here) dominant language would necessarily emanate from a culture that is radically different from the dominant culture.

With the degree of difference aside, the level of commitment necessary to build relationships that are vital to learning to use the language is often much greater than one would expect with the cognates. Walker (1989) said that "experienced and successful students of East Asian languages often remark on the way their lifestyles change in order to accommodate the prolonged contact that is necessary for maintaining and increasing their language skills. Central to this indispensable accommodation is the need to establish and maintain relationships in the learned language" (p. 121).

Consequently, the student must learn about the culture of the learned language in order to know how to go about building these relationships without offending anyone. Walker continues, "Establishing relationships with foreign people requires that the native speakers of the other culture feel comfortable enough in exchanges, both formal and informal, with the nonnative to continue or repeat the event. If a nonnative disconcerts natives when using their language, the latter find ways to avoid the contact or discontinue the exchanges and relationships do not develop. Culture is the framework within which linguistic behavior is deemed appropriate, or even acceptable" (ibid).

Most experienced and successful students of ASL can probably attest to these lifestyle changes as well as remark on feelings of acceptance when a relationship develops ("I've done/said something, looked, or acted appropriately"). And, conversely, most can relate to feelings of puzzlement, frustration, chagrin, disappointment, or resignation when relationships do not develop ("I did/said something, looked, or acted wrong").

A frustration often experienced by students of ASL is the Catch-22 that acceptance by (and hence interaction with) Deaf people is often dependent upon ASL skills, but ASL skills cannot develop unless Deaf people are willing to talk to and interact with the learner. Negotiating this path and getting over this hurdle takes longer and increases in complexity with the degree of difficulty of the second language, as well as any preconceived notions, perceptions, and attitudes the interactants may have of each other. Attitude cannot be taught (Bienvenu 1992), but it is incumbent upon any teacher to prepare students for the attitudes they may encounter when interacting with target natives, as well as helping them to realize attitudes they may harbor in themselves. When attitudes (byproducts of culture) are unrealized and in conflict, the relationships necessary to build language skills are difficult at best.

According to Walton, even the separation between language and culture is often a moot point in teaching a TFL, as "culture properly subsumes study of the linguistic code from the outset in TFL teaching and learning because of the role that it plays in intercultural communication and pragmatics" (p. 8). If language cannot be separated from culture and the goal is to teach people to actually use the language, how does this necessary inclusion of these two interrelated facets of communication affect the length of a course of study? Walker (1989) explains that, in the teaching of a TFL, "a focus on culture from the start is essential to the pedagogy of these languages. If culture is ignored, it is likely that learners will never reach the point of using the language in the way intended when embarking upon the course of study; when it is included, it consumes inordinate amounts of instructional time (p. 122).

Extending this overlay of language and culture to those who use a second language professionally (i.e., interpreters), it becomes evident that having a firm grounding in the culture and pragmatics of the second language is paramount. Otherwise, if one attempts to use a language without knowing how to talk about what with whom in a given social situation, one is essentially forcing the recipient of the interpreter's second language to conform, or even just to understand, a message given in the interpreter's native language paradigm. That is, if someone is functioning as a "sign language interpreter," yet they do not have a firm grounding in ASL or Deaf culture and/or do not have training in a theoretical model of interpretation, when a hearing person is speaking and the interpreter is "signing," the Deaf person who is the recipient of the interpretation is being forced to follow a message that has not made the transition into his or her language or cultural framework. Therefore, if the Deaf person does indeed succeed in understanding the message, it is because he or she is doing the interpretation in his or her own head, rather than the interpreter doing the work. If an interpreter's job is to make a message presented with one world view intelligible to someone with a different world view, then the interpreter is basically functioning as a "paradigm shifter." In order for this to happen effectively, interpreters must know the pragmatics of both languages with which they are working. This often is not the case. It seems, then, the dividing line between the highly skilled interpreter and the merely adequate (or inadequate) interpreter is pragmatics.

Although linguistic and cultural factors are the main determinants for deciding just how difficult a language is to learn, pedagogical factors determine how difficult a language is to teach. Pedagogy here refers not only to the actual classroom teaching but also to the much larger academic picture. This includes student motivations, the history and values of the pedagogical tradition, developments within the field and the approach to pedagogy, and issues regarding the teachers themselves.

As with the Truly Foreign Languages, students don't generally sign up for ASL because it is a graduation requirement, as is often the case with cognates. There often is some specific reason, whether it be to become an interpreter, to work with Deaf people, to talk with Deaf people, or because it looks like fun. Likewise, "the typical TFL student comes with curiosity and a plan, however vague, to use the language in some way as part of his or her postgraduate career" (Walton, p. 10). Whatever the reason, the ultimate objective is to *use* the language, not just be exposed to it. It is for this reason that teachers of ASL consider themselves as teachers of a second language as opposed to teachers of a foreign language–with foreign and the implications of that pedagogy being equivalent to cognate pedagogy (Dively 1994). That is, students often study cognate (foreign) languages merely for exposure and do not intend to actually use the languages, whereas students often take up second languages for just that purpose: to have and use a second language. Motivation, then, is not an issue for teachers in the initial stages of a program, but it does become an issue "in maintaining and strengthening the learner's initial motivation as the complexity of the TFL [in this case ASL] becomes apparent" (Walton, p. 10).

The history and values of the American pedagogical tradition, specifically, the American university, are essentially European in origin. Therefore, if one is to have a well-rounded liberal arts education, one must study (though not necessarily be able to use) one of the cognate (European) languages (Walton, pp. 7–8). In the past several years, this canon mentality has been challenged in English literature departments across the country with the recognition that American history and values do not obtain only from Western Europe and that education, in order to reflect our society, must become more global.

However, if one insists on going outside the canon of languages, other languages historically have been considered languages, exotic perhaps, but languages all the same. The history of ASL has not even enjoyed this status. It has been just over thirty years since Stokoe recognized ASL as a language in its own right. Moreover, historically, ASL users have been looked at from a pathological point of view. Since a language is accorded only as much status as the people who use it, ASL is still struggling for acceptance as a language in many places (including Gallaudet University). This situation is rapidly changing[13] as more and more ASL classes are being offered, particularly with the passage in 1990 of the Americans with Disabilities Act (ADA). But this latter fact, the increased recognition and visibility of ASL partially due to the ADA (which requires the provision of interpreters under the heading of "reasonable accommodation"), only serves to reinforce a pathological mindset. It is difficult for a language to achieve recognition on its own merit when its users are seen as disabled by the larger society. Indeed, "one only has to examine the legislation affecting the rights of Deaf people to see that Deaf people are still classified as handicapped. Deaf people are almost never classified with other minority groups" (Woodward 1982, p. 75).

It is a Catch-22 that more and more people are seeing ASL–English interpreters and recognizing the reality of ASL, yet they are associating this recognition with the ADA, which reinforces the disability mindset. Even those (hearing people) who study ASL and use it are often seen as "benevolent," "altruistic," or at best "fascinating," rather than as learners studying a second language/culture and its people, and accorded the requisite value. When was the last time anyone told a student of Spanish or even Japanese, "Wow, that's fascinating, so do you plan to teach Spanish/Japanese children?" as if that were the logical extension of studying the language? Interpreters and students of ASL are asked this question regularly. Alternatively, ASL is seen as a fun elective, not something valued as appropriate to complete a liberal arts education. (This also is slowly starting to change.)

This valuation is evident on a societal level as well. For example, why are United Nations interpreters seen as highly valued language/culture experts (and paid accordingly) and ASL–English interpreters seen as social service providers? Indeed, the very universities that are trying to decide whether or not to accept ASL as a foreign language, either for

13. Currently, sixteen states have enacted laws regarding the recognition/acceptance of ASL as a foreign language, although specifics vary. See appendix C for the status of ASL in each state.

university admission or graduation requirements, are at the same time often teaching sign language through the departments of audiology, special education, communication disorders (occasionally modern languages), or are not sure where to put it—it's not "Romance," it's not "East Asian." Although there are several universities that have established interpreting departments/majors with ASL courses as part of the curriculum, there is no university, as stated previously, where one can major in ASL specifically. Moreover, virtually all of these universities provide interpreters through the office of Disabled Student Services or Disability Support Service (DSS). The University of Maryland at College Park DSS has tried to rectify this problem by renaming themselves the Disability Support Service and Interpreting Service, but technically the office is still called Disability Support Service and is a branch of the Counseling Center. Attempts to change this categorization have not been successful mainly due to funding-source constraints. There are a great many social and political consequences when a group that identifies itself as a cultural/linguistic minority is seen by the larger society as part of a group labeled disabled. The struggle for language status/recognition is one of them.

This problem extends far beyond the world of academia. Indeed, the World Federation of the Deaf (WFD) must move its home office because its funding is being cut in Finland and has only been offered money (and a substantial amount at that) from a disability fund. There is no culture fund, and the United Nations is not an option as Deaf people do not represent a country (Padden 1994).

The historical tradition, then, of the American university reflecting European values and norms, combined with the history of Deaf people in America, in which Deaf people have been seen by the larger society from a deficit perspective, serves to create the situation of a language being truly foreign to that which is accorded value in academia. That is, for a student to be considered to have a well-rounded liberal arts education that includes foreign language study, those foreign languages have generally been chosen from a short list of European languages. As our society has become more global in nature, that list has in many places expanded to include languages such as Russian or Japanese. As countries become more vital to American interests, economically and politically, their languages become more highly valued, and students are encouraged to take them in order to succeed in today's economy. Compare this view with how society has looked at Deaf people:

One cannot deny that over the last few years there has been some improvement in attitudes towards Deaf people and American Sign Language and that there have been some economic benefits to Deaf people, but Deaf people are still far from being equal to Hearing people in U.S. society ... It is very improbable that Deaf people will ever achieve equality, unless Hearing society depathologizes deafness: that is, unless Hearing society rejects the handicapped classification of Deaf people ... Value change must accompany the economic benefits if permanent social benefit is to accrue to Deaf people. (Woodward 1982, pp. 75-76)

If one were to place languages on a continuum of importance to learn, due to the academic, economic and political importance of people who use these languages, French and Japanese would appear at one end of the spectrum, and ASL at the other "since access to social and economic success is controlled by a culture with an ideology that tends to consider Deaf people as inferior" (ibid).

Several other factors have been mentioned by Walton, Jorden and Walton, and Walker as common to Truly Foreign Languages and as issues in their pedagogy, that seem also to be present in the case of ASL. For example, many TFLs have teaching associations that represent either single languages or a group of languages (Walton, p. 2). ASL has ASLTA (The American Sign Language Teachers Association). From these teaching associations, the more frequently taught TFLs have developed their own pedagogical traditions and, along with other LCTLs, "have their own world within American foreign language education: their own history, infrastructure, pedagogical traditions, financial support structures (however weak), and, of course, their own problems. However, it is a small world compared to that of French, German, and Spanish language instruction and one that operates largely on the fringes of foreign language education as a national endeavor" (ibid). Although I speak as an ASL second language learner and observer, and not as an ASL instructor, this situation also seems to obtain in the case of ASL instruction.

Another example is that the emphasis on teaching culture in the TFL classroom is almost exclusively behavioral rather than "achievement" or "informational." In this breakdown (Hammerly 1982, pp. 513-15), "achievement culture" refers to "high culture" (e.g., history, arts, literature), "informational culture" to factual information (geography, political systems), and "behavioral culture" to "conventions for interpersonal communication or pragmatics." For example, coursework on behavioral culture would include "what should and should not be said in particular social interactions, which topics should and should not be discussed, and how topics and discourse should be tailored depending on the social status and the familiarity of the interlocutors." Furthermore, the amount of time it takes to teach the "linguistic code and the pragmatic system is so great" that the other areas of culture are generally best left to be taught in separate culture courses, and generally the whole evolves into an "area studies model" (Walton, p. 4). This again seems to be the case with ASL, where, in good programs, the pragmatics of behavioral culture are embedded within the ASL courses. Presently, there are four universities in the United States that offer a total of four undergraduate and two graduate degree programs in Deaf studies.

A pedagogical practice that has been shown to be quite effective for teaching behavioral culture in the TFLs and is imperative for ASL students who plan to become interpreters is that of contrastive pragmatics (Ellis 1985). This practice requires "that learners be made aware of their native pragmatic system as a way of modifying this system to fit in the new and quite different pragmatic system of a TFL" (Walton, p. 6). Conversely, an interpreter whose second language is ASL must have enough knowledge and awareness of his or her native pragmatic system (i.e., English) to manipulate the message being interpreted into one that sounds comfortable and appropriate to the listener. Indeed, contrastive pragmatics is one of the cornerstones of the master's program in teaching interpreting, formerly housed at Western Maryland College.

One methodological issue of concern in the TFL classroom is that of students practicing with one another. Although common practice in the cognate language classroom, in the TFL classroom, as Walton points out, this practice may be "of questionable value . . . and may even be pedagogically harmful . . . [as] such practice may well encourage learners to continue using the English pragmatic system, though using it with the target language linguistic code" (Walton, pp. 4–5). Although I have heard this concern expressed by students of ASL, it is not known how this issue plays itself out in ASL classrooms around the country. However, the concern seems to be even more relevant to an ASL classroom since both the base and target languages are native to the same country; hence the tendency for learners to communicate in a manner that is familiar to them. As Walton warns, "premature emphasis on students' speaking to one another in the target language must be seen for what it is, not intercultural communication, but 'same culture' communication with a different linguistic code" (ibid). When this type of communication is applied more broadly to Deaf-hearing interactions, it can result in what is now termed *contact signing* (Lucas and Valli 1992). When applied to the interpreting context, as mentioned earlier, this leads to interpreters who, knowing the linguistic code but not the pragmatic system, force Deaf consumers to adjust themselves to the English/hearing pragmatic system, rather than the interpreter doing his or her job, which is to make the transfer between pragmatic systems as well as linguistic codes.

Likewise, the concept of "negotiating meaning" (Walton, p. 5) is that process by which users of different languages and from different cultures try to communicate, where one tries to make oneself understood and to understand the other. In order for this process to truly happen, the interactants must actually be from different cultures. If two students, or a student and teacher, from the same culture are interacting, then they are technically not negotiating meaning.

"For the TFLs, it is the negotiating of meaning across different cultures that should form the heart of the instructional process, for we are supposedly educating our students to interact successfully with members of another culture, not our own" (ibid). Replacing TFLs with ASL, the same holds true.

Since it is this cross-cultural interaction that is the heart of the instructional process, a grave concern arises regarding the use of nonnative teachers in the classroom. The situation is slightly more complex in the case of ASL since there are hearing people who are native signers of ASL. Although a hearing person may be technically/linguistically competent to teach ASL, as Bienvenu (1992) advises, "it is not politically correct." But again, linguistic competence is only half the picture,

> since non-native teachers will not intuitively provide authentic pragmatic responses, the student will not be properly prepared for authentic intercultural communication with native speakers. The instructional process simply loses validity if it is not geared to genuine intercultural communication. A great fear in the teaching of the TFLs is that a learner will excel in the linguistic code, thus increasing native speaker expectations about the foreigner's control of the pragmatic system, but will fail in the pragmatic domain, thus creating more damage in intercultural situations than if the student were poor in both domains. (Walton, p. 5)

Another issue regarding nonnative teachers is that of testing. A native vs. nonnative teacher administering tests is even more of an issue for signed language teachers than spoken language teachers (for those spoken languages with writing systems). For spoken language teachers, at least a portion of tests given will be paper-and-pencil tests. For signed language teachers, where the language in question has no written system, the majority of tests will be "live," although answers may be recorded on paper. For the cognate languages, "it is common . . . for both tester and student to be American. [However] If the purpose of the test is to gauge the learner's ability to conduct intercultural communication, can there be any test validity when a member of one culture judges another member of the same culture? This is not a test of intercultural communicative ability but rather of 'same culture' communicative ability" (ibid).

Accepting the premise, then, that the teacher should be native, the next question is, is native good enough? Prospective ASL students in search of a teacher are often advised to make sure they find a Deaf teacher. This may be good advice for the reasons mentioned above, but is being Deaf adequate qualification to teach? As Walker (1989) puts it, "Being a native of a culture no more prepares one to teach others to behave in that culture than being a native speaker of a language is sufficient background to teach others to function in that language" (p. 123). Or, from the administrative point of view, especially with the ever increasing demand for ASL classes, what must an administrator require when looking for a qualified ASL teacher? The situation is the same with the TFLs.

Administrators, working to get things going, may not require that standards for accountability and teaching credentials for TFL teachers be identical to those of cognate language teachers. Some college, community college and high school programs are so desperate for teachers of Chinese and Japanese [read: ASL] that normally required teaching standards are being by-passed through special certification procedures. As a result, one finds the incredible situation that strict certification procedures are required for a Category 1 cognate language, but are slighted for teachers of a Category 4 TFL. Thus, complex languages that require a high degree of pedagogical sophistication and teacher training have less stringent certification procedures than the instructionally less demanding Category 1 cognate languages. . . . [Rather], programs and administrative decision makers are placing emphasis on finding "experienced" teachers rather than pedagogically trained teachers. There is a difference, since experience alone is no guarantee of quality or pedagogical sophistication. (Walton, p. 13)

If one insists on pedagogically trained teachers of ASL, luckily, there is a small cadre of those who have received master's degrees in teaching ASL from the only (and now defunct) program that provided such training; but is this supply sufficient to meet the demand? With the numerous accredited programs in the country now teaching ASL, it seems the answer is no. It is not my intention to solve this problem, merely to state that it is one also faced by the TFLs.

The goals of this chapter have been to show that ASL is indeed difficult to learn, and, in comparison with other languages, is more on a par with learning Chinese or Japanese than learning French or Spanish, and to explain the concept of Truly Foreign Languages and show that this concept and the issues faced by the TFLs are virtually identical to those faced by ASL. It is the author's hope that seeing ASL within this framework will have an effect on the structure and length of ASL programs, the entrance requirements for ASL–English interpreting programs, the standards for teacher qualification, and the information presented to those aspiring to a career in interpretation.

REFERENCES

Baker, C., and R. Battison, eds. 1980. *Sign language and the deaf community.* Silver Spring, Md.: National Association of the Deaf.

Bienvenu, M. J. 1992. Personal communication, class lecture. Western Maryland College.

Bowen, D., and M. Bowen. 1985. Entrance examinations for translation and interpretation students. *ADFL Bulletin* 17(1):31–34.

Dively, V. 1994. Personal conversation.

Ellis, R. 1985. *Understanding second language acquisition.* New York: Oxford University Press.

Hammerly, H. 1982. *Synthesis in second language teaching.* Blaine, Wash.: Second Language Publications.

Johnson, R. E., and S. K. Liddell. 1984. Structural diversity in the American Sign Language lexicon. In *Papers from the parasession on lexical semantics,* ed. D. Testen, V. Mishra, and J. Drogo. Chicago: Chicago Linguistics Society.

Jorden, E., and A. R. Walton. 1987. Truly foreign languages: Instructional challenges. *Annals of the American Academy of Social and Political Science* 490:110-124.

Lucas, C., ed. 1989. *The sociolinguistics of the Deaf community.* San Diego: Academic Press.

Lucas, C., and C. Valli. 1992. *Language contact in the American Deaf community.* San Diego: Academic Press.

Olsen, G. 1988. Acceptance of American Sign Language: An American groundswell. *Sign Language Studies* 59:107-108.

Padden, C. 1980. The deaf community and the culture of deaf people. In *Sign language and the deaf community,* ed. C. Baker and R. Battison. Silver Spring, Md.: National Association of the Deaf.

Seleskovitch, D. 1978. *Interpreting for international conferences.* Washington, D.C.: Penn and Booth.

Stokoe, W. C. 1960. *Sign language structure: An outline of the visual communication system of the American deaf.* Studies in Linguistics, Occasional Papers Vol. 8. Buffalo, N.Y.: University of Buffalo Department of Anthropology and Linguistics.

Walker, G. 1989. The less commonly taught languages in the context of American pedagogy. In *Shaping the future: Challenges and opportunities,* ed. H. Lepke. Middlebury, Vt: The Northeast Conference on the Teaching of Foreign Languages, Inc.

————. 1991. Gaining place: The less commonly taught languages in American schools. *Foreign Language Annals* 24(2):1-26.

Walton, A. R. 1992. Expanding the vision of foreign language education: Enter the less commonly taught languages. Occasional Papers, No. 10. Washington, D.C.: The National Foreign Language Center. Reprinted from *Critical issues in foreign language instruction,* ed. E. Silber. New York: Garland Publishing, Inc., 1991.

Wilcox, S. 1993. Personal conversation.

Wilcox, S., and P. Wilcox. 1991. *Learning to see: American Sign Language as a second language.* Center for Applied Linguistics. ERIC Clearinghouse on Languages and Linguistics. Englewood Cliffs, N.J.: Prentice Hall.

Woodward, J. C. 1972. Implications for sociolinguistic research among the deaf. *Sign Language Studies* 1:1-7.

————. 1973. Some characteristics of Pidgin Sign English. *Sign Language Studies* 3:39-46.

————. 1982. *How you gonna get to heaven if you can't talk with Jesus: On depathologizing deafness.* Silver Spring, Md.: T. J. Publishers.

APPENDIX A

Expected Levels of Speaking Proficiency in Languages Taught at the Foreign Service Institute (1993)

Language Group	Length of Training	Speaking Proficiency Low/Average/Superior		
Group 1: Afrikaans, Danish, Dutch, French, German, Creole, Italian, Norwegian, Portuguese, Romanian, Spanish, Swedish	8 weeks (240 hours) 16 weeks (480 hours) 24 weeks (720 hours)	0+/1 1/1+ 2	1 2 2+/3	1+ 2+ 3/3+
Group 2: Indonesian, Malay, Swahili,	16 weeks (480 hours) 24 weeks (720 hours) 36 weeks (1080 hours)	1 1+ 2/2+	1/1+ 2 2+/3	1+/2 2+ 3/3+
Group 3: Amharic, Bengali, Bulgarian, Burmese, Czech, Dari, Farsi, Greek, Finnish, Hebrew, Hindi, Hungarian, Khmer (Cambodian), Lao, Mongolian, Nepali, Pilipino, Polish, Russian, Serbo-Croatian, Sinhala, Thai, Tamil, Turkish, Urdu, Vietnamese	16 weeks (480 hours) 23 weeks (690 hours) 44 weeks (1320 hours)	0+ 1+ 2/2+	1 2 2+/3	1+ 2+ 3/3+
Group 4: Arabic, Chinese Japanese, Korean	16 weeks (480 hours) 23 weeks (690 hours) 44 weeks (1320 hours)	0+ 1 1+	0+ 1/1+ 2	1 1+/2 2+

Note: The number of hours is the theoretical maximum of 30 hours a week. The data is adapted from L. Hart-González and S. Linemann 1993.

Interagency Language Roundtable
Language Skill Level Descriptions
Speaking

PREFACE

The following proficiency level descriptions characterize spoken language use. Each of the six "base levels" (coded oo, 10, 20, 30, 40, and 50) implies control of any previous "base level's" functions and accuracy. The "plus level" designation (coded o6, 16, 26, etc.) will be assigned when proficiency substantially exceeds one base skill level and does not fully meet the criteria for the next "base level." The "plus level" descriptions are therefore supplementary to the "base level" descriptions.

A skill level is assigned to a person through an authorized language examination. Examiners assign a level on a variety of performance criteria exemplified in the descriptive statements. Therefore, the examples given here illustrate, but do not exhaustively describe, either the skills a person may possess or situations in which he/she may function effectively.

Statements describing accuracy refer to typical stages in the development of competence in the most commonly taught languages in formal training programs. In other languages, emerging competence parallels these characterizations, but often with different details.

Unless otherwise specified, the term "native speaker" refers to native speakers of a standard dialect.

"Well-educated," in the context of these proficiency descriptions, does not necessarily imply formal higher education. However, in cultures where formal higher education is common, the language use abilities of persons who have had such education is considered the standard. That is, such a person meets contemporary expectations for the formal, careful style of the language, as well as a range of less formal varieties of the language.

SPEAKING 0 (NO PROFICIENCY)

Unable to function in the spoken language. Oral production is limited to occasional isolated words. Has essentially no communicative ability. (Has been coded 5-0 in some nonautomated applications.) [Data Code oo]

SPEAKING 0+ (MEMORIZED PROFICIENCY)

Able to satisfy immediate needs using rehearsed utterances. Shows little real autonomy of expression, flexibility, or spontaneity. Can ask questions or make statements with reasonable accuracy only with memorized utterances or formulae. Attempts at creating speech are usually unsuccessful.

Examples: The individual's vocabulary is usually limited to areas of immediate survival needs. Most utterances are telegraphic, that is, functors (linking words, markers, and the like) are omitted, confused, or distorted. An individual can usually differentiate most significant sounds when produced in isolation, but, when combined in words or groups of words, errors may be frequent. Even with repetition, communication is severely limited even with people used to dealing with foreigners. Stress, intonation, tone, etc., are usually quite faulty. (Has been coded S-0+ in some nonautomated applications.) [Data Code 06]

SPEAKING I (ELEMENTARY PROFICIENCY)

Able to satisfy minimum courtesy requirements and maintain very simple face-to-face conversations on familiar topics. A native speaker must often use slowed speech, repetition, paraphrase, or a combination of these to be understood by this individual. Similarly, the native speaker must strain and employ real-world knowledge to understand even simple statements/questions from this individual. This speaker has a functional, but limited, proficiency. Misunderstandings are frequent, but the individual is able to ask for help and to verify comprehension of native speech in face-to-face interaction. The individual is unable to produce continuous discourse except with rehearsed material.

Examples: Structural accuracy is likely to be random or severely limited. Time concepts are vague. Vocabulary is inaccurate, and its range is very narrow. The individual often speaks with great difficulty. By repeating, such speakers can make themselves understood to native speakers who are in regular contact with foreigners but there is little precision in the information conveyed. Needs, experience, or training may vary greatly from individual to individual; for example, speakers at this level may have encountered quite different vocabulary areas. However, the individual can typically satisfy predictable, simple, personal, and accommodation needs; can generally meet courtesy, introduction, and identification requirements; exchange greetings; elicit and provide, for example, predictable and skeletal biographical information. He/she might give information about business hours, explain routine procedures in a limited way, and state in a simple manner what actions will be taken. He/she is able to formulate some questions even in languages with complicated question constructions. Almost every utterance may be characterized by structural errors and errors in basic grammatical relations. Vocabulary is extremely limited and characteristically does not include modifiers. Pronunciation, stress, and intonation are generally poor, often heavily influenced by another language. Use of structure and vocabulary is highly imprecise. (Has been coded S-1 in some nonautomated applications.) [Data Code 10]

SPEAKING 1+ (ELEMENTARY PROFICIENCY, PLUS)

Can initiate and maintain predictable face-to-face conversations and satisfy limited social demands. He/she may, however, have little understanding of the social conventions of conversation. The interlocutor is generally required to strain and employ real-world knowledge to understand even some simple speech. The speaker at this level may hesitate and may have to change subjects due to lack of language resources. Range and control of the language are limited. Speech largely consists of a series of short, discrete utterances.

Examples: The individual is able to satisfy most travel and accommodation needs and a limited range of social demands beyond exchange of skeletal biographic information. Speaking ability may extend beyond immediate survival needs. Accuracy in basic grammatical relations is evident, although not consistent. May exhibit the more common forms of verb tenses, for example, but may make frequent errors in formation and selection. While some structures are established, errors occur in more complex patterns. The individual typically cannot sustain coherent structures in longer utterances or unfamiliar situations. Ability to describe and give precise information is limited. Person, space, and time references are often used incorrectly. Pronunciation is understandable to natives used to dealing with foreigners. Can combine most significant sounds with reasonable comprehensibility, but has difficulty in producing certain sounds in certain positions or in certain combinations. Speech will usually be labored. Frequently has to repeat utterances to be understood by the general public. (Has been coded S-1+ in some nonautomated applications.) [Data Code 16]

SPEAKING 2 (LIMITED WORKING PROFICIENCY)

Able to satisfy routine social demands and limited work requirements. Can handle routine work-related interactions that are limited in scope. In more complex and sophisticated work-related tasks, language usage generally disturbs the native speaker. Can handle with confidence, but not with facility, most normal, high-frequency social conversational situations including extensive, but casual, conversations about current events, as well as work, family, and autobiographical information. The individual can get the gist of most everyday conversations but has some difficulty understanding native speakers in situations that require specialized or sophisticated knowledge. The individual's utterances are minimally cohesive. Linguistic structure is usually not very elaborate and not thoroughly controlled; errors are frequent. Vocabulary use is appropriate for high-frequency utterances, but unusual or imprecise elsewhere.

Examples: While these interactions will vary widely from individual to individual, the individual can typically ask and answer predictable questions in the workplace and give straightforward instructions to subordinates. Additionally, the individual can participate in personal and accommodation-type interactions with elaboration and facility; that is, can give and understand complicated, detailed, and extensive directions and make non-routine changes in travel and accommodation arrangements. Simple structures and basic grammatical relations are typically controlled; however, there are areas of weakness. In the commonly taught languages, these may be simple markings such as plurals, articles, linking words, and negatives or more complex structures such as tense/aspect usage, case morphology, passive constructions, word order, and embedding. (Has been coded S-2 in some nonautomated applications.) [Data Code 20]

SPEAKING 2+ (LIMITED WORKING PROFICIENCY, PLUS)

Able to satisfy most work requirements with language usage that is often, but not always, acceptable and effective. The individual shows considerable ability to communicate effectively on topics relating to particular interests and special fields of competence. Often shows a high degree of fluency and ease of speech, yet when under tension or pressure, the ability to use the language effectively may deteriorate. Comprehension of normal native speech is typically nearly complete. The individual may miss cultural and local references and may require a native speaker to adjust to his/her limitations in some ways. Native speakers often perceive the individual's speech to contain awkward or inaccurate phrasing of ideas, mistaken time, space, and person references, or to be in some way inappropriate, if not strictly incorrect.

Examples: Typically the individual can participate in most social, formal, and informal interactions, but limitations either in range of contexts, types of tasks, or level of accuracy hinder effectiveness. The individual may be ill at ease with the use of the language either in social interaction or in speaking at length in professional contexts. He/she is generally strong in either structural precision or vocabulary, but not in both. Weakness or unevenness in one of the foregoing, or in pronunciation, occasionally results in miscommunication. Normally controls, but cannot always easily produce, general vocabulary. Discourse is often incohesive. (Has been coded S-2+ in some nonautomated applications.) [Data Code 26]

SPEAKING 3 (GENERAL PROFESSIONAL PROFICIENCY)

Able to speak the language with sufficient structural accuracy and vocabulary to participate effectively in most formal and informal conversations on practical, social, and professional topics. Nevertheless, the individual's limitations generally restrict the professional contexts of language use to matters of shared knowledge and/or international convention. Discourse is cohesive. The individual uses the language acceptably, but with some noticeable imperfections; yet, errors virtually never interfere with understanding and rarely disturb the native speaker. The individual can effectively combine structure and vocabulary to convey his/her meaning accurately. The individual speaks readily and fills pauses suitably. In face-to-face conversation with natives speaking the standard dialect at a normal rate of speech, comprehension is quite complete. Although cultural references, proverbs, and the implications of nuances and idiom may not be fully understood, the individual can easily repair the conversation. Pronunciation may be obviously foreign. Individual sounds are accurate, but stress, intonation, and pitch control may be faulty.

Examples: Can typically discuss particular interests and special fields of competence with reasonable ease. Can use the language as part of normal professional duties such as answering objections, clarifying points, justifying decisions, understanding the essence of challenges, stating and defending policy, conducting meetings, delivering briefings, or other extended and elaborate informative monologues. Can reliably elicit information and informed opinion from native speakers. Structural inaccuracy is rarely the major cause of misunderstanding. Use of structural devices is flexible and elaborate. Without searching for words or phrases, the individual uses the language clearly and relatively naturally to elaborate concepts freely and make ideas easily understandable to native speakers. Errors occur in low-frequency and highly complex structures. (Has been coded S-3 in some nonautomated applications.) [Data Code 30]

SPEAKING 3+ (GENERAL PROFESSIONAL PROFICIENCY, PLUS)

Is often able to use the language to satisfy professional needs in a wide range of sophisticated and demanding tasks.

Examples: Despite obvious strengths, may exhibit some hesitancy, uncertainty, effort, or errors which limit the range of language-use tasks that can be reliably performed. Typically there is particular strength in fluency and one or more, but not all, of the following: breadth of lexicon, including low- and medium-frequency items, especially sociolinguistic/cultural references and nuances of close synonyms; structural precision, with sophisticated features that are readily, accurately, and appropriately controlled (such as complex modification and embedding in Indo-European languages); discourse competence in a wide range of contexts and tasks often matching a native speaker's strategic and organizational abilities and expectations. Occasional patterned errors occur in low frequency and highly complex structures. (Has been coded S-3+ in some nonautomated applications.) [Data Code 26]

SPEAKING 4 (ADVANCED PROFESSIONAL PROFICIENCY)

Able to use the language fluently and accurately on all levels normally pertinent to professional needs. The individual's language usage and ability to function are fully successful. Organizes discourse well, using appropriate rhetorical speech devices, native cultural references, and understanding. Language ability only rarely hinders him/her in performing any task requiring language; yet, the individual would seldom be perceived as a native. Speaks effortlessly and smoothly and is able to use the language with a high degree of effectiveness, reliability, and precision for all representational purposes within the range of personal and professional experience and scope of responsibilities. Can serve as an informal interpreter in a range of unpredictable circumstances. Can perform extensive, sophisticated language tasks, encompassing most matters of interest to well-educated native speakers, including tasks which do not bear directly on a professional specialty.

Examples: Can discuss in detail concepts which are fundamentally different from those of the target culture and make those concepts clear and accessible to the native speaker. Similarly, the individual can understand the details and ramifications of concepts that are culturally or conceptually different from his/her own. Can set the tone of interpersonal official, semi-official, and non-professional verbal exchanges with a representative range of native speakers (in a range of varied audiences, purposes, tasks, and settings. Can play an effective role among native speakers in such contexts as conferences, lectures, and debates on matters of disagreement. Can advocate a position at length, both formally and in chance encounters, using sophisticated verbal strategies. Understands and reliably produces shifts of both subject matter and tone. Can understand native speakers of the standard and other major dialects in essentially any face-to-face interaction. (Has been coded S4 in some nonautomated applications.) [Data Code 40]

SPEAKING 4+ (ADVANCED PROFESSIONAL PROFICIENCY, PLUS)

Speaking proficiency is regularly superior in all respects, usually equivalent to that of a well-educated, highly articulate native speaker. Language ability does not impede the performance of any language use task. However, the individual would not necessarily be perceived as culturally native.

Examples: The individual organizes discourse well, employing functional rhetorical speech devices, native cultural references and understanding. Effectively applies a native speaker's social and circumstantial knowledge. However, cannot sustain that performance under all circumstances. While the individual has a wide range and control of structure, an occasional non-native slip may occur. The individual has a sophisticated control of vocabulary and phrasing that is rarely imprecise, yet there are occasional weaknesses in idioms, colloquialisms, pronunciation, and cultural reference, or there may be an occasional failure to interact in a totally native manner. (Has been coded S-4+ in some nonautomated applications.) [Data Code 46]

SPEAKING 5 (FUNCTIONALLY NATIVE PROFICIENCY)

Speaking proficiency is functionally equivalent to that of a highly articulate well-educated native speaker and reflects the cultural standards of the country where the language is natively spoken. The individual uses the language with complete flexibility and intuition, so that speech on all levels is fully accepted by well-educated native speakers in all of its features, including breadth of vocabulary and idiom, colloquialisms, and pertinent cultural references. Pronunciation is typically consistent with that of well-educated native speakers of a nonstigmatized dialect (Has been coded S-5 in some nonautomated applications.) [Data Code 50]

States That Recognize American Sign Language as a Foreign Language

The following list identifies the status of American Sign Language as a foreign language in each state. In most cases, the description has been quoted from the legislation or developed from information provided by the state commission on deafness or office which serves deaf and hard of hearing people. Asterisks identify the 16 states with such legislation. Each law is different. In some states the legislation affects elementary school through university offerings; in others, sign language may be offered only in elementary and secondary schools. In some cases, boards of education (state- or county-wide) or individual school districts have authority to approve credit for American Sign Language classes. Readers having specific questions regarding legislation must contact each state directly. This information is current as of June 1993.

Alabama   American Sign Language as a foreign language has never been proposed to the state legislature. However, American Sign Language is taught in several colleges, and academic credit is granted. American Sign Language is taught in high schools on a limited basis.

Alaska   If a course in American Sign Language is offered, the course shall be given credit as a foreign language.

Arkansas   A committee is in process of drafting a proposal. Sign language classes are taught on a state-wide basis to state employees, and American Sign Language is taught in several colleges and given credit on a limited basis.

Arizona   American Sign Language as a foreign language has never been proposed to the state legislature. The University of Arizona accepts American Sign Language for foreign language credit. Other postsecondary pro-

Reprinted by permission of the National Information Center on Deafness, Gallaudet University, Washington, D.C.

grams and high schools also accept American Sign Language for foreign language credit.

California*	Effective July 1, 1988, high school students are required to complete a minimum number of courses in specified subjects in order to receive a high school diploma. This law provides that for the purposes of satisfying this requirement, a course in American Sign Language shall be deemed a course in foreign language.
Colorado	American Sign Language as a foreign language has not been proposed to the state legislature. Several community colleges and universities offer American Sign Language for foreign language credit.
Connecticut	American Sign Language as a foreign language has been proposed to the state legislature but was not passed. It is under consideration for future legislation. If American Sign Language is offered at the secondary level, students receive academic credit for language arts.
Delaware	American Sign Language as a foreign language has never been proposed to the state legislature. The University of Delaware offers American Sign Language as a foreign language and grants academic credit. Secondary programs do not offer American Sign Language.
Florida*	Effective August 1, 1991, each student who is admitted to a state university must have completed two credits of sequential foreign language study at the secondary level or the equivalent of such instruction at the postsecondary level. Students shall be exempt from the provisions of this subsection if they can demonstrate proficiency in American Sign Language equivalent to that of students who have completed

two credits of such instruction in high school. For the purposes of this section, American Sign Language constitutes a foreign language. Florida high schools may offer American Sign Language as a for-credit elective or as a substitute for any already authorized foreign language requirement.

Georgia*   American Sign Language has been accepted as a foreign language in limited circumstances: for deaf students as one unit elective credit; for other students as the third unit of foreign language credit. American Sign Language is taught in several colleges both for credit and non-credit. American Sign Language is taught only at the post secondary level.

Hawaii   American Sign Language as a foreign language has never been proposed to the state legislature. Schools do not offer academic credit for American Sign Language.

Idaho   American Sign Language as a foreign language has never been proposed to the state legislature. Some secondary schools recognize American Sign Language as a foreign language and offer academic credit.

Illinois*   American Sign Language is recognized as a foreign language for high school credit. This allows up to 4 years of class credits and one year of credit for demonstrated proficiency.

Indiana   The Indiana Association of the Deaf will propose the American Sign Language Bill in the 1994 General Assembly. American Sign Language is taught in some elementary education classes.

Iowa*   A law enacted by the General Assembly of the State of Iowa stipulates that instruction in American Sign Language shall be in addition to, and not in lieu of, provision of instruction in other foreign languages. Foreign language means spoken and written languages other than the English language and includes American Sign Language. This relates to the teaching of American Sign Language in accredited schools.

Kansas*

The state legislature passed a bill stating that American Sign Language is recognized by the state of Kansas as a language. The state board of education shall provide for the teaching of American Sign Language in accredited schools and all students whether hearing or hearing impaired may be given instruction in American Sign Language. Any state educational institution may offer an elective course in American Sign Language. Students enrolled at any of the state educational institutions which offer a course in American Sign Language may enroll in such course and with the concurrence of the state educational institution may count credit received for the course toward satisfaction of foreign language requirement of the institution.

Kentucky*

If a course in American Sign Language is offered by a state university or community college, it shall be accepted as foreign language credit. Successful completion of any American Sign Language course in the common schools shall satisfy the foreign language entrance requirements for a state institution of higher education.

Louisiana*

Any public high school shall offer instruction in a course in American Sign Language as an elective course provided a sufficient number of students desire to enroll in such course. Any public high school offering a course in American Sign Language shall provide instruction to any pupil wishing to participate in such course. The State Board of Elementary and Secondary Education shall establish by rule criteria for each parish or city school board to determine whether a sufficient number of students desire a course in American Sign Language and shall develop appropriate procedures for submittal of such determinations by any parish or city school board wishing to offer such instruction. The board shall prescribe suitable teaching materials for the instruction and provide for teacher qualifications. American Sign Language shall mean a visual language which has emerged from the Deaf Culture and is composed of handshapes, movement, and body and facial expression, and possesses an identifiable syntax and grammar specific to visual languages which incorporates spatial relationships as a linguistic factor.

Maine*   American Sign Language is the official state language of the deaf community. Each school administrative unit may offer American Sign Language as a foreign language and offer credit at the elementary and secondary levels.

Maryland   County boards of education in the state are authorized to give academic credit for the study of American Sign Language.

Massachusetts   In all public elementary and secondary schools, American Sign Language shall be recognized as a standard, independent language with its own grammar, syntax, vocabulary, and cultural heritage. Courses in American Sign Language may be taught for the purpose of contributing to a greater understanding of the social and cultural dimensions of the language, and to encourage and enable increased interaction between hearing persons and deaf and hard of hearing persons in society. School committees may credit such courses toward satisfaction of foreign language requirements.

Michigan*	The board of a school district may grant high school credit in a foreign language to a pupil enrolled in high school who has satisfactorily completed a high school course offered in American Sign Language or who has attained proficiency in American Sign Language outside of a public or private high school curriculum.
Minnesota	American Sign Language as a foreign language has never been proposed to the state legislature. However, some secondary and postsecondary programs recognize American Sign Language as a foreign language and grant academic credit.
Mississippi	American Sign Language as a foreign language has never been proposed to the state legislature. However, some postsecondary programs offer American Sign Language for credit.
Missouri	A proposal to recognize American Sign Language as a foreign language is being developed for the FY94 legislature.
Montana	American Sign Language as a foreign language has never been proposed to the state legislature. Sign Language is taught at the high school and postsecondary levels and in community adult education programs. Credit may be given in high school and postsecondary classes.
Nebraska	American Sign Language as a foreign language has never been proposed to the state legislature. Students may take American Sign Language at community colleges and postsecondary programs and receive credit.
Nevada	Acceptance of American Sign Language as a foreign language has never been proposed to the state legislature. Educational programs do not offer credit for American Sign Language.

New Hampshire	American Sign Language as a foreign language has never been proposed to the state legislature. However, some high schools and colleges offer American Sign Language and give academic credit.
New Jersey	American Sign Language as a foreign language has never been proposed to the state legislature. Educational programs do not offer credit for American Sign Language.
New Mexico	American Sign Language as a foreign language has never been proposed to the state legislature. When American Sign Language is offered at the university and postsecondary level, students receive academic credit.
New York	Elementary and secondary schools offer instruction in American Sign Language for second language credit. Students will earn credits to meet second language requirements upon graduation, and higher education institutions will be encouraged to establish teacher training programs in American Sign Language.
North Carolina	American Sign Language as an official language has not been proposed to the legislature. Some secondary programs offer American Sign Language and grant academic credit.
North Dakota	American Sign Language as a foreign language has never been proposed to the state legislature. However, American Sign Language is accepted as a foreign language statewide and academic credit is given in school.
Ohio*	American Sign Language is recognized as a foreign language, and any public or chartered non-public school may offer a course in American Sign Language.

A student who successfully completes a course in American Sign Language is entitled to receive credit for that course toward satisfaction of a foreign language requirement of the public or chartered nonpublic school where the course is offered. American Sign Language is hereby recognized as a foreign language, and any state institution of higher education may offer a course in American Sign Language. An undergraduate student who successfully completes a course in American Sign Language is entitled to receive credit for that course toward satisfaction of an undergraduate foreign language requirement of the state institution of higher education where the course is offered.

Oklahoma*

American Sign Language is hereby recognized as a language and may be taught in the public schools of the state in educational programs for both hearing and deaf students. Academic credit will be granted for courses in American Sign Language.

Oregon

During the 1991 legislative session, a bill was introduced recognizing American Sign Language as a separate modern language. The bill did not pass. Some postsecondary programs offer American Sign Language, but no foreign language credit is given.

Pennsylvania

A proposal is currently pending in the General Assembly of Pennsylvania. It states that every secondary school, both public and private, established and maintained in the commonwealth may offer courses in sign language to all interested students to be taught as an elective course for credit.

Rhode Island

American Sign Language as a foreign language has never been proposed to the state legislature. Some postsecondary programs offer American Sign Language for academic credit.

South Carolina	American Sign Language as a foreign language has been proposed to the state legislature. Academic credit is not currently given in schools where American Sign Language is offered.
South Dakota*	Sign Language is hereby recognized as a language. Any high school may offer American Sign Language as a for-credit elective pursuant to rules adopted by the State Board of Education. The teaching of American Sign Language is encouraged at the elementary level. Any postsecondary educational institution controlled by the State Board of Regents may offer an elective course in American Sign Language according to policy adopted by the Board of Regents.
Tennessee*	American Sign Language is recognized as a language. Educational programs are encouraged to offer American Sign Language for academic credit.
Texas*	American Sign Language is recognized as a language, and any public school may offer an elective course in American Sign Language. For the purpose of satisfying any requirement in the public schools for two units of study in another language, a course in American Sign Language may be deemed another language.
Utah	The 1992 legislature established a task force to study interpreting issues. They will study the possibility of recognizing American Sign Language as a foreign language. A state board of education motion allows American Sign Language to be taught in schools if the school administration wishes it to be.
Vermont	American Sign Language as a foreign language has been proposed and is pending in 1994 state legislation.
Virginia	American Sign Language as a foreign language has

never been proposed to the state legislature. Some academic programs offer American Sign Language and foreign language credit is granted.

Washington*
Pursuant to any foreign language requirement established by the state board of education or a local school district, or both, for purposes of high school graduation, students who receive instruction in American Sign Language shall be considered to have satisfied the state or local school district foreign language graduation requirement. Minimum admission standards will be established for four-year institutions, including a requirement that coursework in American Sign Language shall satisfy any foreign language requirement the board or the institution may establish as a general undergraduate admissions requirement.

West Virginia
American Sign Language as a foreign language has been proposed to the state legislature. Educational programs do not offer American Sign Language for academic credit.

Wisconsin
School boards in individual districts may grant foreign language credit to a pupil who successfully completes a course in American Sign Language.

Wyoming
American Sign Language has never been proposed to the state legislature. Some postsecondary programs offer American Sign Language for academic credit but this does not fulfill the foreign language requirement.

Index

American Sign Language (ASL)
(*continued*)
Narrative structure in ASL
storytelling
nonmanual grammar, 193–94
polysynthetic language as, 194
register variation, 6
students practicing with each other,
203–4
teaching of, 199–206
American Sign Language Teachers
Association (ASLTA), 202
Americans with Disabilities Act
(ADA), 200
Aramburo, A., 6
ASL. *See* American Sign Language
ASLTA (American Sign Language
Teachers Association), 202
Attention of addressee
visual and tactile methods of
getting, 115–16
vocal methods of getting, 114–15
Attitudes toward
Deaf persons, 200
gay, lesbian, and bisexual signs, 4–
5, 8–17, 24–26, 28–29, 31
interpreters, 200
Austin, J.L., 133

Baer, A., 115
Bahan, B., and S. Supalla, 155, 167
Bali, Indonesia, sign language in a
deaf village, 39–57
aid to Deaf as disabled persons, 48
culture of Bali, 45–46
description of village, 41–42
facial expression, 43
iconicity, 43–44
image of Bali, 45–46
independence from oral language,
40
kata kolok (the signed language of
the village), 42–44, 54–56
life of Deaf villagers, 41–42, 44–

49, 54–55
linguistic environment, 49–52
literacy, 49, 52–53
marriage, descent, and inheritance
as factors in village life, 46–
48
mimesis, 43
name signs, 43
nonliterate society's oral language
vs. sign language, 40
normality within village, 44–45
oral culture, 50–52
schooling for Deaf students, 42,
48–49, 54
Signed Indonesian, 42, 49, 54
Singaraja school, 42, 48–49, 54
sociocultural structures of Bali, 45–
46
space, use of, 43
work and education as factors in
village life, 48–49
Yucatec Mayan village's use of sign
language compared with,
40–41, 54
Bateson, G., 133
Bickel, J., 147
Bienvenu, M.J., 204
Bilingual deaf education
ASL and English, 80–83, 96–99.
See also American Sign
Language, comparison of
English word and ASL
definitions
Venezuelan Sign Language and
Spanish, 61–79
Bisexual signs. *See* Gay, lesbian, and
bisexual signs
Black Deaf signing, 6
Body shifts in ASL constructed
dialogue, 113
Bourdieu, P., 46, 48
British vs. American fingerspelling,
193
Bruner, J.S., 135